The Loving Parent Guidebook

This ACA WSO Publication is under fellowship review, with a goal of eventual conference approval.
Fellowship comments are invited. To submit feedback, please visit:
http://litreview.adultchildren.org

For additional reparenting resources, please visit:
https://adultchildren.org/literature/loving-parent-guidebook
https://adultchildren.org/lovingparentguidebook/studyguide_LTR

Adult Children of Alcoholics®/Dysfunctional Families

The Loving Parent Guidebook

ISBN: 978-1-944840-14-3

Printed in Canada
1st edition, 4th printing, 2022

4 5 6 7   25 24 23 22

Table of Contents

Appendices

ACA Serenity Prayer

_____, [god, higher power, life, universe, etc.]

grant me the **serenity** to accept the people I cannot change,

the **courage** to change the one I can,

and the **wisdom** to know that one is me.

The Solution

The solution is to become your own loving parent.

As ACA becomes a safe place for you, you will find freedom to express all the hurts and fears you have kept inside and to free yourself from the shame and blame that are carryovers from the past. You will become an adult who is imprisoned no longer by childhood reactions. You will recover the child within you, learning to accept and love yourself.

The healing begins when we risk moving out of isolation. Feelings and buried memories will return. By gradually releasing the burden of unexpressed grief, we slowly move out of the past. We learn to re-parent ourselves with gentleness, humor, love and respect.

This process allows us to see our biological parents as the instruments of our existence. Our actual parent is a higher power whom some of us choose to call God. Although we had alcoholic or dysfunctional parents, our higher power gave us the Twelve Steps of Recovery.

This is the action and work that heals us: we use the Steps; we use the meetings; we use the telephone. We share our experience, strength, and hope with each other. We learn to restructure our sick thinking one day at a time. When we release our parents from responsibility for our actions today, we become free to make healthful decisions as actors, not reactors. We progress from hurting, to healing, to helping. We awaken to a sense of wholeness we never knew was possible.

By attending these meetings on a regular basis, you will come to see parental alcoholism or family dysfunction for what it is: a disease that infected you as a child and continues to affect you as an adult. You will learn to keep the focus on yourself in the here and now. You will take responsibility for your own life and supply your own parenting.

You will not do this alone. Look around you and you will see others who know how you feel. We will love and encourage you no matter what. We ask you to accept us just as we accept you.

This is a spiritual program based on *action coming from love*. We are sure that as the love grows inside you, you will see beautiful changes in all your relationships, especially with God, yourself, and your parents.

The ACA Twelve Steps

1. We admitted we were powerless over the effects of alcoholism or other family dysfunction, that our lives had become unmanageable.

2. Came to believe that a power greater than ourselves could restore us to sanity.

3. Made a decision to turn our will and our lives over to the care of God as we understand God.

4. Made a searching and fearless moral inventory of ourselves.

5. Admitted to God, to ourselves, and to another human being the exact nature of our wrongs.

6. Were entirely ready to have God remove all these defects of character.

7. Humbly asked God to remove our shortcomings.

8. Made a list of all persons we had harmed and became willing to make amends to them all.

9. Made direct amends to such people wherever possible, except when to do so would injure them or others.

10. Continued to take personal inventory and, when we were wrong, promptly admitted it.

11. Sought through prayer and meditation to improve our conscious contact with God, as we understand God, praying only for knowledge of God's will for us and the power to carry that out.

12. Having had a spiritual awakening as the result of these steps, we tried to carry this message to others who still suffer, and to practice these principles in all our affairs.

The ACA Promises

1. We will discover our real identities by loving and accepting ourselves.

2. Our self-esteem will increase as we give ourselves approval on a daily basis.

3. Fear of authority figures and the need to "people-please" will leave us.

4. Our ability to share intimacy will grow inside us.

5. As we face our abandonment issues, we will be attracted by strengths and become more tolerant of weaknesses.

6. We will enjoy feeling stable, peaceful, and financially secure.

7. We will learn how to play and have fun in our lives.

8. We will choose to love people who can love and be responsible for themselves.

9. Healthy boundaries and limits will become easier for us to set.

10. Fears of failure and success will leave us, as we intuitively make healthier choices.

11. With help from our ACA support group, we will slowly release our dysfunctional behaviors.

12. Gradually, with our higher power's help, we will learn to expect the best and get it.

A Special Note

This Loving Parent Guidebook began as a ballot proposal to the Annual Business Conference of the Adult Children of Alcoholics/Dysfunction Families World Service Organization (ACAWSO) in 2017. A writing group began work in January 2018. After several drafts and input from members of Adult Children of Alcoholics/Dysfunctional Families (the ACA fellowship), this book was published in September of 2021. For a period of up to three years thereafter, the ACA fellowship is invited to read and use the book and share their feedback. Feedback and suggestions can range from errors in typing and punctuation to questions and comments about content. A survey form has been created to provide feedback, which members can access as follows: **http://litreview.adultchildren.org**.

Fellowship review comments will be evaluated by the Literature Committee of ACAWSO, and any recommended changes will be made by ACAWSO. After any revisions are made and approved, the Loving Parent Guidebook will be submitted to an Annual Business Conference to become Conference Approved Literature. For information on additional resources, please see: **https://adultchildren.org/ literature/loving-parent-guidebook**

Stylistic Choices

The Loving Parent Guidebook has adopted several style decisions regarding terms. We encourage you to use the terms that work for you if these don't resonate with you:

- We use "they" as a singular pronoun, rather than "he or she," to make the text gender neutral, except in fellow traveler shares.
- We use the words para-alcoholism and codependency interchangeably.
- We do not capitalize "higher power" in order to support the spiritual, not religious, nature of the ACA program. ACA supports each of us to find a higher power of our understanding. Some of us choose to call a higher power by traditional religious names or by terms such as Universe, Spirit, etc. Others may use no name at all or choose a secular force, such as the love and wisdom of their recovery community. By sticking with a neutral term, we aim to support your unique spiritual journey. (*Note: this does not apply to standard ACA readings such as The Solution.*)
- We capitalize "critical parent," "loving parent," "inner child," and "inner teenager" when they begin a sentence. Otherwise we use lower-case letters.
- We use the terms "parents" and "caregivers" interchangeably to refer to the people or the person who raised you. We acknowledge that not everyone knows their biological parents or lived with both parents. Some of us were adopted, raised by a single parent, grandparents, or relatives, or were in foster care or raised in some other manner.
- By "family of origin" or "family" we mean the family in which you were primarily raised.
- Dysfunction can occur in a family without the presence of addiction. To welcome and include adult children from all family backgrounds, we use the term "dysfunction" and "dysfunctional," instead of referring to any particular manifestation of dysfunction, such as alcoholism.

Inner family work and certain words may trigger old pain. If feelings come up when you read certain words or suggestions, we hope you can discover opportunities to reparent and be gentle with yourself.

---

1   WSO is the World Service Organization of ACA (Adult Children of Alcoholics®/Dysfunctional Families). It acts as the central agency of the program, gathering and disseminating meeting information; creating and distributing literature for use in meetings, and provides information to the general public. To learn more, visit www.adultchildren.org.

Preface: About This Guidebook and How to Use It

Meditation / Prayer
May I remember that reparenting is a journey. I don't need to figure this out right now.
I can read, pause, and take a gentleness break when needed.

How This Guidebook Came About

The Solution in the Adult Children of Alcoholics®/Dysfunctional Families (ACA) program is to become our own loving parents. However, until 2021, our program didn't have a workbook focused on reparenting. The ACA World Services Organization (WSO) created this book to fill that need.

This book was inspired by the reparenting check-in: a four-part process designed to help you tend to your inner family whom you'll meet in Chapter 1. The check-in was adapted from a practice used by a counselor skilled in working with adult children. This guide is designed to help you do the check-in and reparent your inner family so you can become your own loving parent.

The Benefits of Reparenting

Becoming your own loving parent is a process. You may struggle at times and face resistance, but the process is ultimately liberating. Consistent reparenting will help you:

- Discover who you truly are and live more often from your true self.
- Learn to give yourself the safety, trust, care, guidance, and unconditional love you needed as a child to know that you are enough just the way you are.
- Learn how to recognize, allow, and feel all your feelings and honor your needs.
- Free yourself of codependent behaviors and rely less on The Laundry Lists.
- Recognize and reframe distorted thinking.
- Relate in a radically different way to the things you cannot control, such as the critical parent.
- Learn to effectively set boundaries and develop other skills suited to your adult needs and interactions.
- Foster healthy relationships in the outer world.
- Experience more joy, fun, and creativity.

The exercises and guidance in this book will help you learn to put your innate qualities of love, compassion, and kindness into action. You will need support from others, and you may need to try things out and make adjustments as you go. Yet, the more you take *action coming from love* by connecting with your inner family, the more your life will change. You can apply everything you learn in this guidebook to parenting, interacting with children, and interacting with adults. When you become a friend to yourself, you're naturally a friend to others.

> ### *Inner Family:*
> *the parts of yourself that make up **your inner life**, such as the critical parent, inner child, and inner teenager.*

Working with Doubts and Misgivings

Reparenting can be challenging. As we come to believe that our inner loving parent loves us unconditionally and that we're supported by a higher power of our understanding, we begin to break the "Don't Talk, Don't Trust, Don't Feel" rule of family dysfunction. This is a radical shift from how we were raised. We may have judgments, doubts, and misgivings about reparenting. It is natural to have reactions about this work. We may also believe we're being disloyal to our families by working the ACA program—this is what the Big Red Book refers to as "False Loyalty."

> **Parents:** As you become **your own loving parent**, acknowledge your inner children's wounds, and make healthy behavioral changes, you give **the healing gift** of living amends to your own children.

Appendix A lists some common doubts, misgivings, and areas of struggle, along with resources to help you work through them if they arise.

How This Guidebook is Organized

This guide is a companion to the Big Red Book and other ACA literature (*Steps Workbook, The Laundry List Workbook, Strengthening My Recovery*). If you're unfamiliar with the concepts in this guidebook, this can be an opportunity to review ACA literature and tap into the experience of recovering adult children.

The book is structured to help you access the love inside you and grow the awareness and skills you need to become your own loving parent:

- Chapter 1 introduces you to the inner family and your inner loving parent.
- Laying a Foundation for Reparenting: In Chapters 2-9, you will awaken your loving parent and identify and connect with your inner family.
- Deepening Your Reparenting Skills: Chapters 10-16 help you deepen your reparenting skills to protect, nurture, support, and guide your inner family.
- Nurturing a Loving Inner Home: In Chapters 17-21, you'll connect more deeply with your inner family to nurture a loving inner home.
- Reparenting as a Way of Life: Chapter 22 concludes the book with an example of how to approach reparenting as a way of life.

This guide includes fellowship submissions condensed and edited for clarity. To help you integrate reparenting into your daily life, the guide also includes:

- Sample loving parent messages that you can adapt to your particular style and voice. Consider keeping handy phrases that resonate with you by making a list or by copying them onto a blank page at the back of this guidebook.
- Exercises, questions for reflection, and guided practices. You might not relate to all the questions. Use your discernment and skip those that don't apply.
- Sample meeting scripts.
- Images by *The Loving Parent Guidebook* artist team that you can color.
- A link for additional reparenting resources.

Tips to Get the Most Out of This Guidebook

This book is not a one-size-fits-all approach and the examples are suggestions, not instructions. Please give yourself the freedom to use the options (including the meditations, prayers, and affirmations) that work for you and leave the rest.

You may consider using a separate notebook to journal, record in-depth reflections, and explore the suggested practices. Please use additional paper as needed for exercises, reflections, and worksheets. How you feel answering the reflection questions is as important as the content of your answers themselves. You may not have answers. That's okay too. If that's the case, perhaps describe how it feels not to have an answer or to dislike your answer. The following additional suggestions help you approach this book, and reparenting more broadly, in a way that is safe and adapted to your needs.

Work through This Guidebook with Others

"ACA offers a road map for learning how to become a loving parent to myself; it offers a community of like-minded people to travel with so that I do not have to do it alone." -Fellow Traveler

ACA is a "we" program. This guidebook is written to be used with a fellow traveler, sponsor, therapist, or private ACA study group or public meeting, not to be read straight through or in isolation. Sharing our answers and challenges can help connect us to our feelings and uproot isolation and shame. Hearing other people's reparenting experience, strength, and hope can support our journey. Others in the program can helpfully model how to put our inherent loving parent qualities into action. Love is inside of us; yet, we may not know how to direct that love to ourselves. We will need help from others, but the help will be there, and we are worth it.

Appendix I contains sample meeting scripts. Some groups practice the reparenting check-in, which you can find listed at www.adultchildren.org. These meetings offer an opportunity to hear others model reparenting skills. They create a safe space to witness others—and be witnessed—connecting with the inner family. This act can validate your inner child and inner teen (your inner children).

Honor Your Learning Style

We each have different primary learning style(s). Understanding your primary learning style(s) can help you better connect with your inner family. For example:

- Kinesthetic learners learn through physical touch. You may be aware of your inner family as various sensations throughout your body.
- Emotional learners learn through their feelings. Your emotions may be the doorway to your inner world, since your inner family members may have different primary emotional qualities. Sitting with these feelings can be illuminating and can help you identify and connect with your inner family members.
- Visual learners learn through pictures. You may see your inner family members as images, or they may communicate with you visually.
- Auditory learners learn by hearing. You may hear your inner family members as thoughts, voices, or music.

As you begin to work with your inner family, notice how you interact with them. Which learning style do you use most? Experiment to see what helps you connect.

Finding Your Own Pace

Reparenting is a new skill that we develop and practice over our lifetimes. Practice at your own pace and remember to take gentleness breaks as needed. Each chapter prepares you for the next. Do the exercises and give them time to sink in, repeating exercises as needed.

We recommend regularly pausing to feel what comes up for you as you work through this guidebook. Building in your own gentleness breaks may help you adjust the intensity of the work and keep you from feeling overwhelmed.

It's said that we can go further when we walk slowly. We need willingness to reparent. Yet, if willingness veers into urgency or striving, some inner family members may push back. It helps to approach the process in a way that allows us to feel safe as we challenge ourselves.

If we camp out in the *comfort zone*, we avoid the healthy risks that can lead to growth. We learn best in the *challenge zone*, where we have enough safety to navigate the discomfort of trying something new and different. Knowing that we have our ACA support network can give us the courage to venture into the *challenge zone*.

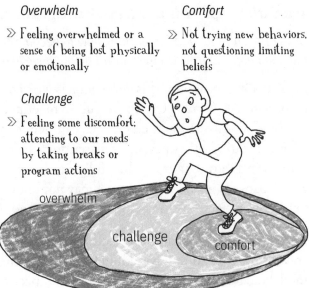

Overwhelm
» Feeling overwhelmed or a sense of being lost physically or emotionally

Challenge
» Feeling some discomfort; attending to our needs by taking breaks or program actions

Comfort
» Not trying new behaviors, not questioning limiting beliefs

If we stretch ourselves too far, we may find ourselves in the *overwhelm zone*, where learning isn't as easy. In that case, we might call a fellow traveler or take a break from active reparenting work. Our guiding question can be, "What do my inner children need in order to feel safe enough to try this out?"

When to Begin The Loving Parent Guidebook

"As I gave my inner child a voice, I gave myself more power to connect with my higher power." -Fellow Traveler

Deciding when to begin your reparenting journey with *The Loving Parent Guidebook* is a personal choice that can be useful to discuss with others in the fellowship. Reparenting and The Steps work together to help us learn to love ourselves and connect with a power greater than ourselves. Each invites us to meet our childhood pain from a unique point of view: with compassion and clear, loving eyes. We encourage you to find the approach and adjustments that best support you, whether that's starting with this book or starting with the Steps. Another option is to complete the first part of this book to create a reparenting foundation for Step work and return to parts two and three later. We don't believe it's possible to make a wrong choice.

> *Sometimes **reparenting "work"** is taking a walk, calling a friend to catch up, having a cup of tea, or doing nothing. **Our mindset** is as important as what we do or don't do.*

> *"Although I saw recovery victories in my life, I didn't understand how the Steps were contributing to reparenting until several years into the program. When it came to making amends, things started to make sense. I had many amends to make to myself, and I could do better at loving myself because of all the work I had put into the program." -Fellow Traveler*

Learning to Reparent Yourself with Gentleness, Humor, Love, and Respect

As we begin the work of reparenting, we may become more aware of the old hurts and trauma stored in our bodies. This can show up as excess tension, tightness, and headaches. We can balance this work with self-care, such as gentleness breaks whenever they're needed, eating well, resting, and taking time to do something fun. We may need to soothe our pain-racked bodies to feel calm. Yoga, meditation, gentle stretching, prayer, massage, tai-chi, art, music, movement, dance, poetry, comedy, play, being in nature, spending time with animals, and connecting with supportive resources can help us do this. Self-care is an expression of our loving parent's gentleness, humor, love, and respect.

gentleness break

Reflections: *Identifying Your Supportive Resources*

Identifying supportive resources early in your reparenting journey helps you call on them more easily at stressful times. Some supportive resources: nature, animals, a sponsor, fellow travelers, movement, poetry, singing, humming, whistling, the sky, calming sounds like those of running water or chimes, movement, holding something comforting, placing your hand on your heart.

- Walk outside
- Contact support
- Listen to music
- Take a bath
- Meditate
- Observe nature
- Do a jigsaw puzzle

Fellow Traveler calling mobile

1. Do you have a "go-to" supportive resource? If so, what is it?

2. List a few resources that can help your body feel more physically calm.

3. If you freeze up or your body wants to shut down, what resources could help your body feel more alive?

When we're triggered or out of balance, it can be hard to discern what we need. Tip: transfer your answers from the questions above to a list that you can carry with you and use when you get triggered.

Reflections: *Creating Nurturing and Safe Conditions for Your Reparenting Work*

Reflect on the questions below to make your space as comfortable and safe as possible while you work through this guide and begin reparenting:

1. What safe physical environment can you use to support your inner children in this work? (e.g., a relatively quiet and private area of your living space.)

2. What objects can you surround yourself with to create a sense of comfort and safety when you do the exercises in this guide? (e.g., cushions, blanket, calming pictures, an image of a safe being or place, symbols that recall connection and comfort, plants, flowers, etc.)

3. What soothing rituals would you like to incorporate before, during, or after working in this guidebook? (e.g., a cup of tea, a warm bath, lighting a candle, looking at a photo of yourself as a child, saying the Serenity Prayer, etc.)

4. What are some things you can do if you find yourself outside your *challenge zone* while doing this work? (e.g., do something you enjoy, do something that nourishes you spiritually, play music, reach out to a fellow traveler or sponsor.)

Safety is personal. Continue to check your sense of safety and take care of yourself as you move through this guide.

Exercise: *Gathering Your Reparenting Supplies*

To mark the beginning of your journey, consider getting some basic art supplies to use with your inner child and to support later activities in this guide. Crayons, colored pencils, glitter, glue, stickers, finger paint, markers, and construction paper can help your inner child express their creativity.

Expectations in the Reparenting Process

If we believe there's something wrong with us, reparenting may become an attempt to "fix" ourselves. An inner loving parent can remind us that we don't need to strive. We are already enough. Little by little, we will heal.

Similarly, when we experience the power of reparenting, we can feel tremendous relief. We may see the practice as the answer to our problems. As with all new practices, however, the initial magic can start to fade. What led to a deep connection with the inner child yesterday may leave us feeling neutral tomorrow. What happened to those waves of compassion? Where is the joy? If reparenting starts to fail us, we may take it as proof that we're too broken to heal, or we may abandon the process and seek out another technique or self-help book.

This natural stage of disillusionment or doubt is not a setback. If we expect to return to specific states of mind, such as compassion, we will be disappointed. States of mind come and go. The only constant is our true self, which reemerges as we shed our reactive behaviors and nurture ourselves with reparenting.

> We can reparent not because we "have to" or because we want to get rid of the pain, but because **it is the kindest response to pain.**

Reparenting works when our intention is to be compassionate towards our suffering. Wanting to avoid pain is natural, but having an agenda—reparenting to get rid of the pain or "improve" ourselves—doesn't work. Paradoxically, real progress happens when we let go of results and release specific ideas about where we want reparenting to take us. The goal of reparenting isn't to become better but to become better at loving ourselves.

Moving Forward by Taking Action Coming from Love

"I started this journey six months ago. I am not healed; however, the burdens are starting to lift. I see that the road is hard, the road is painful, but there is a destination worth reaching. That destination is me."
-Fellow Traveler

Experience shows that we cannot read, think, or wish ourselves into true change. To recover, we must take *action coming from love.* We must develop trust with the inner family by showing up repeatedly, the best we can.

As you continue in this guide, is it possible to approach the work as if you were an explorer on a journey? It's okay to be unsure about the terrain; it's okay to get lost; it's okay to feel fear or dread about what lies ahead. It's okay to be wherever you are. You're on a healing path with many seen and unseen supports, no matter what reservations you might have right now.

Your Key Chapter Takeaway(s):

Affirmation / Meditation

I allow myself to experiment with reparenting , knowing that a higher power of my understanding supports me.
If I lose my way, I can remember the principles of gentleness, humor, love, and respect.

Introduction to Reparenting the Inner Family

Meditation / Prayer
May my connection to a power greater than myself support me as I find the words, images, and actions to nurture my inner family. May I make the life-changing miracle of reparenting an active part of my day.

When the authors of The Solution said that "The Solution is to become your own loving parent," they really meant it. Becoming your own loving parent by developing your reparenting skills can change your life. In his book, *The Laundry List*, ACA pioneer Tony A. wrote, "We cannot return to childhood and ask our parents to love us in the way we needed to be loved. It just can't be done. We need to learn how to nurture and fulfill ourselves. We need to look within, find the origins of our feelings, and come to understand our difficulties and the role we play in causing them."

Reparenting is this "looking within": giving ourselves what we needed to receive as children. To admit you did not learn this basic skill, and need to learn it, is a turning point. We recommend reading this chapter to get a bird's eye view of the process.

You may ask, "How can I reparent myself when I didn't have a good role model?" This book is designed to help you learn how to find and give yourself the love that is already within you. In addition, you have the Steps, the meetings, the telephone, and a higher power to draw on as you learn to reparent yourself.

"I found ACA after reaching a bottom in trying to care for my 2-year-old. His tantrums and emotional outbursts were painfully triggering for me. I often feel split by the competing demands of parenting my son and reparenting myself. Yet, I feel motivated to stick with it to heal the cycle of dysfunction, and not pass along my traits to my son." -Fellow Traveler

Learning to Reparent Ourselves as Our Own Loving Parent

Our parents (or the people who raised us) were children of trauma. They did not receive the love and guidance they needed from their parents, and so they could not pass this love and guidance down to us. They probably did some things well, but they were not able to be good role models for healthy parenting.

At the beginning of this journey, we might wonder if our parents loved us or why they couldn't love us in the ways we needed to be loved. The more we reparent, the more we come to see ourselves through our inner loving parent's eyes. We realize we are lovable and worthy—and always have been. Our parents' inability to love us consistently was never about us but rather about their dysfunction and what they didn't get in childhood.

"Finding my loving parent turned out to be the hardest component for me. I didn't have a lot of good modeling. I had to imagine what to do in situations by asking myself, 'If I were trying to help someone else's child, what would I do or say?' or 'What would a loving parent do in this situation?'" -Fellow Traveler

Recognizing Your Loving Parent

The inner loving parent can be seen as an aspect of our true self that we can awaken and strengthen to tend to our inner family members with wisdom and compassion. Our loving parent possesses deep love, compassion, and kindness. We may need to learn how to recognize and act towards ourselves with these qualities, but there is no doubt they live inside us.

Our loving parent meets our unmet childhood needs of protection, nurturance, support, and guidance. We can recognize our loving parent by noticing when we:

- Care for our physical, mental, spiritual, and emotional well-being.
- Feel the physical sensations associated with openness, softness, lightness, stillness, and ease.
- Offer ourselves comforting words or touch.
- Have loving thoughts or mental images/movies that reflect kindness and compassion.

We want to get our loving parent in the driver's seat of our awareness. Whenever another inner family member takes over, we can pause and access our loving parent's qualities to tend to them.

"In the beginning, it was hard to connect with my loving parent. But I kept practicing with phrases like, 'I'm here for you.' 'I'm sorry you feel so sad.' 'We're going to get through this.' Over time, it got easier to connect with my loving parent." -Fellow Traveler

Meeting Your Inner Family

Our childhood experiences shape our inner life. To understand our inner life more clearly, we can identify our different inner family members and what each needs. We each experience our inner world in unique ways. In this guidebook, we describe inner family members as representations of commonly recognizable patterns of behavior. These descriptions aren't meant to limit your own experience but are offered to give you a starting point for working with your inner life:

- An inner critical parent—a part of us that tries to control our behavior and our life.
- An inner child—the young, vulnerable part of us on an age spectrum from infant to pre-teen.
- An inner teenager—the teen-aged inner child.

We may also experience our loving parent as a part of us, as a healthy inner family member.

"Inner children" refers to the inner child *and* inner teenager together.[1] This guidebook helps us work with these inner family members as an inner loving parent. We may wonder why the program encourages us to work with our inner children rather than simply connect with our emotions. Our abandonment, neglect, and abuse happened within a childhood relationship when we lacked the skills and safety to express our hurts and fears. At the moment of the wounding, parts of us froze and became trapped in the past with a fixed set of beliefs, emotions, unmet needs, childhood reactions, and memories. By establishing a relationship with the frozen parts of ourselves and meeting their needs, we create the conditions for them to heal and release false beliefs. In so doing, we free ourselves from the shame and blame that are carryovers from the past.

---

1 You may hear "inner kids" used in this same way in the fellowship.

Each of our inner family members has a different experience of the world, colored by our family environment in childhood. In stressful adult situations, our inner child may be the one to react, mistaking the person in front of us as a person from the past. This can trigger the helplessness and fear we felt back then. At other times, we may sulk or lash out, like a defiant teenager. No matter where we go, we carry our inner family members inside us. We might not be aware of how some of our actions are in fact driven by these wounded inner family members. When we find ourselves reacting from our inner child or inner teenager, we can recognize that these reactions are the lasting impacts of early childhood trauma. This recognition can make it easier to be gentle toward ourselves. There is nothing wrong with us. Our coping mechanisms are a response to not getting what we needed then, and we can release them now since they have outgrown their usefulness.

Until we reclaim and heal our inner child and inner teen, they remain frozen in cycles of repeating childhood reactions. Our loving parent can help thaw our frozen inner children, nurturing and guiding them so they stop "reacting and reenacting" past situations and harms.

Reparenting helps us revisit and nurture each inner family member, allowing us to gradually teach them newer and healthier responses to life. Our loving parent can soothe the inner child and understand and support the inner teen.

Through reparenting, the inner children learn that it is okay to express their feelings and needs. We stop listening to the critical parent and break the "Don't Talk, Don't Trust, Don't Feel" rule of family dysfunction. Our loving parent's healing love frees our inner children, allowing their natural joy, playfulness, and creativity to shine forth. They can also help the inner critical parent be helpful rather than harmful–trying not to eliminate them but learning to work with them. We replace the fear- and shame-based reactions we learned from our families with unconditional love towards ourselves and others.

Newcomers may find the notion of an inner family uncomfortable or "out there." Yet, many therapy models accept that human beings are made up of distinct and often competing "parts." Even people raised in healthy families sense distinct internal "parts" of themselves. We hear this in everyday conversation: "A part of me is angry, and another part of me is hurt," or "I feel torn between staying home and going out."

These inner family members, or parts of us, interact inside. For there to be emotional balance, these inner family members need to function well together, like passengers

*Our inner family members want to be **heard**.*

*They want to be **seen**.*

*They have **positive intentions**.*

on a bus, with our loving parent in the driver's seat. This way, our actions are a result of clarity, love, and cooperation–and not directed primarily by our wounded and reactive inner family members.

Our inner family members helped us survive our dysfunctional environments. They are trying to help us, even if their actions are sometimes counterproductive or cause pain. They may not realize that we are no longer dependent children caught in a dysfunctional family system. We can thank them and teach them through words, touch, and actions that it's okay to let go of their survival mechanisms. As loving parents, we can help them work together and show them more effective ways to love and protect us today.

As much as anything we can do in our program, creating a safe and loving world for our inner family to co-exist in harmony restores our hearts, our spirits, and our sense of what is possible in life.

Your Inner Family Members

Critical Parent

We can sometimes spot the critical parent from self-talk, such as: "You are so stupid!"; "Why did you do that?"; "Why are you feeling that way?"; "Don't take a chance. You'll fail," and so on. Our critical parent uses the strategies our childhood caregivers used to try to control our behavior but to help us cope with our feelings and prevent further abandonment. For example, imagine that we felt nervous about an upcoming test as a child, and our caregivers told us to stop worrying and study harder. Rather than empathize with us, our caregivers denied our feelings and tried to control our behavior so that we would perform well. Our inner critical parent will repeat that strategy in similar circumstances.

Our critical parent's efforts today can be so painful that we may see them as an enemy. Yet, they're trying to help–just with ineffective strategies. They think other people can still abandon the inner child, so they try to prevent that by any means necessary. Reparenting helps our critical parent trust that they don't need to control the inner child and inner teenager anymore, because a loving parent is there to be with their feelings and support them. As children, we relied on our inner critical parent's directives so we wouldn't do or say something that would lead to unwanted consequences. As adults, we no longer need to rely on the critical parent.

Becoming aware of the critical parent is an essential step in awakening the inner loving parent. The critical parent may be active, if you notice:

- Physical sensations of constriction, rigidity, restricted breathing, tension, or of being restrained/held back,
- Being controlling, pessimistic, striving, perfectionistic, judgmental, having all-or-nothing thoughts, people-pleasing, doubting, scrutinizing—essentially acting out of The Laundry Lists traits, or
- Feeling anxious, worried, discouraged, scared, ashamed, hopeless.

*One critical parent message is: "Don't **Talk**, Don't **Trust**, Don't **Feel**."*

With consistent reparenting, this inner family member can become more reasonable—a partner rather than an enemy. Mindfulness, which we'll learn more about later in this guidebook, can help us detect the critical parent and recognize the need to bring our loving parent into the driver's seat.

It's okay to take a *gentleness break* *whenever you need to.*

"A breakthrough enabled me to reveal my inner critic, separate from them, and start the reparenting process. It made room for my inner-loving parent to meet my inner child and teenager with love and support. After this, when I noticed my inner critic was loud, I could ask myself, 'What would a loving parent say or do?" -Fellow Traveler

Inner Teenager

The inner teenager is the inner family member who can be rebellious, angry, and react quickly— attempting to distract from and defend the inner child's uncomfortable feelings. They may try to set boundaries but in teenage ways that don't usually work well. The inner teen can engage in compulsive behaviors and use substances to try to numb unpleasant feelings. Our inner teenager can react in anger toward us when we disregard our inner knowing or aren't true to ourselves.

The inner teenager we describe is a representation of an angry and defensive part of ourselves, not a replica of how we were as teenagers. We may not have rebelled or expressed anger, but our inner teenagers can. However, they might also have learned to stuff their anger and comply in order to cope with family dysfunction.

The inner teenager has had to fend for themselves after enduring repeated boundary violations and receiving little guidance about healthy coping skills. Watch for the times when you want to lash out, argue, defend yourself, or prove yourself. These cues can signal that the inner teenager is activated. Adrenaline, anxiety, anger, frustration, resentment, and impulsiveness are other cues. In those moments, the loving parent needs to nurture the inner teen and set an internal boundary, such as "I'll handle this for you." We'll explore internal boundaries later in this guidebook.

We may not see a difference between our inner child and our inner teenager at first—or ever. That's okay. The healing actions remain the same: to listen and offer compassion and deep understanding to whichever part of us is present. Just as with an actual teenager, building a trusting and healthy relationship with our inner teenager can be challenging. Once we build a safe and loving place for them, however, they have much to offer to the inner family: strength, courage, and authenticity.

"My inner teenager is angry, frustrated, impatient, and fed up with having to take care of everyone and everything. She's different than the teenager I was, who had to be "good" for mom's sake. She's strong and brave, smart, and sassy. She's not afraid to speak her mind and set boundaries. She's getting stronger every day with the loving parent." -Fellow Traveler

Inner Child

"When I connected with my inner child, he thought he was lazy and no good. He seemed encased in a belief system that told him he could not do anything at all. I noticed a little chink in his armor when I reminded him that he was very bright. He had figured something out. He figured out how to survive a violent, alcoholic upbringing." -Fellow Traveler

The inner child is the innocent part of us who feels awe and wonder but was forced into hiding by dysfunctional parenting. As children, we observed our caregivers and learned to present a false self to cope with the abandonment, abuse, and neglect we experienced. This part of us interpreted the way we were treated to mean that we were unlovable, unworthy, and didn't matter. These false beliefs live on in the inner child today. The inner child is our dissociated self, the child who could have been if it were not for family dysfunction.

The inner child is also the part of us where our joy, playfulness, creativity, and spontaneity live. We can come to understand our inner child in many ways: as our true self, as an essential aspect of our true self, as the part of ourselves connected to something greater, or in some other way.

Your inner child and inner teenager long to be seen and heard. They want to release the pain and grief they carry. We can have one or many inner children who range in age. They communicate through words, feelings, physical sensations, dreams, images, and behavior. When something doesn't go well, they may speak to you with comments such as, "I guess I'm not good enough," or "I was dumb to try."

Some signals the inner child needs love and attention include:

- Overwhelming emotions or sensations, emptiness, depression, shame, sadness, embarrassment, fear, helplessness, hopelessness, and at times, frustration and anger.
- Physical sensations such as numbness, heaviness, constriction, lethargy, or pain.
- Thoughts, images, or movies in the mind's eye of being unworthy, bad, or wrong.

Many people want to unite with their inner child immediately but establishing this connection takes time. We need to build trust with our inner child.

By freeing the inner child, we begin to feel our grief and other emotions from childhood. This transformation opens us to spontaneity, playfulness, intuition, trust, and joy. Once your inner children can emerge from hiding, share their pain, and heal, they will be free to express their natural, delightful qualities more often.

Note: Over time, our inner family can shift. At first, we might have one inner child. Later in recovery, we may encounter others. At some point, one or more inner teenagers might appear. We can have inner family members of any age. For simplicity, we refer to each inner family member in the singular. We use the plural "inner children" to refer to both the inner child and inner teen.

Relating to Our Inner Family Members to Build Cooperation

Our inner family members each have their perspective and believe they are doing what's best for us. This doesn't mean we need to give any one inner family member the right to behave in destructive ways or the power to make all our decisions for us. Instead, we can seek to understand and support our inner family members rather than ignore, belittle, argue with, or try to eliminate them. The more you connect with your inner family members and allow them to speak directly to you, the more you'll understand their different feelings, needs, and positive intentions.

The healing is in the relationship between your loving parent and inner family members. This relationship allows you to be with them. Your loving parent can respond to their pain. These inner family members can share their perspective and emotional truth in their own words and finally be seen and heard.

> *We cannot help our inner families heal by only reading about or talking about them.* **We need to connect with them.** *When we truly grasp this fact and connect with our inner family, we recover more fully.*

Loving Parent

Loving, compassionate, curious, connected,

Spacious, gentle, supportive, calm.

Wounded/Reactive State (Dysfunctional)	Healthy/Healed State

Critical Parent

>> Critical
>> Controlling
>> Fear-based, shamed-based

Critical Parent

>> Part who can relax
>> Supportive

Inner Teenager

>> Rebellious, impulsive, reactive
>> Inner child defender
>> Resentful, angry, shut down
>> Compulsive behaviors, use of substances

Inner Teenager

>> Authentic
>> Direct
>> Brave

Inner Child

>> Isolated, hidden away, guarded
>> In pain from trauma, neglect and abandonment (sad, scared, worried, in shame)
>> False beliefs

Inner Child

>> Spontaneous
>> Sensitive, vulnerable
>> Playful, creative
>> Loving

Exercise: *Inner Family Portrait*

Draw a picture of your inner family. If you notice judgments about your artistic ability, you can gently yet firmly ask your critical parent to give you some room, perhaps by saying "This is a healing exercise. Your judgment hurts the inner child, and I'd appreciate it if you could give me some space." A persistently intrusive critical inner parent might require a stronger boundary, such as saying "Not now" and returning to your drawing. You can tell your inner critical parent that using stick figures is an excellent way of engaging with this activity.

You're welcome to use pencil, ink, crayons, paint, collage, or any other medium. Be as detailed or abstract as you'd like. Draw the inner family members you're aware of now or draw them how you imagine them. If you'd like to try this with your non-dominant hand to access a more subconscious part of yourself, see Appendix G.

The Importance of Building a Solid Foundation

Before we jump into making contact with the most vulnerable inner family member—the inner child—we need to lay a strong foundation. We can remember that it is natural that a child or teen who experienced chronic trauma may not trust any adult, including ourselves. We suggest initially working with inner family members in the following order:

- First: Awaken the loving parent to support, guide, and set boundaries with the critical parent and inner teenager, as needed.
- Next: Learn to identify the critical parent. This is an essential step in developing the loving parent and in creating safety for the inner child. The critical parent can block access to the inner child if we try to bypass them. Understanding what the inner critical parent is trying to achieve can help us have a more cooperative relationship with them.
- Then: Learn to identify and connect with the inner teenager. Their attempts to protect the inner child or keep them numb and out of awareness can lead to undesired consequences. We earn their trust so that they're less likely to intervene when the inner child is triggered by a situation. If the teenager trusts the loving parent to provide care, guidance, protection, and support, we can support the inner child more quickly and directly.
- Lastly: Once we've established our reparenting foundation, we can open ourselves to working more deeply with our inner child.

Reparenting work is not linear. We may meet inner family members in a different order than the one described here. If we begin to get overwhelmed, we can take a gentleness break.

"I dove head first into inner child work without first cultivating a loving parent. I might have scared the child into hiding. I needed to learn to be a gentle and kind adult who could sit patiently nearby. I let my inner child know, often through my presence and posture rather than via words: 'I'm here when you're ready.' My inner child did not come out at first, but over time they learned to trust that I wouldn't hurt or abandon them. They come to me more naturally now that I've cultivated physical and emotional sobriety through daily spiritual practices. I pray for a soft, slow recovery. This is what helps my inner child trust, feel, and then talk." -Fellow Traveler

From Critical Parent to Loving Parent

"I realized I did much of my physical self-care roughly and with anger and resentment. It was the way I had been treated as a child. I started being gentler and began to see that this 'me' that was being gentler and kinder might be my inner loving parent." -Fellow Traveler

You can begin to recognize your inner loving parent by noticing how a loving parent interacts with a child differently than a critical one does. Critical parents often deny feelings. Denial of feelings is a form of control and "fixing." Loving parents make space for feelings. You can cultivate your inner loving parent by naming and empathizing with your inner child's feelings. In this way, you break the "Don't Talk, Don't Trust, Don't Feel" rule.

The following comic strips illustrate the cost of denying feelings. The unspoken message in the first strip is that it's not okay to feel sad or share feelings. Notice how you react to reading the first strip. Then notice the feelings you experience when reading through the same situation in the second strip–this time with a loving parent.

In the second comic strip, the parent listens. They name and make space for the child's feelings and needs. The child can "have" their feelings with a present and supportive person.

The unspoken messages from the loving parent are that:

- It's okay to talk about feelings.
- You can trust others.
- Difficult situations are survivable.

The overall message from the loving parent is: **You are not alone.**

Cultivating Ease Through Reparenting

Reparenting involves tending to our inner family and caring for the physical, emotional, mental, and spiritual health of our whole being. We need to nourish ourselves, so that we have more to give to our inner family members.

Tending to the inner family means that we protect, nurture, guide, and support our inner family members when they're triggered, but as a regular practice. Reparenting is a simple practice that requires consistency, love, and patience. Yet, it is not easy. Because our inner family members are in survival mode, they will try to take over:

- Through judgments and doubt (the critical parent)
- Through substances, compulsive behaviors, and by lashing out (the inner teenager)
- Through fear, false beliefs, not acting, freezing (the inner child)

Your job as the loving parent is to drive the bus and provide the parenting. When you realize you're not at the wheel you quickly and gently move into the driver's seat. Over time, your inner family members trust that it is safe to let go of the wheel. When your inner family members are relaxed and calm, you are more likely to engage with the world from your true self and as a healthy adult.

Our inner family members have spent years taking over the wheel in urgent and desperate attempts to have a sense of safety and control. Over time, our brains can form new grooves, helping us make different choices. The tools and skills in the coming chapters help us form these new grooves. We travel this path accompanied by the experience, strength, and hope of adult children before us: adult children who have learned, as we hope to, to become their own loving parents.

Healing through Conscious Contact with the Inner Family

Connecting with our inner family can bring up old pain. It may feel like we're re-experiencing past pains as we make ourselves present for our inner family members' feelings. While unpleasant, this is a healthy and normal part of the healing process. Reparenting doesn't create this pain; it merely unlocks it. Our inner family members can finally share and unburden themselves of the pain they've been carrying. They now have a loving parent to nurture them.

To support gentleness as we work with this pain, we can balance "working" with and "being" with our inner children. We don't always need to "work" with our inner children by nurturing, supporting, or guiding them. Sometimes we need to "be" with them and their feelings without "doing" anything. Mindfulness, meditation, prayer, play, relaxing, being in nature, and other creative activities help us make conscious contact with our inner life.

Slowly and gently inhabiting our loving parent allows us to show up more regularly for our inner children. We give ourselves the gift of a safe inner world that resembles a healthy family. We create a welcoming environment for our inner family to be heard, to be seen, and to heal. Our inner family members cooperate more readily and let go of their survival mechanisms when their fears are addressed and they can sense our loving parent in the driver's seat. Their distrust melts away and trust grows. The future becomes more inviting.

Even more profoundly, this emerging partnership between our loving parent and inner family relieves our deepest fears: our hearts might have been hurt in our past, but they were never broken. Despite what happened, we find that we are capable of love and of being loved. Our loving parent's compassion, the support of a higher power, and our inner children's emotional authenticity come together to heal our wounds and make us whole.

Guided Practice: *Creating a Safe Inner Space for Your Inner Family*

This guided practice can help you create an internal refuge for your inner family before you move on to the next chapter. Your inner family can visit this space when you need to handle adult issues such as challenging conversations or work assignments. This safe space can also provide a home for the loving parent to visit with the inner family.

Note: As with all guided practices in this book, please refer to the "Guided Practice Preparation" in Appendix B for suggestions and precautions, and to access the opening script. [Begin recording, read the opening script, and continue reading the script here...]

As you begin this healing journey, it can be helpful to have a safe inner space for your inner family to return to where they feel safe and where you can check in on them throughout your day. Imagine yourself showing up in a place that is just right for you at this moment. This can be a place in nature or indoors. You may have visited this place and felt a healing connection to it. It may be a place you long to visit. Maybe it exists only in your mind's eye. (Pause) This is your healing, nurturing safe space. Let yourself settle into this healing space. (Pause) Allow yourself to look around.

(Slow pace with pauses) Notice the quality of the light. Take in the shapes and outlines of what you see. What colors are in your safe space? Absorb the qualities of this place. Notice the sensation of the air on your skin. It may be warm or cold, dry or moist. Feel your body in this space and notice any sensation of textures. What sounds are in your healing space? Notice what aromas, if any, are present.

Picture, if you can, your inner child and inner teen finding cozy spots in this space where they can relax and feel safe. This is their personal space where they can feel nurtured. Take a moment to observe them. Notice what they're doing, how they feel. Do they have everything they need? Give them whatever they need to feel comfortable–perhaps a blanket, stuffed animal, cozy pillows, or a hammock.

Now, notice if there's a spot in your space where the critical parent can hang out. Perhaps that spot is in a separate room or section of the space or where the inner child and inner teen can't see them. See where your critical parent wants to be and keep adjusting until it feels right for the inner child and inner teen or drop this part if it doesn't work for you. (Pause)

Where in your body do you experience the effect of this safe space? (Pause) Your safe place is always within reach. When you're in your everyday life, you can recall the bodily sensations you felt when connected to this safe space. These sensations can unfold within you, allowing you to carry this space's qualities as you go through your day.

For now, take a last look around and savor the experience and feeling of this place. (Pause) Notice how your body feels and say a temporary farewell to this place. (Pause)

Bring your awareness back to yourself in the here and now. Take a couple of deep breaths. Wiggle your fingers and toes. This healing energy is here for you whenever your inner family needs it. Open your eyes or lift your gaze when you're ready and reconnect with the world around you. [End recording]

Reflections: *Your Inner Family's Safe Space Guided Practice*

1. What was the guided practice like for you?

2. In what ways might you use a safe internal space (created through this visualization or some other method) as your reparenting journey unfolds?

Below are some additional techniques that you can use to create a safe inner family space:

- Draw your inner family's safe space.
- Build something to represent the space, using wood, paper mâché, felt, construction paper, clay, or whatever else inspires you.
- Search in magazines or on the internet to find an existing image that represents your healing environment. Place the image where you'll regularly see it.
- Find a song or create a playlist that will help you feel safe.
- Memorize a prayer or phrase to recite when you need a sense of safety.

Consider sharing your experience[2] of creating your inner family's safe space with a sponsor, fellow traveler(s), or therapist.

Your Key Chapter Takeaway(s):

Affirmation / Meditation

I can learn to connect with my inner family members. I can experience the love, compassion, intuition, and purpose that comes with getting to know them.

---

2   In future chapters, you'll see the text "The Power of Sharing," which will serve as a reminder to consider sharing your work with a sponsor, fellow traveler(s) or with a therapist.

Awakening Your Loving Parent

Meditation / Prayer
May I open my heart and recognize the love that is already inside me. May I trust that with that love I can become my own loving parent.

Our inner loving parent can be seen as an aspect of our true selves, embodying qualities including compassion, curiosity, love, and wholeness. Our loving parent can also be seen as an expression of a higher power working through us in a practical way. Our loving parent never goes away, but we can lose sight of it—like a sky obscured by clouds. We can learn to regularly access our loving parent and connect with all our inner family members in new, healthier ways. This is possible at any age and even after years of recovery.

By becoming our own loving parent we can begin to discover our own separate adult identity and individuate from our family of origin. We may have distanced ourselves by moving away, getting a job, and creating our own family. However, unconscious habits, beliefs, and behaviors passed down through the generations might continue to drive our choices. Individuation allows us to recognize and release patterns that no longer serve us. We feel freer to practice new ways of being that help us live healthy lives that are more aligned with our true selves.

When we first start to reparent, our loving parent may seem inaccessible because the loudest, most urgent, or most compelling inner family members can absorb our attention and take over. The more aware we become of the unconscious patterns in our inner life, the more we can individuate from our wounded and reactive inner family members so that we can tend to them as their loving parent. As a loving parent, our role is to nurture a relationship with our inner child, inner teen, and critical parent, so they no longer take over when childhood wounding gets triggered.[1]

Becoming our own loving parent is a process. Each one of us will define and express our loving parent uniquely, though healthy parenting examples can guide us. We can learn how to use the compassion, empathy, love, and kindness we all have—and have probably directed toward others—to reparent ourselves. We will need to practice with our inner family and fellow travelers. Just as we can't recover alone, we can't reparent in isolation. We need each other.

---

1 Depending on our background, it may be difficult to develop a relationship with our inner child and inner teen (and critical parent). They may take over consistently, making it challenging to strengthen our access to our loving parent. If this is the case, we can consider seeking support from a qualified therapist.

"I try to be sure my loving parent is present before I connect with my inner child. They may want to show me painful, forgotten memories. I want to be prepared with my loving parent, a higher power, a sponsor, and the fellowship to guide me." -Fellow Traveler

Exercise: *Letter to Your Inner Loving Parent*

One way to begin awakening the loving parent is to write a letter. We might say...

"Dear loving parent, I need your help to create a gentler inner world. Please step in to lead if other inner family members take over. Please help me surrender the critical parent to a power greater than myself and show warmth and compassion to my inner child and inner teen. Help my inner family feel loved and whole. Help my inner child release their false beliefs one day at a time."

In the space below or in your journal, write a letter to your loving parent.

Keep the letter handy and read it often until it feels natural for you to contact this aspect of your true self. While this exercise is powerful when done on your own, sharing your letter with trusted others can help you connect with your emotions more deeply. Sharing gives you a chance to be seen and heard.

Reflections: *Accessing the Loving Parent Inside*

1. Can you recall a time in your life when someone you cared about was struggling in some way? A child or a close friend (or an animal)? How did you respond? What did your words, your tone of voice, and your body language say to them? Could you sense them receiving your compassion?

2. How do you usually respond to yourself when you are struggling? What do your words, your tone of voice, and your body language say to you?

3. What similarities or differences do you notice between how you treat others and how you treat yourself?

4. During your childhood, who or what was available to you in ways you needed? A teacher? A relative? Perhaps a pet or treasured stuffed animal? What did they do, say, or give you?

5. Who or what do you think of as modeling loving parent behavior? Historical figures, world leaders, other people you know or learned about, animals, nature, characters, or music? List them:

6. What qualities do the people you listed embody (e.g., kindness, love, wisdom, acceptance, etc.)? List as many qualities as you can, referring to the Feelings, Needs, and Physical Sensations sheet in Appendix D, if you wish.

The people you listed above can serve as loving parent role models. You can draw on their qualities as you practice becoming your own loving parent.

- Post their quotes, pictures, or a drawing of them at home, at work, or in the car.
- Ask yourself what they would do in a given situation.
- Imagine them cheering you on in your reparenting efforts.

"I first got an example of a loving parent by my sponsor modeling what an inner loving parent says with praise, affirmations, and allowing feelings. My sponsor saw the light in me that I now see. That light cannot be accessed when I numb out through 'don't talk/trust/feel' measures." -Fellow Traveler

What Does a Loving Parent Do?

Our inner loving parent attunes, or tunes in, to the inner child and inner teen in ways our parents couldn't. A loving parent's message is: you are enough; you matter; I see you, and I'm so glad you're here. A loving parent also affirms that it's okay to have feelings— both pleasant and unpleasant. They do not judge or react to inner family members. They feel compassion, curiosity, gentleness, calm, connection, acceptance, and patience toward them. Our loving parent does not get scared by situations that frighten our inner children. The loving parent resides in the present, yet can visit the past to give our inner children the love and support we did not receive in childhood.

As loving parents, we protect, nurture, support, and guide our inner child and inner teenager to meet their core needs, regardless of how reactive or wounded they may be. Meeting these needs shows our love and builds their trust so that we can guide the inner family in a healthy way.

The loving parent develops a relationship with each family member over time. For example, the inner child might be hidden, scared, skeptical, or angry because of the abuse or neglect they experienced. It might be a while before the inner child can feel or allow themselves to receive that loving care. The loving parent sees this and is present for the inner child, nurturing them by simply being available.

When you first try to connect with your inner child, they might still hope that "one day" their childhood parents or caregivers will change or love them as they needed to be loved. They are also likely to project this unconscious longing onto a new relationship, which keeps them stuck in false beliefs and can lead to outdated coping behaviors.

If your inner child wants "Mom" or "Dad" and not "you" as their loving parent, try not to take it personally. They might need to grieve before they can accept that it's not possible to go back and get what they desperately needed. When they can accept parents' and caregivers' limitations, they become more open to welcoming you as their new, everlasting loving parent.

Our loving parent accepts all our inner family members but does not tolerate all behaviors. A loving parent can see the critical parent's positive intentions but sets boundaries with unhealthy messages. They know that the critical parent's judgments harm the inner child and bring out the inner teen's reactivity.

We can learn about our inner family members by how we relate to the people around us. It can be easier to notice what we reject in others than what we reject in ourselves. If we reject people who seem needy and vulnerable, we might deny that aspect of our inner child. If we judge people who speak up for themselves or get attention, we might reject the part of us who wants to be seen. Our reactions to other people become clues to where our loving parent needs to shine their unconditional love on the inner family.

The goal of reparenting is for our inner family members to trust the loving parent to lead them through life. To achieve that, the loving parent needs to work with each inner family member separately, helping them release their survival traits and pain. This allows them each to heal and play a productive role in our inner family. We can then live more often from our true self.

Worksheet: *Reframing Critical Parent Messages with Affirmations*

The inner loving parent can protect the inner child by counterbalancing the critical parent's judgments with affirmations. For example, if the critical parent says, "You're too much," the inner child might feel ashamed, believing in that moment that there's something wrong with them. Direct contradictions, such as saying, "You're not too much," can make the critical parent defensive. Instead, your loving parent can reframe the sentiment in a more expansive way, such as, "You're just the amount you need to be."

Affirmations can also help your loving parent nurture the inner child after a critical parent message. Experiment with the "It's okay" affirmations found on page 329 of the Big Red Book, and those listed in Chapter 14 of this guidebook. In the worksheet below, list any inner critical parent messages you're aware of and then choose an affirmation to help counterbalance each one.

Worksheet: *Reframing Critical Parent Messages with Affirmations*	
Critical Parent Message	**Affirmation**
Example, "You screwed that up."	It's okay to make mistakes and learn.
Example, "You will look weak."	It's okay to ask for help.
Example, "Those people are losers."	It's okay to think about things differently than my family.

What Core Needs Does a Loving Parent Meet?

As inner loving parents, we create the conditions for our inner family member's wounds to heal by meeting their core needs. Just like with physical wounds, we take the needed steps to help our body heal—applying ointment, protecting the area from further harm, gently nurturing it to health. Yet, like with physical wounds, the healing and pace of healing is in the hands of a power greater than ourselves. Take a look in more detail at the core needs the loving parent meets and how those are accomplished:

Protects

- Sets and upholds internal and external boundaries.
- Checks to see if the inner children feel comfortable in particular settings and with certain people.
- Chooses relationships with emotionally available people who behave in healthy ways.
- Assures the inner children they are safe today. While situations might remind them of the past, they are not in the same situation today.

Nurtures

- Notices when inner children get triggered by paying attention and "tuning in" to them (attunement).
- Accepts the inner children as they are, where they are.
- Makes space to feel feelings.
- Offers compassion, empathy, love, commitment, respect, and care.
- Recognizes and appreciates strengths and qualities. Gives approval on a daily basis.
- Addresses grief and helps inner family members heal.

Supports

- Helps to create balance so there's room for fun, play, and spiritual work.
- Speaks up for the inner child's and inner teenager's feelings and needs and helps them break dysfunctional rules and take healthy risks.
- Notices and supports interests and talents. Provides opportunities to explore them in supportive ways.
- Makes amends to the inner child and inner teenager when necessary.

Guides

- Helps the inner children identify and release false beliefs and survival traits.
- Helps them break the "Don't Talk, Don't Trust, Don't Feel" rule.
- Assists inner family members out of the past and into the present, by helping them release stored grief, parentified roles, and survival mechanisms.
- Offers perspective to counteract distorted thinking and false beliefs.
- Negotiates with the various inner family members and sets healthy boundaries.
- Determines the best way to meet needs and makes decisions that take your whole being into account, not just the most vocal inner family members.

"I set a firm boundary that my inner child/teen does not need to do adult work. Even if I have no idea how to solve a problem, I know one thing for sure, that it's not my 12-year-old's job to figure it out. I get all 'mama/ papa bear' to let my inner child know that they can push up against that boundary, but it will not break. They are safe from adult responsibilities here." -Fellow Traveler

Reflections: *Tapping Your Imagination*

As a child, you may have used imaginative play so that you could be someone or somewhere else. Today you can tap that ability to imagine what a loving parent would do or say in various situations. Just asking the question can open the door to resources beyond your awareness. As you get to know your inner children better, they'll be able to let your loving parent know what they need. Answer the following questions with that in mind.

1. What might a loving parent say to a 6-year-old who calls themselves stupid because they can't tie their shoes?

2. How might a loving parent support an 8-year-old who gets a C on a report card and bursts into tears?

3. How might a loving parent nurture an 11-year-old who is visibly shaken from hearing their parents fighting?

Exercise: *Letter from Your Future Loving Parent*

Write a letter to yourself from your future loving parent, for your eyes only if you wish. Pick a date a few months or years ahead. Imagine yourself as a loving parent who has overcome some of the reparenting challenges you now face. What encouraging words would your inner loving parent say to you? What would they tell you about some of your worries and fears today? What is life like for you in the future? Engage your emotions as you write. Use prompts such as, "What I want you to know is..." or "What you can't see now that I see is...." Focus on the emotions you'll feel as your future loving parent.

You could put the letter in an envelope to revisit whenever you need encouragement. Here's an example:

Date (future): _____

Dear ___,

It's been a whole year since you started practicing becoming your own loving parent. You're in the driver's seat more often now. Your inner family trusts you more, and the critical parent has lowered its volume. You're feeling more serenity. When inner family members take over, you know how to help them relax so you can take the lead. The promises are coming true. You're awakening to a wholeness you never knew was possible. And there's so much more in store. Keep going, you're worth it!

I love you, Future You

If you don't connect with this exercise right now, consider returning to it at a later time.

Reflections: *Description of Your Loving Parent*

1. Write a description of the loving parent you'd like to be for your inner family and how you envision spending time with them:

2. A goal of this guide is to help you expand your toolkit. What program tools could help you become the loving parent you described? (See Appendix H for more ideas.)

3. If you could ask for anything from a power greater than yourself to help you be the loving parent you described, what would you ask for?

Seeing Our Blind Spots

"At first, I acknowledged my inner child's feelings by talking to him but with the subtle intention to get him to feel better so that I could return to whatever task I was involved in. This wasn't conducive to fostering a loving and trusting relationship with my inner child. " -Fellow Traveler

Blind spots—denial—are the areas we have trouble seeing. Our brains created these "blind spots" in childhood to help us survive. We could not take in the abandonment, neglect, and abuse we experienced. Creating blind spots was the best option we had.

We can learn to recognize *how* we're reparenting, so we can identify if reactive inner family members try to control the process. The inner teen or critical parent can learn the loving parent's language but use it to try to control, thus hindering our ability to develop a relationship with the inner child. This can happen without our awareness. If change doesn't happen over time, it might be due to these inner family members trying to control the process. Admitting our powerlessness and letting go when we practice Steps 1, 2, and 3 is an antidote to this impulse to control. Working a program with others can help us relax our control, recognize who is in the driver's seat, and help our inner family begin to trust again.

Today, we need trusted others to help us see our blind spots because our brains automatically default to our childhood programming. A fellow traveler or sponsor may be able to detect a critical tone or false belief when we can't see it or hear it ourselves. We can mirror one another—listening and reflecting back what we hear. We can encourage each other too. Filling our tank with the empathy and compassion of our fellow travelers makes our inner loving parent more available.

Becoming our own loving parent can be challenging at times, but it is extraordinarily rewarding. Any one who accepts this challenge has the opportunity to experience deepened love, compassion, intuition, and purpose. As adult children separated from our hearts at an early age, becoming a loving parent by embracing our inner children can be our pathway back to emotional and spiritual wholeness.

Exercise: *Portable Loving Parent*

List the qualities of your inner loving parent on a card you can slip into your wallet, journal, or other visible spot or add your list to your phone.

An alternative is to create or obtain an object that reminds you of your inner loving parent. Some people use a bracelet with the acronym WWMLPD (What Would My Loving Parent Do?).

Our Deepening Connection with Our Inner Life

Prior to learning about the loving parent, we might spend our lives mastering "adult skills," without realizing we have a wounded inner child in need of care. Skills such as problem-solving and communicating are important to successful living. But, learning to

Intimacy—

into me you see

function as an "adult" does not fully capture what it means to be a loving parent. We can mistake "high-functioning" behavior for "healthy adult" behavior, while still being in denial, suppressing emotions, or not being honest with ourselves.

What is often missing in "high-functioning" behavior is emotional intimacy with, and awareness of, our inner selves. In a stressful situation, an unrecovered adult child might wither without knowing why, or a "high-functioning adult" might respond intellectually. Through increased self-awareness, our loving parent can comfort our frightened inner child, bringing compassion and deeper awareness to the situation. Doing so allows us to handle adult problems as a healthy adult.

Deep love and commitment to the well-being of our inner children inform our adult skills, not only with ourselves but with others. The benefit of strengthening inner intimacy is life changing; the more we deepen and nurture the bond between our loving parent and our inner family members, the more we naturally operate in the world with a sense of security, maturity, and confidence. Living in The Solution means remembering we have an inner child on board to care for at all times.

We are "expanded" by the love, patience, and generosity we learn to show to our inner child. For example, adult children early in recovery can find it painful to ask for help. Once we establish a connection with our inner child and inner teen, our loving parent appreciates the great value in seeking wisdom and guidance from other adult children, from helping professionals, and from a higher power. We grow in confidence and learn to trust that we can provide or find whatever help our inner child needs.

As we become our own loving parent more fully, we might find that we gently nudge our inner family awake with the message, "No matter how today goes, you're enough." At night, we might remind our inner children, "Even if you got triggered today or reacted, you are enough. I see you; I see your good intentions, and I'll help you heal. I love you."

Guided Practice: *Reparenting Check-in*

The reparenting check-in is a foundational reparenting tool. We'll explore it in greater depth in Chapter 9, and Appendix C contains a worksheet that guides the practice. For now, we encourage you to follow the guided practice to the best of your ability, knowing you can attend reparenting check-in meetings to practice further. You'll also be able to learn the skills to deepen this process in the coming chapters.

Note: As with all guided practices in this book, please refer to the "Guided Practice Preparation" in Appendix B for suggestions and precautions, and to access the opening script. [Begin recording, read the opening script, and continue reading the script here...]

Observe your breath where it's relatively comfortable. What's your breath like in this moment? Shallow or deep? Choppy or smooth? Slow or fast? Let yourself experience your breath just as it is without judging it. (Pause)

What emotions are here right now? Emotions are clues to which inner family member is activated. You might notice fear, anger, sadness, worry, or joy, or you might not know what you're feeling. Allow yourself to feel any feelings you're aware of as best you can. (Pause) Notice any physical sensations you feel, such as warmth, coolness, pulsing, or tightness. Whatever you notice, see if it can be okay. Your body is giving you information.

Who needs your loving parent's attention right now or in the recent past—the inner child, inner teenager, or both? Or maybe you don't know? (Pause) What activated this part of you? Was it people, places, or things? Distorted thinking or the critical parent? Maybe it's a combination, or you don't know.

Notice if you feel curious, compassionate, or interested in connecting with the part of you that needs attention? If not, how can you access these qualities to reparent? (Pause) If more than one inner family member needs your loving parent's attention, you can connect with the one who seems to need your attention the most. Let the other one know you'll connect with them afterward. How can your inner loving parent tend to this part of you? (Pause)

Let this part of you know that it's okay to feel whatever they're feeling. Listen to them. What do they need? Maybe they need to trust that your loving parent will protect them. Maybe they need to know you love them just as they are. (Pause) If this part needs comfort, can you offer that right now in whatever way they need? A hand on the heart, a hug, a gentle caress of the cheek, or a pat on the arm? If other inner family members judge this process or try to fix the feelings that arise, let them know this is not the time, and you'll tend to them later.

As we close, notice how you're feeling. You may feel calm, sad, or the same as when you started. Let your inner child or inner teen (or both) know that you appreciate the time you spent together. Thank them for telling you how they felt. If you can uphold the promise, let them know you'll be checking in with them again soon. (Pause) You can open your eyes or lift your gaze and reconnect with your surroundings. [End recording]

"Awakening the loving parent was the hardest part of the program for me. I knew the loving parent was there, but I couldn't get that connection, continuity, trust, or closeness until I began the reparenting check-in practice." -Fellow Traveler

Your Key Chapter Takeaway(s):

Affirmation / Meditation

With help from my ACA support group, I am learning to become my own loving parent, the loving, gentle, and supportive parent I needed as a child.

The Healthy Family: A Reparenting Model

Meditation / Prayer
Grant me the courage to trust that I can learn the skills to nurture a healthy inner family.

What a Healthy Family Gives a Child

In healthy families, caregivers provide food, love, physical contact, and a safe place for children to thrive. From the start, babies learn that their needs matter. As babies grow, their needs become more complex, but their healthy families continue to reinforce that they matter and that help is available. This security is the foundation for healthy relationships throughout their lives.

Imagine a construction crew receives a blueprint to build a new house. The blueprint provides the order in which the parts of the house should be built. It shows the size and shape each part should be and how they all fit together. A complete blueprint results in a functional home.

The way we learn to interact in our families becomes the blueprint we use to guide our adult lives. This blueprint affects all our relationships and, perhaps most importantly, our relationship with ourselves.

Starting life in a dysfunctional environment is like working from a faulty blueprint. The gaps in the blueprint represent unmet needs and missed essential life lessons. Moreover, the family environment itself was a source of stress, pain, and confusion. Any form of abuse (emotional, verbal, physical, and/or sexual) further complicates the faultiness in the blueprint.

Even if you doubt your ability to reparent yourself now, you can learn how to access and express the love that is already inside you. You can draw on a power greater than yourself and outside resources like the model of healthy families, just as you use the Steps, the meetings, and the telephone.

We Can Create a Healthy Inner Family Today

By strengthening the relationships with our inner children and a higher power, we free ourselves from childhood reactions. We give our inner children a second chance to be seen and heard and mend our faulty blueprint.

Our loving parent can build and maintain healthy relationships with our inner family members by using the following qualities and principles of healthy families:

- Parents take the leadership role, recognizing their responsibility to protect, love, support, and guide their children.
- Decisions are made in the best interest of all members of the family.
- Adults take responsibility for their relationships with themselves and model these skills for

their children. They are responsible for their feelings, motivations, and reactions.

- Parents make a purposeful effort to nurture relationships with their children. It is not the child's responsibility to establish that relationship.

- Children are kept out of harmful tension between adults but do observe and learn healthy ways to resolve conflict. Parents speak to the person directly involved in the conflict. They also do not divulge details about their sexual relationship with children.

- Family members are allowed to have their own identities. This avoids enmeshment and boundary confusion. Children are given privacy, to the extent it is safe. Adults do not scrutinize or intrude on the children.

Attending to our inner family members in this way helps us find the love and security of those raised in healthy family systems.

Messages We Needed to Hear in Childhood

Revisiting childhood developmental milestones helps us address wounds from those life stages. We can provide our inner children with the love, safety, and support they needed but didn't get. We can help them internalize the life lessons we missed and create a powerful new blueprint for the rest of our healing journey. As we learn to love and support them, our true self emerges more fully, and we can face challenges as healthy, capable adults.

Birth to 18 months

By tuning into our bodies or getting into a meditative space, we can connect with a vision or felt-sense of our inner infant. We can tell them they are loved and perfect just as they are. "I will always love and protect you. You are safe, secure, and I am here for you." We can show our inner infant that they matter by attending to our body's temperature, thirst, hunger, breathing rate, and need for comforting touch. Placing a hand on our chest to feel the rhythm of our heartbeat can connect us with our inner infant.

18 months through Two years

We can tell our inner toddler that it is okay to roam in new places, to play and splash in puddles, and to seek out experiences that make them feel alive. We avoid judging our inner toddler's lively energy and give them a safe home base from which to explore and learn. We validate their sense of joyful wonder about the world and all it has to offer. We remind them, "It's okay to explore," and to say, "I like this," or "I don't like that."

Three through Five years

We can help our young inner child learn to share and cooperate, to value other people's needs, and to respect limits, while advocating for their needs. We can give them room to grow and explore, but we can also set healthy boundaries and offer them choice. We can tell them, "You matter to me," and "There is enough; it's safe for you to share." We let them know that their need to be treated fairly is valid and that it's important to treat others fairly. We can say to them, "It's okay to play and have fun." Most importantly, we can love them and show them that they matter to us by giving them our time and attention.

Six through 12 years

Our six-to-12-year old might need our love and support when we encounter issues working in groups, cooperating, or allowing others to have their space. Our loving parent can assure this inner child that it's okay not to know something and that it's okay to ask questions. Our loving parent can tell them, "It's okay to allow others to show us how to do things." The inner child needs to know that it's okay to make a mistake. We can assure them, "Making mistakes is how we learn and grow." Our inner loving parent promises this inner child that they can always turn to us and that we will seek the help they need if we can't take care of it alone.

Six through 12 years

Our six-to-12-year old might need our love and support when we encounter issues working in groups, cooperating, or allowing others to have their space. Our loving parent can assure this inner child that it's okay not to know something and that it's okay to ask questions. Our loving parent can tell them, "It's okay to allow others to show us how to do things." The inner child needs to know that it's okay to make a mistake. We can assure them, "Making mistakes is how we learn and grow." Our inner loving parent promises this inner child that they can always turn to us and that we will seek the help they need if we can't take care of it alone.

12-18 years

We understand that the first steps toward an independent identity can be strange, confusing, and unpleasant. Our loving parent sets boundaries for our inner teen but also encourages them to speak their mind to us without fear of rejection. They learn that they can rely on their inner loving parent for emotional support and to challenge authority in healthy ways on their behalf. We can let our inner teen know, "You don't have to be responsible for this. I am here to take care of this for you."

Human Development is a rich subject. If you're interested in learning more than this small taste, you'll find many books and online resources to help you deepen your understanding.

"I focus on the gentleness my inner children want; gentleness looks different at different ages, and I've learned that the first step I can take toward gentleness is to earn their trust." -Fellow Traveler

Healthy Families Talk, Feel, and Trust

Healthy Families TALK

A healthy family understands the importance of communication. In a healthy family, the members:

- Share their inner and outer lives. They talk about their wants, needs, dreams, plans, hopes, fears, concerns, and uncertainties.
- Ask questions and take a genuine interest in one another, listening to what they hear with an open mind.
- Communicate directly. They do not communicate for one another or talk behind anyone's back. Parents work things out with each other rather than venting to a child. They don't ask kids to act as messengers or involve children in their relationship problems or discuss their sex lives.

- Compliment, celebrate, and encourage each other. They notice and share the things they like and appreciate about each other.
- Understand communication can be difficult and messy. They give each other space and make time to resolve misunderstandings.

Children of all ages in a healthy family are encouraged to speak about what they think, feel, and want. They also learn the importance of listening to others.

Healthy families know that conflict is unavoidable. They make time to talk about issues and problem-solve until they reach a resolution. The resolution may not be everyone's preferred outcome, but the family honors each member's feelings and needs in the process.

Healthy families do not:

- Silence any member or criticize "how" they communicate. They focus on the feelings and needs behind the words.
- Use the "silent treatment."
- Mock, tease, belittle, insult, or shame one another for their opinions, behavior, or for expressing themselves as individuals.

Parents in a healthy family guide and support the children by setting and maintaining healthy boundaries. The way they set boundaries respects all of the members' fundamental worth, no matter their age.

Healthy Families FEEL

Healthy families accept and allow all feelings and discuss their feelings with each other. They do not condemn, judge, ridicule, or reject any feelings. A healthy family knows deep in their hearts that "feelings aren't facts." Given the proper space to exist, be felt, and be communicated, feelings will eventually change, if necessary. Healthy families don't see any particular feeling or set of feelings as "good" or "bad." Some feelings are more pleasant than others, but that does not make the unpleasant ones "wrong" or the comfortable ones "right."

Healthy Families TRUST

Healthy families are safe and secure from infancy to adulthood, fostering a sense of consistency and respect for everyone. The family members see their family as their "base camp"—a place where they are welcomed and valued. There they can reliably find love, protection, nurturance, support, and guidance. Whatever challenges any member of a healthy family may meet out in the world, they know they can turn to their family for unconditional love, protection, and guidance.

Because healthy families talk and feel, the trust they have in each other is strengthened over time. Promises and commitments are kept. No one in the family tries to "win" by lying, looking for loopholes, gossiping about each other, keeping hurtful or dangerous secrets, or breaking confidences.

Children raised in a healthy family trust that their families will listen to their feelings, value their needs, and respect their boundaries. They will face consequences if they cross anyone else's boundaries. All members of a healthy family are subject to the same norms of personal space and respect. No one member misuses their power.

Exercise: *Family-of-Origin Inventory*

The following statements reveal where our families lacked healthy parenting skills. Similar to some of the Step 4 work we do, taking this inventory can show us where we internalized unhealthy behaviors. Using the healthy family principles discussed in this chapter can help us change the course of intergenerational family dysfunction. Check all the statements you relate to and notice how you feel as you read them:

☐ One or some of my family members shamed, belittled, mocked, or otherwise rejected some of my feelings, needs, or characteristics or those of other family members.

☐ One or some of my family members' feelings were more important than other family members' feelings.

☐ One or some of my family members used the "silent treatment" or withholding as a communication method or a punishment.

☐ Conflict was not addressed openly in my family, resulting in grudges, gossip, or unaddressed tensions. Rather than resolve conflicts directly, one or some family members vented to others about conflicts.

☐ Instead of treating emotions as something that naturally arise and eventually pass, difficult feelings were treated as something that needed to be "fixed."

☐ The adult(s) in my family needed emotional support from me or my siblings, or I was put in the position of meeting my caregiver's emotional or physical needs.

☐ It was difficult or impossible to trust one or some of my family members. One or some of my family members consistently told lies, stole, broke the rules, broke promises, or were violent or abusive without consequence.

☐ I did not understand the rules in my family. There either were no rules, or the rules were unclear or inconsistent.

☐ The adult(s) in my family did not make time to have a relationship with me.

☐ Decisions seemed to be made for the benefit of only one or some of my family members, and everyone else was expected to go along with those decisions.

List any other behaviors or patterns you recall from childhood that enforced the "Don't Talk, Don't Trust, Don't Feel" rule.

While our families passed down dysfunctional behaviors and patterns, they may have also passed down healthy characteristics such as humor, generosity, or a strong work ethic. Part of creating a healthier inner family involves learning to identify not just the dysfunctional characteristics we want to release but also the characteristics that we may want to keep.

List any healthy characteristics that family members passed down that you'd like to keep:

Guided Practice: *Loving Kindness for Your Inner Family Members*

In this guided practice, you will offer loving phrases to your inner family members to begin building a healthy inner foundation. Loving kindness meditation can boost well-being and strengthen your ability to feel love and affection toward your inner family members. Loving kindness meditation invites you to break the "Don't Talk, Don't Trust, Don't Feel" rule and takes practice. It's okay if you don't feel anything at first or if parts of you react.

You can repeat this guided practice as many times as you like or return to it later. You can offer the phrases below to one inner family member per session or focus on one inner family member for a few minutes and move to the next during the same session.

Note: As with all guided practices in this book, please refer to the "Guided Practice Preparation" in Appendix B for suggestions and precautions, and to access the opening script. [Begin recording, read the opening script, and continue reading the script here...]

Bring to mind a person or being who loves you to invite the feeling of loving kindness into your heart. You can feel this person or being's love in the way they greet you or listen to you, or wag their tail, or cuddle up to you. Let yourself take in that feeling for a moment. If it's not available, think of someone friendly or compassionate, around whom you feel comfortable and at ease—you need not know them personally. (Pause)

Decide if you want to first focus on your inner child or inner teenager. Bring that part of you to mind, sensing their presence in whatever way you can. That may be through emotions, images, words, or physical sensations.

Repeat the following phrases to this part of you in silence. Pause between each phrase to feel whatever you feel. Notice if this part of you responds in any way. It's okay if there is no response.

May you be safe
May you be happy
May you be healthy
May you be at ease in your heart

Continue to repeat the phrases for the next few minutes, adjusting the words to find the ones that help this inner family member feel loved and seen. There is no right or wrong way to do this, and there is no rush to find the response right now. Allow this part of you to be where they are. Continue to repeat the phrases for the next few minutes, switching to another inner family member if you wish. *[Repeat the four phrases above a few times for the recording, allowing space to say the phrases to yourself in silence]*

As this guided practice closes, take a moment to appreciate yourself for making time to reparent yourself. This is The Solution—to become your own loving parent. (Pause) When you're ready, open your eyes or lift your gaze and reconnect to your surroundings. [End recording]

Neuroscience teaches us that our brains can change as we practice new habits, like cultivating loving-kindness. We can repeat this guided practice often, caring for the inner child and inner teenager and perhaps even the critical parent. We can even say these phrases as we go about our day. Each time we practice, we incline our heart toward kindness and compassion, awakening and strengthening our inner loving parent.

> ### Take a **moment**
> *to appreciate yourself for your courage and the action you are taking to heal.*

Reflections: *The Healthy Family: A Reparenting Model*

1. What feelings and physical sensations are you aware of after working through this chapter?

2. What stood out to you about healthy families? What principles of healthy families did you recognize in your various relationships, past or present?

3. How might you use the example of healthy families to help you reparent?

If you felt overwhelmed or discouraged while reading this chapter, it can help to remember that we work at relationships with ourselves and others all day, every day. We simply work at them using the faulty blueprint handed down by our families. You are not alone in having this blueprint.

You will not be alone as you work to transform it either.

Your Key Chapter Takeaway(s):

Affirmation / Meditation

I am learning to mend the dysfunctional blueprint I received in childhood
to build a happier and healthier inner home, one day at a time.

Mindfulness: An Essential Loving Parent Tool

Meditation / Prayer
*May my ability to be mindful and present grow so
I can build a strong foundation for my reparenting work.*

Living in the here and now is a fundamental spiritual concept that our program offers. It's also part of The Solution: "You will learn to keep the focus on yourself in the here and now." Mindfulness is one way to put this spiritual concept into action and strengthen access to your loving parent. Mindfulness is non-judgmental, present-moment awareness. It means we notice what's happening in the present moment without needing it to be different. This simple shift can give us serenity, and a greater sense of awakened connection to ourselves and the world around us. Like the 12 Step healing principle we commonly hear—"one day at a time"—mindfulness helps us be present "one moment at a time."

Coming out of denial and dissociation is needed to reparent effectively.[1] We learned to dissociate or disconnect from ourselves and the world around us early in life to cope with dysfunction. We did this by daydreaming, getting lost in a book or movie, or spacing out. We might have instinctively disconnected from our bodies or feelings during traumatic events. To heal, we can learn to accurately name the elements of our inner life as they happen. That is what mindfulness teaches us. We learn to gradually become more aware of our physical sensations, our senses of sight, sound, smell, taste, touch, of the mind (thinking). We also become increasingly conscious of our emotions and needs and our inner family members.

Every moment of mindfulness builds our ability to be with discomfort so we no longer need to avoid or medicate it away. We can't change something if we're not aware of it. If we are unaware of our thoughts, emotions, or inner family members, we react to them automatically. The critical parent might go undetected, causing us to feel shame or to people-please, or we might act from our inner child's false belief that we're not enough and isolate. If we wish to become our own loving parent, we can practice a new way of life. Mindfulness is a tool that teaches us to live with greater awareness, choice, and serenity. The ability to be mindful enhances Step work, reparenting, and can be practiced at any time.

1 See Big Red Book, page 87 for more on dissociation.

Strengthening Our Mindfulness Capacity

Mindfulness is both a simple daily way of being and a specific practice. Mindfulness can be practiced formally as part of certain types of meditation where we are aware of our senses without judging them. We notice sounds, sights, touch, taste, smell, and the mind (thinking). Informal mindfulness practice happens when we notice our senses as we go about our day. While washing dishes, for example, we can notice the feel of the warm water on our hands. We notice, too, if our mind wanders into the past or future, gently returning to the task at hand. Mindfulness means not running, numbing, or distracting.

Formal mindfulness practice strengthens our capacity to be mindful in our daily lives. Each time we practice mindfulness, formally or informally, we build our ability to be mindful as we go about our day. Mindfulness gives us choice.

Mini-Mindfulness Break

To try mindfulness out, choose two minutes to sit in silence. Select an object to pay attention to—your breath, physical sensations, or sounds. Your eyes can be open with a soft gaze on one spot or closed. Let yourself feel your breath, your physical sensations, or notice any sounds that arise. When your attention wanders from your chosen object (which it inevitably will), gently bring it back without judging yourself. It's okay if your attention wanders many times. That is what minds naturally do. Noticing when your attention wanders is a moment of mindfulness. Over time, you can learn to be mindful of any experience that arises. Consider writing about what the experience was like for you.

Ways to build your mindfulness muscle include:

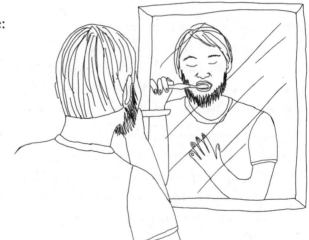

- Throughout the day, ask yourself, "What am I aware of right now in the form of thoughts, bodily sensations, emotions, judgments, or needs?"
- Pick a weekly focus—opening doors, getting dressed, washing dishes, showering, eating, brushing teeth— and practice mindfulness each time that happens.

Meditate for a short time each day. Studies show that 12 minutes a day is the threshold for seeing benefits. Yet, even practicing a few minutes a day builds the mindfulness muscle. We can increase the length of practice little by little.

Navigating Our Challenge Zone with Mindfulness

As adult children, our nervous systems have learned to be on guard all the time to keep us safe. Even in adulthood, our attention tends to fixate on reminders—sensations, memories, thoughts, people, places, things, sounds, smells, or sights—of past threats. It's as if we're back in those situations. This can happen unconsciously, and we might feel suddenly overwhelmed without knowing why.

Our old survival modes kick in, causing a flight, fight, or freeze response.

Mindfulness helps us regulate our attention so we can notice and attend to a trauma reaction before we get overwhelmed. This, in turn, helps regulate our nervous system. The sympathetic (accelerator/activating) and the parasympathetic (brake/calming) nervous systems help regulate our energy throughout the day. At times, energy can be low. We might feel sleepy, foggy, or low in energy. At other times, our energy might be high. We might feel agitated, shaky, or caught up in racing thoughts. Just like when driving, one needs to use both the accelerator and the break to navigate life.

When we work with all the practices in this guide, it helps to know how to put on the brakes or apply the accelerator so we can learn to spend more time in our challenge zone. If we notice we're too focused on what's painful, or if we're in a fight, flight, or freeze reaction, we can shift our awareness. This doesn't mean we redirect our attention every time we feel pain to avoid discomfort. We're learning to feel some discomfort. Yet, if we become overwhelmed, gentleness can help us return to our challenge zone. We can adjust the intensity by opening our eyes, taking a breath, and shifting our attention outside our body on an external object or sounds. Allow the intense feelings to be, gently observing them. We might not like or want to work with these feelings. However, learning to tolerate their presence and merely observe them deflates the power they have held over us.

> *We disconnected to stay **safe**.*
>
> *If paying attention to anything in the body is too much, **take small steps**. It's okay to **shift focus** if needed.*

In recovery, we develop many tools to help regulate our nervous system. That might be putting a hand on our heart or on our arm or pausing what we're doing to call a sponsor or fellow traveler. As The Solution states, "We learn to reparent ourselves with gentleness, humor, love, and respect." Those qualities, along with mindfulness and the practical tips in this section, can help you pace yourself and navigate any intensity that arises:

- Change your posture. Stand up to generate a bit more energy, for example.
- Ask for support from a power greater than yourself.
- Placing your attention on your breath can be supportive when you shut down or become agitated. However, the breath might not be grounding, due to trauma or other physical issues. If being with the breath adds to your overwhelm, you can let it go and focus on sounds instead.
    o Take a couple of deep breaths if you need to increase your energy slightly.
    o Take slower, deep breaths if you need to reduce feelings of agitation.
- Get outside to be in nature.

When you begin to have intense feelings, it's okay to make adjustments rather than push yourself to overwhelm. At any point you can stop what you're doing and use one of the supportive resources you identified in the preface or just allow yourself to do nothing and "be."

The field of neuroscience has made remarkable breakthroughs in recent years, bringing insight into how the nervous system functions, how our bodies remember pain and trauma, and how our brains can change. A wealth of research and techniques to work with trauma and emotional regulation are available. While those areas of study can be quite valuable, we leave those for us each to discover independently. The focus of this book is to support us to be in The Solution of reparenting.

What Mindfulness Is Not

The misconceptions below can make us think that mindfulness is not for us. But mindfulness is a capacity we all have.

Mindfulness is not:

- A blank mind. Mindfulness is knowing what is happening, including thinking. We learn to become aware of our thoughts and take them less seriously or personally. This is different from pushing thoughts away or trying to eliminate them. Mindfulness helps us more skillfully relate to our thoughts.
- A specific feeling, like calm, still, or blissful. While we might experience a sense of peace, calm, or relaxation while practicing mindfulness, these are not guaranteed outcomes. Mindfulness is about noticing whatever experience we're having, including uncomfortable thoughts, feelings, or physical sensations that arise.
- Positive thinking. Mindfulness isn't about having positive or negative thoughts. It is simply about noticing when thoughts arise. It doesn't take long to realize we have no control over thoughts. They come and go. We learn to relate to our thoughts differently and give them less power.
- Complacency. Acceptance does not mean agreement or complacency. It means acknowledging whatever is going on—life on life's terms. We take action when appropriate, but we do so out of compassion and understanding versus reactivity.
- Disengaged. Mindfulness trains the mind, but it also trains the heart. The more intimate and accepting we become with our inner life, the more loving we become. Mindfulness is sometimes referred to as heartfulness. Heartfulness is how our loving parent engages.
- Religious. Mindfulness practices are useful for all people, regardless of their spiritual or religious backgrounds or beliefs. It's a human capacity that taps the awareness and compassion within each of us.

How Mindfulness Serves Reparenting

We Learn to Identify the Critical Parent

The Big Red Book stresses that, "Becoming aware of the critical parent is essential for the development of the loving parent." Mindfulness helps us recognize when and how the critical parent arises.

We Break through the Don't Feel Rule

We know that in dysfunctional families, children learn to deny, stuff, and numb their feelings. Avoiding our emotional truth might have helped us cope, but it has kept our hearts, and other people, at a distance.

Our literature underlines the importance of feeling our feelings so we can build our adult lives on a healthier foundation. This means we must go within. Mindfulness helps us do that and recognize when our inner children's emotions take over. This is an essential step in our inner loving parent's quest to make our feelings safe to feel.

We Learn to Identify Triggers & Takeovers

Triggers are events or circumstances that can evoke unpleasant emotional and physical symptoms, often returning us to childhood emotional states. External triggers take many forms, such as people, places, or things. Internal triggers include the critical parent and distorted thinking. When triggered, we can regress to a childhood stage and believe we're wrong, faulty, or undesirable.

Triggers generally signal unmet needs or that we're perceiving a person or situation as a threat. Our emotional brain reacts as if the perceived threat is in the present before our rational brain can tell us, "This is not the past; this is not that old, painful experience." When we are not mindful of triggers, we tend to overreact. If that occurs, we experience what's known as a takeover. We lose our perspective and can't stay grounded. Mindfulness helps us slow this process down and helps us prevent takeovers. We'll explore takeovers in more depth in subsequent chapters.

Signs of a trigger include:

- Over-reactions; the intensity of your feeling doesn't match the current situation
- Hyper-vigilance
- Fight, flight, or freeze reaction
- Acting out The Laundry List or The Other Laundry List traits (people-pleasing, etc.)
- Intense Feelings (anger, hopeless, ashamed)
- Engaging in compulsive behaviors or reactivity
- Reactions that seem "old" and familiar
- Spacing out
- Avoidance or seeking distractions
- Using words a child would use; a sense of being physically smaller, like a child; feeling "young"

Once we identify a trigger, we can pause and take a few breaths. Then we can turn our attention away from the trigger and tend to our triggered inner family member(s). If that is a challenge, we can call a fellow traveler or sponsor to talk through the trigger and get more space to reparent.

When we're mindful, we notice distorted thoughts, false beliefs, and inner family members before they take over. As our mindfulness grows, we have more space for our loving parent to lead. Our inner children dissociate, ruminate, and react less, leading to fewer takeovers. If their reactions do take over, mindfulness gives us more space to make healthier choices about that reaction. Eventually we can come to see triggers as opportunities to be free from carried pain and shame and rewrite our generational family script.

Reparenting *is an **inside** job.*

Reflections: *Creating Space when Triggered*

1. What physical sensations, thoughts, and emotions tell you that a part of you is triggered?

2. What are some practical actions your loving parent can take when your inner child and inner teen get triggered?

3. What are your thoughts, feelings, and actions when you're fully aware in the present moment?

4. What are your thoughts, feelings, and actions when you revert to survival mechanisms (control, perfectionism, all or nothing thinking, judgment, fear, shame, survival traits, etc.)?

5. What would tell you that a part of you has taken over? How is that different than when a part of you is triggered and you're able to be present and grounded?

Your answers in questions four and five above can help you check which mode you're in throughout the day. When stressed, pause and check the practical actions you listed in number two and three above. Taking one of those actions might create more space to pause, get present, and tend to your inner family.

> *Make a list* of the practical actions you listed in #2 and #3 to carry with you.

Mindfulness Can Help Us Reduce Our Suffering

There's a saying that pain is inevitable, but suffering is optional. Pain is everything we are powerless over—for example, our past, our age, others' words and actions, our critical parent, our pace of healing, and loss. Suffering is the tension we add to the original pain by resisting, judging, denying, and pushing reality away. "I don't like these wrinkles," "I need that person to acknowledge me," "I should be further along...."

Even though mindfulness doesn't eliminate pain, it reduces suffering by helping us be with our experience rather than resist it. While we might prefer times when our critical parent is quiet, judging the critical parent when they appear will not make them retreat. Instead, mindfully accepting a situation can help us realize we do have a choice about how we respond. We can accept, in the moment, that the critical parent has arisen. That acceptance can give

Pain **X** *resistance* **=**

Suffering

us more space to choose not to listen to the harsh voice of the critical parent and, instead, lovingly nurture our inner child. As in the Serenity Prayer, we gain the wisdom to change the things we can and accept the things we can't.

Guided Practice: *Body Scan*

Body scans allow us to increase awareness of our body and befriend our physical sensations. This is meant to be a gentle, comfortable exercise which will take about 15 minutes. You can try it now or pick it up when you have the time. You can do this seated, standing, or lying down. If you feel sleepy at any point, open your eyes or sit up straight to encourage more alertness. If you start to feel over-activated, use the tips from earlier in this chapter, such as moving your body, opening your eyes, or taking a break. You might wish to skip or move more quickly through areas of the body that can be activating to you, being respectful of your needs; everything offered is optional.

Note: As with all guided practices in this book, please refer to the "Guided Practice Preparation" in Appendix B for suggestions and precautions, and to access the opening script. [Begin recording, read the opening script, and continue reading the script here...]

Take three deep breaths, allowing your attention to drop into your body. Bring your attention to the top of your head and see if you can notice any sensations. Maybe you feel tingling, pressure, or tightness— perhaps temperature or vibration. If you don't notice any sensations, you can notice that too. Tune in to what's present, as best you can, without judgment. Anything you feel is okay; you might feel pleasant, unpleasant, or neutral sensations. At any point, you are welcome to make gentle contact with any parts of your body that might need reassurance. That might be placing a hand on your heart, belly, or arm.

(Internal note: pause during the recording/guiding for at least a few seconds before moving to the next area in the body scan, whether a pause is indicated or not.) Feel your face. (Pause) Your forehead. Pay attention to your eyes. Your cheeks. Your nose. Your ears. Feel your jaw. Your chin. See if you can make room for your experience, whatever it is. Be aware of the back of your head. Notice your neck and throat. If your mind wanders, gently return your attention to your body.

Bring your attention to your left shoulder and any sensations you notice—moving down your left shoulder to your upper arm. (Pause) Elbow. (Pause) Forearm. Feel your left hand. Feel your fingers. (Pause) Move your attention to your right shoulder. (Pause) Move your awareness down your upper arm. (Pause) Feel your elbow. (Pause) Your right forearm, hands. Feel your fingers. Allow your attention to scan your shoulder blades. Move your attention to your back. Give yourself the possibility that whatever you're feeling, or not feeling, is okay. Scan your attention down to your lower back. (Pause) Take a moment to notice where you are right now and what time of day it is. Know that you're doing a body scan, learning to be with yourself and in the present moment. Become aware of your chest. (Pause) Feel your belly. (Pause) Feel your left hip. Place your attention on your left thigh. (Pause) Knee. (Pause) Calf. Your ankle (Pause). Feel your foot and your toes.

(Pause). Move your attention to your right hip. (Pause) Notice your right thigh. (Pause) Your knee. Your calf. Notice your foot and your toes. (Pause) Now become aware of your whole body, allowing your attention to take in your full body all at once. (Pause)

Consider the following questions silently. How do you feel right now? (Pause) What part of your body was easiest to focus on? (Pause) What part was the most difficult? (Pause) See if it's possible to allow your experience to be okay just as it was. (Pause) You might like to wiggle your fingers and toes, letting your body know you'll be shifting out of this practice. Open your eyes if they've been closed, taking in your surroundings. [End Recording]

Body scans can help us ground[2] our attention in the present moment. We can do body scans as we did here, starting with our head and moving to our feet, or the reverse. We can also randomly explore sensations, inviting our attention to go wherever it wants to go in our body, gently bring our awareness back to our physical sensations if it wanders into thought.

Your Key Chapter Takeaway(s):

Affirmation / Meditation

Underneath the busyness of my mind is a stillness where my loving parent and
a spiritual force are available to support me in order to reparent myself with a gentle, loving heart.

---

2 Ground: to bring yourself back in contact with the present moment, often by paying attention to the direct experience of your senses (sight, sound, smell, taste, physical sensations, touch, thoughts

Identifying the Critical Parent

Meditation / Prayer
I can learn to notice when my critical parent shows up. I can pause when I notice them.
I can build compassion for my critical parent and can simultaneously stop them from hurting my inner children.
I can ask instead what a loving parent would say or do.

Please note: This chapter is longer than usual and has several substantial exercises, any of which might be triggering. Please allow yourself to go slowly and to take gentleness breaks as needed (which could be a couple days or a week). If you're working through this guidebook in a study group, trying to complete this chapter in a week would not allow for the gentleness and depth needed to work with this challenging part of ourselves. You might need to refer to Chapter 4 at times to support your challenge zone, use supportive resources, and connect with fellow travelers as you go. In the latter part of this chapter you will develop specific loving parent practices to support your work with the critical parent.

It's okay to take a
gentleness break
whenever you need to.

A Necessary Step

As we strengthen access to our inner loving parent, it is essential that we learn to become aware of our inner critical parent. If we're not aware of our critical parent, we're likely to believe their messages and try to hide or "improve" what they see as our "deficiencies." This happens because we're not able to recognize that the critical parent, whether it appears as a voice, physical sensation, or mental image, is merely one part of us. The critical parent is not the truth or the totality of who we are. Once we can recognize the critical parent as an inner family member who has their own motivations, we can get a little space. As we feel able, we can learn about who the critical parent is and what they want for us. Eventually, we may come to appreciate their efforts — however misguided — to protect us from abandonment, shame, criticism and rejection.

You can take a break, critical parent. I'm here now.

The goal in reparenting is not to eliminate the critical parent. The goal is also not to spend time arguing with them, whether in word or in spirit. Instead, we can learn to detach with love. We can recognize the criticism and step back so we stop reinforcing it. We might still hear or sense the criticism, but we gain enough distance so that we don't believe it or get swept away by it.

As we are detaching from these critical messages, we are also learning to treat ourselves—in word and deed—the way a loving parent would treat us. The more we do that, the clearer the contrast between critical messages and loving messages becomes.

At our own pace, we can transform our relationship to the inner critical parent so we're guiding them to relax their control, not fighting with them. To do so, we need to understand how they're trying to help. We will explore how to do that as this guidebook unfolds.

Step 1 teaches us that life becomes unmanageable when we try to control what we can't control. We are powerless over the critical parent arising. When we find ourselves trying to control the critical parent, we might realize that it is still our critical parent in the driver's seat—relying on their lifelong habit of control to try to "fix" this new "problem" that they have identified. Instead, our loving parent can move into the driver's seat. We can practice gentleness, humor, love, and respect when the critical parent appears, as counter-intuitive as that might seem. In this way, we put our inner loving parent's qualities into action.

The critical parent wants to help us stay safe, be lovable, avoid abandonment, and fit in. They try to accomplish that by getting us to do things "right" and not show any vulnerable feelings—essentially asking us to present a false self. Yet, like an unwitting parent who tries to teach a child not to hit others by hitting the child themselves, they use a strategy that is doomed to repeat the cycle. Just as Step 4 encourages us to take a "blameless" approach to understanding our family's actions, we take a "blameless" approach to understanding how the inner critical parent hurts our inner child.

We share this newfound, blameless understanding with the inner critical parent to help them release their control-based behaviors. It's crucial to let the critical parent know that, unlike in our childhood, the *inner child* can't be abandoned by caregivers or other adults today; we aren't dependent children anymore. However, **we** can abandon our inner child emotionally when we lack awareness, and when other parts of ourselves take over and convince us there's a higher priority than the inner child. When the critical parent becomes controlling, we might say, "Thank you for your concern. I've got this now." If the critical parent persists, we can ask, "What are you trying to protect the inner child from?" We can set an internal boundary—something we will begin to practice later in this chapter—to give ourselves more space.

We can also take Steps 1, 2, and 3:

1. "I am powerless over having a critical parent. My life becomes unmanageable when I believe them or fight with them."
2. "I believe I can be restored to clarity, to unconditional love, and acceptance of myself."
3. "I am making the decision to turn the critical parent over to the care of a power greater than myself."

"The critical voice in my head is not as loud as she once was, and she is now joined by this new loving, forgiving, accepting voice. Is my critical parent gone? No, she is still there. But when I hear her, I make the loving choice not to listen or take her advice. I choose to listen to my loving parent." -Fellow Traveler

What is The Critical Parent?

A home life filled with abandonment, neglect, and abuse sent the inner child into hiding, buried deep within our unconscious. An inner critical parent emerged to manage our behavior and feelings. This part of us believed they needed to control our feelings, impulses, and behaviors so that we could function, stay safe, and be acceptable in the outside world and our family. They learned to work tremendously hard to avoid further abandonment from our childhood authority figures. Our critical parent moved into the driver's seat, taking on an adult-sounding voice or persona to help us cope and survive. We began to rely on our critical parent for guidance to manage everyone's perceptions of us, abandoning our true self.

Take the hypothetical example of feeling disappointment about a grade you got in school when you were a child. Rather than empathize and reassure you that it's okay to try and do the best you can, your caregiver may have communicated, "You're lazy. You should have studied harder." The shame and abandonment that your inner child felt in this moment might've been too overwhelming for you to handle without support and guidance from an adult.

In an attempt to shield you from experiencing this kind of shame and abandonment again, your critical parent steps in and tries to manage your feelings and behavior. Adult situations that resemble this childhood situation activate the inner critical parent—in this example, that might be tests in higher education or performance reviews at work. The critical inner parent would rather that you anticipate these criticisms than be blindsided by them: and so, they try to protect you by directing these same judgments your way: "You're lazy. You need to be studying harder. Get it together."

The critical parent often judges more than just actions – they can attack our thoughts before we even act, or can deny our feelings and needs. They can bombard us with questions and statements that fill us with shame and doubt: "Why are you feeling this way?" "You're making a big deal out of nothing." "Don't be like that." They can fill us with a false sense of danger about the future or chronic regrets about our past. "See, I told you that would happen." The critical parent also judges others silently or through words or body language. "Those people are so stupid; they don't know anything..."

> The next time your critical parent is active, **take a deep breath.** Remind yourself that this is the critical parent. Observe them. This may be all you need to do to lessen their impact.

In all these instances, the critical parent is acting out their fear of what might happen if we break the rules. They do this through shame, blame, and criticism. This ends up enforcing the unspoken "Don't Talk, Don't Trust, Don't Feel" rule.

Thus, the critical parent might seem more like a perpetrator, than like a well-meaning part of you. The sad irony is that the critical parent doesn't always understand the pain its judgments cause the inner child. Your inner critical parent's judgments might even be so vicious that they make it harder to get work done. Chronic trauma has frozen the inner critical parent into their role; it will take time, patience, and the steadfast care of a loving parent to help them release their unhelpful behaviors. When we develop compassion for the critical parent and the traumatic experiences that have shaped their worldview, we can understand how they tried to keep us safe, and how their strategies no longer serve our adult lives. We are now older, wiser, and more mature, and our program is helping us become our own loving parent. We can replace critical parenting with loving parenting and invite our loving parent into the driver's seat.

Adult children use a variety of names for the critical parent—inner critic, critical voice, the critic, protector, judge, manager, and the like. Some choose to use a name with personal meaning.

The critical parent can appear in many forms, some obvious and others subtle. Some hear a parent or caregiver's voice in their head. Others might hear the critical parent as their own voice. Others might recognize the critical parent through their emotions, physical sensations, physical contraction, or tone of voice. The critical parent can also appear as images in the mind's eye: of past behavior, what could happen in the future, or how others perceive them.

Some adult children discover their critical parent is a younger version of themselves, a parentified or "hero" child. Others experience their critical parent on an age spectrum, varying from young to old, or as ageless.

Identifying the inner critical parent is the first step to being able to interrupt their misguided attempts to protect us. *How* the critical parent shows up is less important: what matters is noticing *when* they're present. The exercises in this chapter can help you build this practice of noticing.

Even though our inner children might dislike the critical parent, we acknowledge that they helped us survive under painful circumstances. The safety our loving parent creates for our inner children allows the critical parent to take a break, retire, or in some cases, assume a role that better serves our adult lives.

What the Critical Parent Fears

The critical parent fears the following could happen if it doesn't try to control or suppress your inner child's feelings:

- The inner child will overwhelm you with shame, fear, or other painful feelings.
- You will break the "Don't Talk, Don't Trust, Don't Feel" rule and reveal to others what happened in childhood, which could lead to overwhelm, shame, and more abandonment.
- The inner child will feel their feelings only to be judged or shamed by others or left alone to deal with them, like in childhood.
- That healing the inner child could cause changes to relationships, situations, or family of origin dynamics. The changes are good for the true self, but the critical parent believes the false self is the only way to be safe.

"I made a mistake that I thought made me look stingy in front of colleagues and manager. I spiraled, hot with shame. My parents always said cheapness is the worst thing. My critical parent berated me, telling me these relationships were in tatters and that I was unforgivable—with no proof." -Fellow Traveler

Detecting the Inner Critical Parent

You might recognize the critical parent in your physical sensations, in a cruel inner voice that you hear, or in images and movies in your mind's eye.

Critical parent messages can be harsh and scrutinizing, such as "You're bad," "They're phonies," and can even get destructive: "You're a loser"; "Your body doesn't look right." Critical parent messages like these – that make us question and doubt our worth – might cause us to isolate and avoid taking healthy risks. Working with an experienced therapist, along with calling on a higher power or our loving parent for support, can help this kind of critical parent.

> *We might recognize the critical parent immediately. At other times, the critical parent might slip under our radar. **Recognizing** the critical parent and choosing **not to engage** is a significant first step.*

Critical parent messages can also be more subtle: "Are you sure you're qualified to do this?" "Who do you think you are?" In situations that are new and therefore naturally challenging, critical parent messages can also evaluate and judge our efforts too early or too harshly: "You don't know what you're doing"; "You're no good at this." The sinking feeling that follows can make us give up. This kind of criticism can be the critical parent's attempt at keeping us safe from disappointment or rejection.

> *If you're not sure if a message is coming from your critical parent, you can ask yourself,*
>
> ## "If I were in a good space, **would I say this to a dear friend?**"

Sometimes the inner child sounds like the critical parent because they're parroting a parent or authority figure. These are false beliefs the inner child internalized, which we'll explore later in this book. You'll gain clarity the more you connect with your inner family members. This is also why it's helpful to approach inner family members with compassion and curiosity, since we're not always sure who is communicating with us. If our critical parent is actually a younger version of ourselves, like a "hero child", they need the love and care that we did not get at that age.

"For a long time, I thought I didn't even have an inner critic, since it is commonly described to communicate in words or sentences—and mine never has!" -Fellow Traveler

Exercise: *Critical Parent Field Notebook*

"My critical parent is a hedgehog—very prickly, judgmental, and reactive (often to others)." -Fellow Traveler

Birdwatchers keep field notebooks to improve their bird-identification skills. We can do the same as we learn to spot our critical parent. Once we can clearly see painful patterns, it becomes possible to break them.

For several days or weeks, keep a journal, notepad, or note app handy.

- Record any critical thoughts or images you experience.
- Track your critical parent's tone and volume.
- Jot down when and where the critical parent gets activated.
- Identify where you feel the critical parent in space (e.g., inside or outside your body, close by or far away; on your shoulder, head, etc.)

Filling journal pages with critical thoughts can trigger your inner child and your inner teen. Keep it simple. Inventory the various ways your critical parent appears, writing a sentence or two at a time. Take a moment to consider what a loving parent would say in response. If jotting down critical parent "sightings" during the day isn't practical, you could choose a regular time each day to do this exercise. This time is not for the critical parent to vent but for your loving parent to take the driver's seat and inventory the critical parent messages you recognized that day. If the critical parent appears during this time, let them know you're trying to understand them better and need some quiet to do that. If they persist, you might need a firmer boundary statement, such as "Not now."[1] Setting a timer for this activity might be useful.

> *Don't focus on the content of the critical parent's messages. Instead, **focus on spotting** your critical parent when they emerge. Acknowledge them, **then turn your attention away.***

"I learned to be judgmental from my mother. Now that I understand where my critical parent learned this behavior, I have more compassion for myself every time I find my critical parent going on in my head judging others." -Fellow Traveler

Reflections: *Identifying Your Critical Parent*

"I was surprised to discover my critical parent acting like a smokescreen or distractor to hide my inner child." -Fellow Traveler

1. What are some critical messages (or feelings or images) that you notice within yourself often?

2. What is your emotional experience of your critical parent? Is the critical parent matter-of-fact, angry, doubting, questioning, urgent, and/or shaming? Describe how you experience them.

3. What has been your relationship to your critical parent? (e.g., not aware of it, experience it as "you", experience it as an abuser and have had to fight for distance, fear it, rely on it as a voice of "reason," etc.)

---

1 The end of this chapter discusses boundary statements in more detail.

4. How might you describe the physical sensations that you have when your critical parent is active? (e.g., a weight on your shoulders, a foot in your back, being boxed in or trapped, etc.)

5. When do you experience your critical parent as focused inward, on you and your thoughts, feelings, and actions? What are these situations like?

6. When do you experience your critical parent as focused outward, on others and their thoughts, feelings, or actions? What are these situations like?

7. What image(s) describes your critical parent (e.g., a judge, lion tamer, you at a certain age, cartoon, movie character, a figure from your childhood, etc.)? What do they look like? What do they wear? If you feel inspired, draw your critical parent.

8. What images does your critical parent show you? Draw them, if you wish.

9. What persona (or avatar) might you create for your critical parent? You might want to ask your critical parent what they want to be called or what they like to wear. If you get no response, you can come up with your own name or persona.

"My critical parent manifests as a teacher with pinched lips and reading glasses hanging off a beaded chain on her bosom. She is not evil. She is strict, but she means well." -Fellow Traveler

Exercise: *Signs the Critical Parent is Active*

Check any of the signs below that you've experienced when your critical parent is active.

☐ Perfectionism

☐ Control

☐ All-or-nothing thinking (never, always, nothing, everything)

☐ Being judgmental toward yourself or others

☐ Worrying, catastrophizing, projecting into the future Could be in words or images of disastrous scenarios

☐ Avoiding healthy risks or vulnerability

☐ Making predictions about what will happen if you don't do what it says. "You'll lose your job"; "You will be shunned from the community." etc.

☐ Rumination (On a past event/conversation, imagining "do-overs.")

☐ Comparing

☐ Rehearsing an upcoming event/conversation

☐ Thoughts that dismiss, minimize, invalidate, undermine, cause doubt, scrutinize, argue with feelings, fight reality (I'm not feeling x; is that bad? Am I avoiding my feelings?)

☐ Doubt, questioning your reality

☐ Withholding approval

☐ Gossip

☐ "Shoulds"—statements about what you or someone else should, ought, or must do. ("I should be able to do this without feeling afraid." "I should be over this stuff by now.") etc.

☐ Making assumptions ("They're mad at you. They're blaming you.")

☐ A finger pointing at you, a whip, or other menacing image

> *"Instead of hearing criticism (real or imagined) and considering it, my critical parent shouts that I am bad, wrong, and takes up all my psychic space. Much of the time this is over imagined criticism." -Fellow Traveler*

Your critical parent may communicate through memories, mental images, or physical sensations rather than words. For "You're bad," they might show you an image from your past when you did something you regret. You might see a wagging finger directed at you, or you might feel a clench in your stomach.

Whenever you're aware of your critical parent, give yourself credit for noticing. You might acknowledge it to yourself, "This is the critical parent." You can then ask yourself, "What would a loving parent do or say in this situation?" Other inner family members may express these signs and characteristics too. We will discuss this further in later chapters.

Worksheet: *Common Situations and Times the Critical Parent Shows Up*

Jot down any physical sensations and emotions you remember having in the situations below. Tracking these common cues can help you recognize when the critical parent shows up in the future. The Appendix D: "Feelings, Needs & Physical Sensations Sheet" (page 224) might be a useful reference.

Sometimes, our critical parent is activated before we even engage in the situations below: simply considering or contemplating a vulnerable situation can activate the critical parent. As you move through the following worksheet, try to recall moments you've considered one of these actions and perhaps decided against it: for example, can you recall a time when you have wanted to cry or express emotions in front of another person, and had your critical parent convince you against doing so?

Worksheet: *Common Situations and Times the Critical Parent Shows Up*			
Situation	**Physical Sensations**	**Emotions**	**Memories, mental images, thoughts, or other cues**
You tried something new	*Fluttering in my stomach, racing, heart, shallow breathing, tight jaw*	*Fear, dread, embarrassment*	*Memory of faltering during a speech in the past, image of disgusted faces, thoughts like, "You're going to screw this up," "You're not prepared," "This is dumb."*
You "made a mistake"			
You spoke up and broke the "Don't talk, Don't Trust, Don't Feel" rule			
You wore something different than you usually do			
You cried or expressed emotions in front of others			
You ate in front of others			
You pursued something you wanted			
You didn't get something you wanted			
Someone else did well or got praised in your presence			
Someone showed you how to do something			

Situation	Physical Sensations	Emotions	Memories, mental images, thoughts, or other cues
You had unpleasant feelings or feelings you judge as unacceptable			
You asked for help or contemplated asking for help			
You worked on something important to you			
You set a boundary with someone or said "no"			
You didn't uphold a commitment you made			
You did something silly, playful			

Reflections: *Identifying What Activates Your Critical Parent*

1. What other situations and times generally seem to activate your critical parent?

2. Your critical parent may get more active around certain types of people. With whom do you notice your critical parent getting activated?

3. In what situations is your critical parent more likely to criticize *you* rather than others?

4. In what situations is your critical parent more likely to criticize *others* rather than you?

"When I am around "accomplished" people who are doing things I admire, my critical parent compares me to them and judges me harshly." -Fellow Traveler

The Loving Parent Needs to Intervene

The critical parent can appear powerful and overwhelming to an inner child, because in childhood, our parents had all the power. When we were young, we didn't have an inner loving parent to intervene in the ways we needed. Today, when the critical parent is in charge, the inner child gets hurt by their judgments. It's the loving parent's job to step in and protect the inner child. One quick way to do that is to write down or say a counterbalancing statement to the critical parent's spoken or unspoken message. For example, if they say, "You're wasting your life," you might say, "This is what mom used to tell me; it was wrong then, and it's wrong now."

Left: critical parent in charge; *Right:* loving parent back in charge

The critical parent appears to wield enormous power, but like the Wizard of Oz (just a small person hiding behind a big mean voice), they can't do much. The more frequently our loving parent steps in, the quicker our critical parent will learn to step aside and relax.

Approaching the critical parent with gentleness can diminish their power. It also makes it more possible to let go of the shame of having a critical parent and imagine a new path forward together. When your critical parent gets activated, you can let your inner children know, "Here's the reason why you don't need to believe that right now...." and then offer an alternative perspective. You can place your attention in your body and remind yourself that you have a choice to redirect your attention to helping the critical parent relax, or focus on caring for your inner children.

"I thanked my critical parent for keeping us alive for so long. 'We need you; you know our darkest fears and secrets, but you are no longer in charge. The loving parent is now in charge. Let us know if we are missing something, and we will call an inner family meeting with our higher power and loving parent.' My inner children started coming out to meet me when my critical parent's power over me diminished. I am amazed at my healing; it has been gradual." -Fellow Traveler

N.I.P. - Nip it in the Bud

1. N - Notice when the critical parent arrives on the scene. Take a deep breath to create space.

2. I - Identify the exact nature of the attack. Is your critical parent judging you, blaming you, yelling at you, controlling you, calling you names? Are they judging others, blaming others, yelling at others, calling others names, or wanting to control others? Label the specific behavior. (You will start to see patterns the critical parent uses.)

3. P - Parent yourself by replacing the distorted messages with loving parent messages.

"The more I was able to see the critical parent as a part of myself who was trying to help, I realized how exhausted they must be. That made it easier to be able to say, 'I've got this, I'm okay.'" -Fellow Traveler

It is Okay to Detach from the Critical Parent

"I discovered that I was living according to my critical parent; I had made them my higher power, even though I claimed to have a caring and loving higher power." -Fellow Traveler

In the beginning, we might not be open to the idea of thanking our critical parent or seeing their positive intention. We might have experienced the critical parent as a perpetrator and our inner children might be too angry with them or scared of them for this gratitude to feel accessible. In this case, we can set a boundary of not listening to the critical parent and give ourselves space to consider the critical parent's positive intention at a later time.

While it might seem wise to rebel against the critical parent, this could subconsciously place them in a position of authority and reproduce the pain of our family of origin. Spending precious time and emotional resources arguing with them might unintentionally give them more power.

Instead, we can treat the critical parent the same way we would a friend caught in The Problem. We can have compassion for them, but set an internal boundary when they're not willing to move into The Solution. A neutral tone with the critical parent can be an effective pivot from habitual inner conflict. When the critical parent appears, a simple, "Hi," or "It's okay," or "I see you" works.

Such acknowledgments help you avoid overreacting by either believing the critical parent ("You're right. I'm worthless") or assuming your recovery is ineffective ("My critical parent is still here. I must be doing this wrong"). Instead, you can simply acknowledge the critical parent and invite them to relax. This also allows you to relax, and reduces the impact of your critical parent on your life.

If we've placed our critical parent in a position of inner authority, we might be afraid of detaching. We might believe we need our critical parent's harshness to get things done, not harm others, or stay safe. When these fears arise, we can remember why we came to ACA: because having our critical parent in the driver's seat had made our lives unmanageable. We can take Steps 1, 2, and 3 to practice letting go, and trusting that our higher power will help us find a different way to live.

"To thank my critical parent and say, 'I've got this,' felt very scary but also interesting. By being gentle, they went into the background, which is usually not possible because I fight with them, even when I think I don't." -Fellow Traveler

Building Trust by Becoming Your Own Loving Parent

Whether you see your critical inner parent's positive intention or have detached from them for the time being, they won't stop intervening unless they trust the loving parent will be there to protect, love, support, and guide the inner family. Messages like the following—when heartfelt—can help the critical parent trust that you recognize their intentions and are beginning to become your own loving parent:

- I get why you think that's important.
- I appreciate and respect what you did for me in childhood. It is deeply sad/horrible/painful

that there was no one else around to take care of us the way that you did.

- I understand why you are so hypervigilant. You had to be prepared to handle a lot of unexpected, terrifying situations.
- In order to live our best life, we need to allow the inner children to feel and express their feelings. Trying to control them hasn't worked.

When the critical parent steps back and the loving parent steps in, we can then attend to our inner child's feelings and needs. Over time, we stop trying to manage ourselves by listening to critical parent messages. With a loving parent in charge, we can trust that we will act from clarity and compassion toward our inner children and inner teen. When we don't, we can make amends.

"In early recovery, my inner critic went looking inside for my inner children, which didn't work well. My sponsor suggested I first cultivate my inner loving parent. I inventoried my inner critic and asked my higher power to help me become my own loving parent. I adopted ideas and examples from long-time fellow travelers and TV, like Mr. Rogers. I began to cobble together the loving language and self-care actions that would replace my inner critic's old ways. It took time and a lot of practice, but eventually my inner loving parent began to disarm my inner critic." -Fellow Traveler

gentleness break

As you begin to break the "Don't Talk, Don't Trust, Don't Feel" rule, your critical parent may become more reactive. This is because you're breaking deeply conditioned patterns that conflict with how the critical parent thinks you "should" behave. As you continue to set healthy internal boundaries and care for your inner children, this will lessen. Consider doing something nourishing for yourself as a gentleness break before proceeding.

Setting Boundaries with the Critical Parent

Earlier in this chapter, we learned how the N.I.P. method could help the loving parent intervene when the inner child was being hurt by the critical parent's judgments. Setting gentle internal boundaries with the critical parent is a crucial way for us to diminish their power, relieve them of their burden, and help integrate them into the inner family in a cooperative way.

Guided Practice: *Setting Boundaries with the Critical Parent by Summoning the Loving Parent*

This guided practice helps you connect to what it feels like to set a gentle boundary with your critical parent—a skill that will serve you well on your reparenting journey.

Note: As with all guided practices in this book, please refer to the "Guided Practice Preparation" in Appendix B for suggestions and precautions, and to access the opening script. [Begin recording, read the opening script, and continue reading the script here...]

You awaken from a night's rest to a soft light filtering through your bedroom window. The sheets are soft and pleasing against your skin.

You shift in the bed. Your stomach tightens, and your heart races. Your breathing becomes ragged. You feel confused. You have no pressing appointments today or anything else that would cause you to feel this way.

You remember hearing a fellow traveler share how they try to notice what they're thinking whenever they feel uncomfortable. When you tune in to your thoughts, you notice a running commentary about the day—what you have to do, how little time you have to do it, and the like. This might come as a voice, physical sensations, images, or just a sense of dread.

You call on your loving parent, who knows what to do from a clear, loving place. Your loving parent addresses your critical parent in a gentle but firm tone.

"Thank you for your concern. I'm here now. You can relax and take a break."

You take a deep breath. The critical parent begins to speak again, and your loving parent speaks up. "I know you're trying to protect us, and I've got this." Your body relaxes a bit.

You stretch and prepare to get out of bed. The critical parent shows up again, and you realize you can be free to move on with your day, even if the critical parent is there. You don't need to listen to what they say. The more your loving parent shows up, the more the critical parent will relax.

When you're ready, slowly open your eyes or lift your gaze. Reconnect to the here and now. Look around your space and let this feeling continue into your day. [End recording]

Reflections: *Setting Boundaries with the Critical Parent by Summoning the Loving Parent*

There is no right or wrong way to experience this guided practice. The purpose is to feel what it's like to set a boundary and gently detach from the critical parent. When you are ready, answer the following questions:

1. What was the guided practice like for you? Were you able to create a boundary?

2. If you created a boundary with the critical parent, how did that feel?

3. If you didn't create a boundary, what came up that prevented that? How did that feel?

4. Anything else you'd like to share about your experience?

Critical Parent Boundary Statements

The guided practice gave some examples of internal boundary statements that you can use with your critical inner parent: "Thank you for your concern. I'm here now. You can relax and take a break."

It's good to experiment with different boundary statements to discover what works best for you. Here are some other examples to try out:

- "It's okay" affirmations from the BRB, page 329 (e.g., "It's okay to make mistakes and learn.").
- I know you want to help, but your judgments are making things harder.
- I see your good intention but I need some space right now.
- What are you trying to protect us from? (If you feel curious and can empathize with the critical parent's answer.)
- Here's what I know about the situation _____ (share perspective). I can handle it.
- I'm not comfortable with how you're talking, it's scaring the little one.
- I know you want to protect the little one. I'm in charge of _____ (safety, etc.) now.

"What works for me is to love all the parts of myself. That means listening to the critical parent and responding with 'Thanks for sharing,' followed by a counteracting statement such as, 'And just for today, I think differently.' This works better than trying to kick this part. As a result, my critical parent feels heard, seen and felt, resulting in a reduced amount of intensity and frequency of hearing from that part of myself." -Fellow Traveler

Reflections: *Critical Parent Boundary Statements*

1. What internal boundary statements are effective with your inner critical parent? See if you can come up with at least three or four that feel right to you.

2. What other internal boundaries or ways of practicing healthy detachment from your critical parent can you think of?

"As I said affirmations in the mirror, a voice told me I was getting old and fat. After a few minutes of insulting each other, I told my critical parent to sit on a bench on my deck and said, 'Stay there until you learn how to treat me with respect.' A few days later while driving to work, I looked in the mirror to give myself a positive affirmation. The critical parent judged me again. We had another round of insults. I sent him to the back seat and said, 'Sit there until you learn how to treat me nicely.' To my surprise, he said, 'But I don't know how to do that.' I said, 'We can learn together.'" -Fellow Traveler

Exercise: *Critical Parent Boundary Partner Practice*

Practicing boundary setting with a fellow traveler or sponsor can be helpful and even a little bit fun. Each person will make their own list of critical parent messages. List some of yours below:

_____

_____

_____

_____

Next, share your list with your partner. Your partner role plays your critical parent and says one statement from your list to you. Pause and notice how you feel. Respond to your partner with one internal boundary statements—your own or an example from the previous section. Pause and notice how you feel after setting this boundary.

Have your partner continue through your list until they have delivered all your statements, and you've replied with a boundary statement each time. Take some time to share what the experience was like for you both, then switch roles.

Just as we can role-play difficult conversations with other people ahead of time, we can prepare for critical parent attacks using this exercise and share about our efforts with trusted others.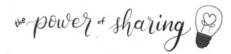

Exercise: *Write a Letter to Your Critical Parent*

We can begin to change our habits by activating our loving parent to work with our critical parent. We can start by writing a letter to the critical parent, recognizing their efforts to help us survive and giving thanks for their helpful intention, if we can. Ask the critical parent how else they would like to serve you today. Perhaps you can ask if they'd like to take a break and relax for a while. Sign the letter in whatever way feels authentic.

Sample letter to the critical parent:

Dear critical parent,

I recognize how hard you worked to keep the little one safe for so many years. There was no place for feelings back then. You did your best to help us cope. You helped us survive. I'm here now, and I'll be in charge of safety from now on. Your criticisms can hurt the inner child and make the inner teenager defensive. You can speak to me directly about your concerns. It's okay to trust me, take a break, and relax.

Love, your loving parent

Your letter:

After you complete your letter, give yourself a chance to be with any feelings that arise, tending to any parts of you who need your loving attention. Consider reading your letter to a sponsor or fellow traveler(s).

Your Key Chapter Takeaway(s):

Affirmation / Meditation

May I have the awareness and courage to practice healthy detachment from my critical parent.
May I trust that love and compassion can guide my inner family toward wholeness.

Discovering Your Inner Teenager

Meditation / Prayer
May I open to my inner teenager, learn to accept
them just the way they are, and support them to heal.

The sometimes turbulent teenage years are an essential time to learn how to establish and test boundaries. Our teenage years are when we begin the process of individuation—learning to separate from our families of origin and discover our own identities. In dysfunctional families, unclear boundaries made it hard to know whether we were living our own life or people-pleasing for the approval of others.

Our inner teen developed reactive ways of coping with these dysfunctional situations and unclear boundaries: sometimes it was panicked heroism and an overdeveloped sense of responsibility; sometimes rage, defensiveness, and cynicism; and in some cases hopelessness and numbing behaviors. Our inner teenager may demonstrate some of these behaviors more than others, or they may rely on some combination of them. This teenager, with their intense feelings and behaviors, still lives inside us and reacts from the pain, resentment, and outrage of not being seen or heard as a person in their own right.

The good news is that we can individuate in a healthy way *now*. We are already doing so, by disentangling from dysfunctional authority figures–even if they operate only in our heads–who undermine our ability to care for our own needs and set boundaries.

As we listen less to critical voices, and rely on our loving parent instead, we create an opportunity to lessen our inner teen's reliance on reactive behaviors. Our inner teenager learned these behaviors when they did not know what they needed. Our loving parent can help them feel their feelings and uncover their needs, the way they would've if our families had been healthy. This will allow our inner teen to release their old patterns.

Becoming our own loving parent allows us to address the buried pain which is the source of our inner teenager's reactivity. By addressing this pain, our inner teen's compulsion to react subsides and trust in our loving parent grows. With the help of our ACA support group, our loving parent can give our inner teenager the support and guidance they've long needed.

Our inner teen then grows into an invaluable member of our inner family. They help us access and honor our inner knowing and stay true to our boundaries. Through this process of nurturance and integration, we can emerge with a liberating sense of who we are, what we need, and how we can get it – through the loving parent's gentleness, humor, love, and respect.

The Inner Teenager

Your inner teenager may not welcome you with open arms. That's okay. Their mistrust, anger, or indifference toward you will soften as you continue to show up for them. Give them space, and they will connect when they are ready.

The inner teen can take many forms. Sometimes, they are the strong, angry, and sometimes impulsive or rebellious inner family member who reacts strongly to emotional triggers. In other cases, they are overly responsible, don't trust others, and try to take care of everything themselves. Some inner teens are hopeless, depressed, and prone to numbing behaviors—they have learned that anger would either be violently suppressed, disapproved of, or simply ignored, and so they have stuffed their angry feelings. Many inner teens rely on a combination of these strategies and patterns—the result of multiple traumas in different areas of our lives and at different ages. Each of these inner teens needs our love, but has trouble admitting it.

Many of us went through our teenager years without the protection we needed. We endured egregious physical, verbal, or even sexual abuse without an adult to keep us safe. We needed someone to be looking out for and caring for us. Other adult children may have been neglected entirely, and left alone for days on end without engagement with any family members.

In all these situations, the important emotional needs of being seen, heard, respected, and valued weren't met for many of us in our teenage years. We needed guidance and support to individuate, learn to set boundaries, and respect others' boundaries. Those unmet needs left us with pain and rage that live on in us today in the form of our inner teenager. With support, our inner teen can release this rage and their positive traits can come to the fore: you may find that your inner teen is authentic, brave, resourceful, or direct: deeply connected to your inner knowing.

Without a loving parent in the driver's seat, the inner teen can try to play a few roles in the inner family:

- They try to fix, distract from, or numb the inner child's painful feelings,
- They defend the inner child's fragile sense of self to anyone who threatens it, and
- They let you know when you – the adult – haven't honored your inner knowing or your own boundaries (which, in turn, abandons the inner child).

The inner teenager might not realize you're an adult, or might not even be aware of your adult self's existence. They became frozen in time: trying to survive life alone and carrying the responsibility of keeping the inner child hidden and safe. When the inner child has painful feelings, the inner teen responds and can act out through you, often without your awareness. The inner teen focuses on "fixing" feelings instead of "feeling" feelings. Until you build their trust, the inner teenager tries to fix these feelings by relying on survival mechanisms, including distorted types of thinking, addictions, compulsions, and traits from either of The Laundry Lists.

If we can identify and connect with our inner teen, we might be able to more easily access our inner child, as we'll do in Chapter 7. Without a clear connection with our inner teen, we may confuse the inner child and inner teen. The inner teen needs different kinds of support and guidance from our loving parent than our inner child.

"I did things like paragliding and flirting for connection, thinking this was exploring my inner child, but it was my inner teen without an inner loving parent." -Fellow Traveler

Some Inner Teenager Patterns

Inner teenagers can accomplish their primary roles by employing many different strategies. Your inner teenager may primarily rely on one set of strategies, or on some combination of strategies.

Below are three kinds of inner teenager patterns and strategies:

- A hero or parentified[1] inner teenager, trying to save the family of origin.
    - o Inner teenagers with this pattern might respond to scary situations with panicked attempts at problem-solving, control, planning, or management. They are scared yet stubborn and resolute in their feeling that no one is capable of or willing to help them. They only trust themselves.
- A rebellious, defensive, or insubordinate inner teenager.
    - o Wants to burn everything to the ground.
    - o Thinks other people are dishonest, fake, incompetent, controlling, unhelpful. Tries to control them as a result.
    - o A stubborn voice that rejects recovery behaviors. "I don't want to, and you can't make me!"
- A shut-down or pleasure-seeking inner teenager.
    - o Seeks out stimulation, adrenaline, sex, or intoxicating substances to numb painful feelings or out of an addiction to excitement.

While these patterns might seem quite dissimilar at first, they have a core characteristic in common: each is a way of relating to anger.

The rebel inner teenager has an explosive relationship with anger, turning to it as the solution to all challenging emotions and boundary violations.

The parentified inner teenager avoids feeling their frustration at their abandoning and unsupportive environment, and instead tries to fix situations for other people. This cultivates resentment and a simmering rage that can explode unexpectedly, often towards ourselves.

The pleasure-seeking or shut-down inner teen numbs their anger because they feel hopeless or depressed. Knowing something at home was amiss in their dysfunctional family, and yet feeling helpless and unable to change anything, might have led them to shut down or "freeze." They might have stopped "fighting" because they learned that anger would be violently suppressed, disapproved of, or simply didn't change anything. They learned to comply to survive, but that meant stuffing

---

1 Parentification happens when a child or teenager is put in the position of parenting their own parent or sibling(s): perhaps by managing adult household tasks, or by providing emotional support to a caregiver(s) as a confidante or mediator.

their anger. This teen is the part of us that can lead us to an abyss of numbing behaviors and chemical substances.

Getting angry might seem pointless to the parentified or shut-down inner teen, but it doesn't mean the anger isn't there. They might need time, reassurance that it's okay to feel anger today, and a safe place, perhaps with a therapist, to access the outrage today. Your inner teen can learn to express their anger to your loving parent, knowing that you—the adult—will stand up for them in healthy ways.

Since each of these inner teens holds a lot of anger, they share many common tendencies, like:

- An adept side-stepper: "yes-but" response to situations requiring vulnerability.
- A sarcastic rebel: smart comments, wise cracks, and an unwillingness to engage in many situations.
- A cynical downer: being hopeless, jaded, or bitter, and having a negative outlook on life. Defensive, judgmental, or critical (similar in some ways to the inner critical parent, which we'll explore later in this guide).boundaries (which, in turn, abandons the inner child).
- Terribly, deeply hurt – and lashing out to cope with or cover the pain.

Our inner teen can get our attention through thoughts, images, and strong physical sensations. We may notice ourselves using The Other Laundry List or The Laundry List traits. The inner teen's anger or rage might appear in our body language, facial expressions, or gestures. We might experience a clenched jaw, heat in the hands and arms, or a rapid heart rate. Our thoughts tend to focus on people, places, and things, rather than on our feelings and needs. Blame arises.

The ability to access and process anger—which can be terrifying for those of us who learned to shut down to survive—can help us reclaim our full range of emotions. We can use the supportive resources we identified in the preface and our fellowship to help us do so safely.

Our inner-family members are unique to each of us, and we can get to know them by observing them and being with them. Mindfulness, which you've learned about in Chapter 4, can help you get to know your inner teen and recognize when they get triggered.

"My inner teenager is the part of me that protects my inner child against the critical parent. He used to be mad at me, too, because I didn't set boundaries or meet his needs or my inner child's needs. Listening to him and changing my behavior means he trusts me more nowadays. I can dialogue with him. And when I fall back on one of my traits, he is more understanding because he knows I care about him, my inner child, and that I'm doing my best." -Fellow Traveler

Guided Practice: *Discovering Your Inner Teen*

Note: As with all guided practices in this book, please refer to the "Guided Practice Preparation" in Appendix B for suggestions and precautions, and to access the opening script. [Begin recording, read the opening script, and continue reading the script here...]

Invite your inner teenager into your awareness. This inner family member is welcome here, whether they're combative or cautious, tired or lively, clear to you or murky. Notice how you feel as you open to this part of yourself. (Pause)

(Pause) Thank your inner teenager for protecting the inner child all these years. Thank them for being here now. Ask if they're willing to share with you what they want to protect the little one from. How do they try to do that? How does your inner teen respond? Make room for silence if they prefer not to answer. If they share something, thank them for sharing it with you.

(Pause between each question) Can you understand how desperately they've been trying to avoid pain? How outraged they feel at not being seen, heard, supported, respected, or valued? How resentful they are of everyone who has failed them? How alone and hopeless they've felt? Let them know that you wish it had been different for them back in the family, that you understand why they've been doing what they've been doing.

Reflect for a moment on how your inner teen has been working for many years to protect the inner child, to defend them, and to distract them from unpleasant feelings. Even if your inner teen's behavior has unpleasant or isolating consequences, you can begin to see that their heart is in the right place. They may not even like playing this role in your inner family, but they believe that they must, in order to ward off the pain (Pause).

Maybe they react at times because they want you, their loving parent, to honor their inner knowing, to set boundaries, to rely on trustworthy individuals/to ask for help, and to be a healthy adult voice for them and the inner child. Maybe they are tired of fighting and being hypervigilant. Maybe they are frustrated by all the people who don't show up for them and who they think they need to manage.

Deep down, they might just want to relax and trust you to lead and take care of the inner family as a loving parent. Ask them what kind of support they need from you. (Pause) See if it's possible to support them in these ways in your everyday life, the best you can.

Let them know that you'll be there to listen as they express all that they've bottled up inside. Reassure them that they can choose when to connect with you and when not to. (Pause) It's okay if they don't trust you yet. You will wait until they're ready. You are never leaving.

See if it's possible to keep your heart open to your inner teen, whether they connected with you during this guided practice or not. Thank them for visiting with you and for their courage. (Pause) Check in with how you're feeling as this practice comes to a close. (Pause) Take a few deep breaths. (Pause) When you're ready, open your eyes or lift your gaze and connect with the world around you. [End recording]

Reflections: *Discovering Your Inner Teen Guided Practice*

Sometimes it can be hard to bring up the inner teenager. They can have powerful energy. We can revisit this guided practice to keep connecting more deeply with this part of ourselves.

1. What was it like to open to your inner teen; what was your experience?

2. What did you learn about your inner teenager?

3. What was difficult? What was easy?

4. Which survival strategies or inner teen patterns does your inner teen seem to rely on most? Do they have behaviors that don't seem to fit any of the patterns?

5. What more would you like to know about your inner teenager?

6. What are some ways you could learn more about your inner teen?

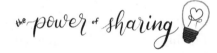

Exercise: *Inner Teen Field Notebook*

You can learn about your inner teenager by keeping track of when they appear through emotions, thoughts, bodily sensations, or other cues. For several days or weeks, keep a journal, notepad, or note app handy.

- Record any reactive, panicked, distrustful, or numbing behaviors or thoughts you experience that seem to come from your inner teenager.
- Track your inner teen's tone, volume, and impulses.
- Jot down when and where your inner teen gets activated.
- Identify where you feel your inner teen in space (e.g., inside or outside your body, close by, or far away).

If you'd rather take an inventory each day, choose from the questions below or use your own:

- Was my inner teenager reactive, panicked, distrustful, or numbing/numb today? If so, how did they feel? What thoughts or trigger led to their response?
- Did my inner teen view anyone as an authority figure and become rebellious, defensive, or impulsive? Did they get frustrated at any situations with other people?
- Did my inner teen try to distract from unpleasant feelings? If so, what feelings did my inner teen want to numb?
- What healthy qualities did I notice in my inner teenager today?

The awareness we gain from observing our inner teen helps us better understand them. We'll then be more likely to notice when they get triggered in the course of a day. Rather than allowing the inner teen to take the lead in situations that trigger them, our loving parent can tend to the feelings and distorted thinking that are driving their reactions. We may even begin to recognize the inner teen in the times we're courageous, funny, witty, clear, direct, protective, and authentic.

Exercise: *Journaling about Your Teenage Years*

Another way to connect with your inner teenager is by writing about your teenage years. Journal or use some other way to explore losses, experiences of peer pressure, your relationships and feelings about sex, and how you experienced and responded to strong emotions, such as anger and resentment.

Was there room for you to be you back then? What was your family role—hero, lost child, scapegoat, or mascot? How did these role(s) become part of your identity? What challenging events happened during those years? What does your inner teenager most need from your loving parent today?

As you revisit your teenage years, reflect on your core wound(s) from that time. What was most painful? Not being heard? Not being seen? Not being supported? Not mattering? Not being respected? Distrust of authority? Shame for having been powerless over changing what happened in your dysfunctional family? Being overly responsible? Or something else?

Inviting your loving parent and a power greater than yourself into the process can help your inner family members feel more comfortable when beginning this exploration. Record your main discoveries below, if you'd like:

_____

_____

_____

Some Common Inner Teenager Triggers and Reactions

"My inner child needs comforting. My inner teen needs to be noticed in her anger." -Fellow Traveler

The inner teen can be triggered by unmet needs—theirs and those of the inner child. Some important inner teen needs are fairness, respect, autonomy, authenticity, integrity, to matter, to be seen, and to be heard. When these needs aren't met, the inner teen can act out in rage, frustration, resentment, contempt, distraction, and/or impatience. Inner teenagers can also feel deep loss about the lack of support and guidance they received during adolescence.

The inner teen's reactions are designed to help provide a sense of power, but it is false power. The inner teen tries to control rather than feel "out of control." Angry or resentful positions like, "I'm right; you're wrong" or "You hurt me; now I'll hurt you" usually come from this acting-out place. If reacting in anger doesn't quiet the unpleasant feelings, the inner teenager might try to

Some ways the inner teen distracts/ numbs out: compulsive shopping, sleeping, work, sex, food (restricting or overindulging), exercise, video games, reading, addictions, self-harm, violence, arguments, dissociation, avoidance, obsession, compulsions, fantasy, etc.

distract from or stuff the inner child's painful feelings and pretend they don't exist. They might also suppress the feelings with substances or compulsive behaviors. Sometimes, inner teens may try to control "out of control" situations by resentfully compensating for absent or unhealthy adults: they take over situations and attempt to control others.

New projects, opportunities, or relationships might trigger the inner child's abandonment fears. The inner teen might spring into action to reduce those uncomfortable feelings. They can become uncooperative and temperamental on teams; they might panic and assume responsibility for more than their share; they might procrastinate, avoid situations and people, and fall short of commitments.

"I thought it was time to meet my inner teenager after finding an old photo of my actual teenage self. I looked angry and depressed, with black eyeliner and a dyed black mohawk. When my inner teenager is activated, I'm right back in the 80s, with two middle fingers raised to any and all authority. My inner-mohawk grows. Leather-spiked armor appears around me, saying "keep a safe distance," or "look at me, I'm special, I matter." I respond to situations the way I did when I was in my family: the solution to just about everything is to burn it down to the ground. I want to engage in self-harm and lash out at myself, instead of directing healthy anger at injustice, expressing my pain, or asking for help." -Fellow Traveler

Inner Teen Trigger: Criticism–Real or Perceived

When someone judges or criticizes us today, the inner child might take it to heart and feel hurt. The inner teenager might then argue and try to prove the other person wrong to distract from those painful feelings and validate the inner child. This might occur only in our head and build resentment, or we might get directly into heated conversations or arguments.

This mental replaying of the situation over and over (rumination) shifts the focus away from the inner child's more vulnerable feelings. Unfortunately, rumination creates anxiety, dread, or being overwhelmed, which eventually causes the inner teen to lash out, withdraw, or withhold.

Inner Teen Trigger: Not Honoring Our Own Boundaries & Inner Knowing

At times, you might engage in codependent behaviors, not set or maintain your own safe boundaries, or not honor your needs or inner knowing. This can happen without being aware that you, the adult, are acting out the reactions of your inner child or critical parent. If these reactions, driven by the inner child or critical parent, compromise your sense of safety and integrity, the inner teen can be angered and can spring into action. The ways that other inner family members respond when they are triggered, can thus end up triggering the teenager in turn.

Observe when the inner teenager gets triggered, using the information in the following chart as cues. Further discussion and examples of boundary issues can be found in Chapter 13. We'll explore these inner teen triggers more deeply in Chapter 18.

Note: The inner teenager can also act out through our behavior in ways that cause us to violate our own boundaries. However, the focus of this section is on boundary violations that trigger the inner teenager, not the boundary violations caused by the inner teen's reactions.

When you as an adult:	**Your inner teen may:**

Your inner teen may:

Isolate, avoid.

Self-medicate compulsively; confuse self-indulgence with self-nurturance.

Try to frantically plan, manage, and control situations to reduce and suppress challenging emotions.

When you as an adult:

Don't end a conversation when you want.

Encounter a situation that the inner child finds scary or overwhelming.

Say *yes* when you want to say *no*.

People-please.

Don't set or maintain boundaries.

Don't "speak up" for the inner child or inner teen's needs.

Don't address or resolve conflicts and issues.

Rebel (passively or actively, through procrastination, perfectionism, "analysis paralysis", sabotage, argumentativeness, conflict).

Get defensive, passive-aggressive, argue, prove others wrong, insist on being "right."

Try to become perfect to avoid or deflect criticism.

Be judgmental and controlling, victimize others.

Dissociate, distract, ruminate, obsess, get lost in fantasy.

Take another person's behavior personally ("They are out to get me," "They are disrespecting me.")

Reflections: *Identifying Your Inner Teenager*

You might find it helpful to imagine you're in a situation that triggers your inner teenager and answer the questions below from that place. Notice any emotions, bodily sensations, thoughts, images, and words that arise. Take gentleness breaks as needed.

1. What does your inner teenager look/feel like? You might wish to draw your inner teenager.

2. List some characteristics that describe your inner teenager. (e.g., assertive, resourceful, tough, defensive, shut down, etc.)

3. Ask your inner teenager what they'd like you to call them. They might give you a name or a title, like Defender, Rebel, or Champion.

4. What reactive thoughts or phrases occur when your inner teen is activated? (e.g., "What do they want from me? Why can't they leave me alone? No one knows what they're doing. Stop trying to control me!")

5. How do you behave when your wounded inner teen takes over? (e.g., distracts me with certain activities, lashes out or blames others, wants to numb)

6. What physical sensations in your body tell you that your inner teenager is activated?

7. What is your inner teenager's role in your inner family (you might ask your inner teenager this question)? How are they trying to help you in their own way?

8. What does your inner teenager want you to know? Feel free to ask them.

"I can feel the rage bubbling up when I'm cut off, ignored, or not validated. Just like in my family of origin." -Fellow Traveler

The Inner Teenager's Positive Intention

Like the inner child, the inner teenager has been alone and without support for years, but with the added burden of protecting the inner child. The inner teenager has done the best they could to figure out how to cope and survive, with limited resources, skills, and guidance. It was never our inner teen's job to care for themselves and the inner child, and it's not their job now. They likely felt compelled to take on that role because no one else did so. By understanding their positive intentions as a loving parent, we can relieve them of their burdens and unfair responsibilities. They will begin to feel the healthy freedom and vitality that they missed out on in their younger years.

Understanding what your inner teen is trying to achieve can help you step in as their loving parent to offer healthier strategies. Instead of numbing to avoid the pain or lashing out, your loving parent can help your inner teen lower the intensity by taking deep breaths and grounding their awareness in the present moment. Try to see their positive intentions and have compassion for how they have had to fend for themselves. Tune in to how they feel and imagine what they need. Alternatively, you can ask them, and make space for their answer. Nurture them.

Your loving parent can help the inner teenager trust that the strategies they learned made sense at the time but are unlikely to meet long-term needs today. The adult you can follow up by addressing the issues that concern them from a place of clarity.

Reflections: *Inner Teen Survival Mechanisms*

1. What activities has your inner teenager historically engaged in to distract from or numb unpleasant feelings (e.g., alcohol, drugs, food, sex, relationships, porn, gambling, internet, television, work, exercise, shopping, etc.)?

2. What numbing or distraction activities does your inner teen engage in today?

3. What feelings does your inner teenager try to avoid, eliminate, numb, or distract from by engaging in these activities (e.g., sadness, fear, guilt, shame, etc.)?

4. What are the short-term benefits of avoiding those uncomfortable feelings? What are the long-term costs?

5. What actions can you take if you recognize your inner teenager is in a reactive state and wants to lash out, procrastinate, control, avoid, panic, distract, manage, numb, or indulge?

The more your loving parent steps in to tend to the inner child's pain, the less your inner teenager needs to engage in these behaviors. Your loving parent can keep showing up for both the inner child and inner teenager to help them feel safe. You'll learn more about the inner child in the next chapter.

"Though my inner teenager gets great satisfaction in the physical (or emotional) slamming of the bedroom door when frustrated, I have better tools now. I can identify when my inner teenager is asking to be heard and lovingly reparent myself by acknowledging my inner teen's feelings and needs, without letting those feelings lead to behaviors that sabotage my adult life. I have learned to integrate, not ignore, my inner teenager as a part of my inner family, and together we stay in emotional sobriety." -Fellow Traveler

Developing a Cooperative Relationship with Your Inner Teenager

You can develop a cooperative relationship with your inner teen by listening to them and making healthy changes, such as honoring your need to say "no" and speaking your truth. The more you "walk the talk" and make an effort to connect with them, they more they will trust you. Until then, they might try to keep the inner child safe and hidden away by relying on survival mechanisms.

To nurture a healthy relationship with the inner teen:

- Give your inner teenager time and attention and try to be gentle. They can be quite tender behind their armor.
- Protect and honor your inner child by upholding healthy boundaries with other people and by addressing boundary violations with others in healthy ways. Jot down when and where your inner teen gets activated.
- Help the inner teenager pause when strong emotions arise. Then choose a course of action as a loving parent rather than reacting as the inner teen.
- Allow your inner teen to express themselves to you and try not to take any reactions personally—even if they're angry or yelling at you. They've had nowhere safe to share their pain, and being with them without needing to fix their feelings can go a long way toward building trust.
- Set healthy internal boundaries with your inner teen, even if they seem to balk at them.
- Give them hope; help them trust you'll care for the inner child so that they longer feel compelled to do so.

The inner child's feelings of helplessness propel the inner teenager to control. You can help the inner teenager trust in a power greater than ourselves and our loving parent. "I see how mad you are and how that person's behavior doesn't meet your needs. We're so powerless over other people. I see how much it hurts. I've got your back and so does a power greater than ourselves." You might then be able to help your inner teen let it go, or you might need to address the issue with the other person.

"When I ask my inner teenager questions, she often yells or swears at me and calls me names. At first, I was so hurt that I took long breaks between communication attempts. Eventually, I developed the ability to hold space for her anger." -Fellow Traveler

Exercise: *Letter of Appreciation to the Inner Teenager*

You can show appreciation for your inner teenager's positive intentions by writing them a letter. Focus on connecting with this part of yourself from your heart and in your own words. They might want to be seen for alerting you to boundary violations or for the needs they're trying to meet. Acknowledge what it has cost them not to have your loving parent's guidance before now.

Sample:

Dear inner teenager,

I admire your bravery and how hard you've worked to survive. Thank you for protecting the little one. I am here now to take the pressure off you. I'm so sorry you were alone for so long and haven't been seen and heard. I see you now, and you matter to me very much.

You don't have to stuff the inner child's feelings. I'll help the little one feel their feelings so they can heal. As much as you can, I want you to relax as I take care of the inner family with help from seen and unseen supports. Let's find ways for you to let off steam and have fun, too.

Love, your loving parent

Your letter:

You might want to record your letter and play it back when you can give it your full attention. Gently witness any feelings or reactions that come up as your inner teen receives the words.

Activity: *Make a Date with Your Inner Teenager*

Consistency is vital for the health of any important relationship. Make time to visit with your inner teenager regularly. Try to do things they enjoy. Here are some activities you might try:

- Listen to music from your teenage years.
- Watch a movie geared toward teenagers, or perhaps a movie you loved as a teenager.
- Reread books you liked as a teen.
- Look over pictures from your teenage years. Try to connect with the feelings that arise.

List some other ways you could connect with your inner teenager:

One way to heal your inner teenager is to meet your inner child's emotional needs. Making your inner child a priority shows your inner teenager that you're taking the lead in life. When they can trust that you are present to parent, they will feel less compelled to take over. They will be free to enrich your life with their authenticity, courage, humor, and passion.

Your Key Chapter Takeaway(s):

Affirmation / Meditation

As my inner teenager learns to trust my loving parent, they will help me honor my inner knowing and stay true to my boundaries. I will emerge with a powerful sense of who I am, what I want, and how I can get it: with gentleness, humor, love, and respect.

Discovering Your Inner Child

Meditation / Prayer
May my inner child find the safety and freedom to express all the hurts and fears they have kept inside,
freeing us from the shame and blame that are carryovers from the past.

While the inner child can be the spark of our creativity, the child is also a deeply hurt part of us. The cycles of abandonment, neglect, and abuse make it hard for children in dysfunctional families to develop self-worth and healthy coping skills. Important core needs are not consistently or sufficiently met or acknowledged, leaving children with survival strategies that they carry into adulthood. The confusion and trauma of childhood can become frozen in the body and mind— waiting for a safer time to be resolved. With the help of an inner loving parent, fellow travelers, and our program, we embark upon the journey of healing these old wounds.

If children aren't supported in developing their relationship with their inner world—like learning how to separate thoughts from emotions or seeing beyond all-or-nothing thinking—the patterns of childhood can become stumbling blocks in their adult lives. For example, it's natural for children to be egocentric and to personalize everything, but this behavior can hurt, rather than help, in adulthood. Healthy parenting helps the child understand how their inner world relates to the world around them. Not only is that support missing in dysfunctional environments, but parents can also shame children for displaying their natural developmental level—calling them selfish or needy, for example—and mistreating them in other ways. Our inner child was forced to develop many survival strategies to cope with a lack of protection, nurturance, support, and guidance.

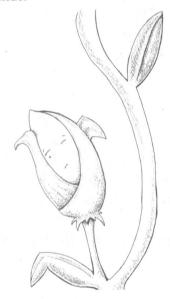

Becoming our own loving parent is at the core of healing from a dysfunctional childhood and the gateway to the gifts of the child within.

"As I have learned to connect with my inner child as part of this fellowship, sometimes I feel that it is nothing short of miraculous that we are here together learning to care for and heal ourselves after all we've been through in childhood." -Fellow Traveler

Note: We can refer to the inner child in many ways: the child within, little one, inner kid, by a name with personal meaning, and others. We might experience having one inner child or many. The gender expression or identity of the inner child might not match one's present-day gender identity. For simplicity in this guidebook, we usually refer to the inner child in the singular. We use the third-person pronoun "they."

Embracing the Inner Child

The child within holds our original loving and trusting nature. This part of us understands feelings and the language of a higher power. Some adult children consider the inner child to be their true self, while for others the inner child is an important aspect of their true self. All of us—no matter how much dysfunction we've endured—still have our inner child's precious vulnerability, intuition, spontaneity, and innocence inside us.

Fortunately, we can now give ourselves the love and support we needed in childhood. We are already doing so by engaging with this guidebook. As we learn to reparent, we accept that our inner child exists, and we prioritize caring for them. We understand that The Solution is not "to fix" but to *embrace* this part of ourselves. Reparenting creates the conditions for frozen feelings and memories to surface and heal. Gradually, our inner child releases the burden of unexpressed grief. They begin to move out of the past, leaving behind the survival mechanisms that can lock us in destructive behaviors, relationships, and dynamics.

Our inner child's natural joy, wonder, and creativity retreated when abandonment, shame, and fear forced them into hiding. By reparenting ourselves with gentleness, humor, love, and respect, our inner child becomes a cherished member of our inner family who brings us lightness and great optimism. They become a guide to creativity, fun, and spirituality. We feel more at peace and have a better grasp of our true feelings and choices. Through this process of nurturing and integration, we emerge with an expanded sense of our worth, our gifts, and our place in the world.

It's natural for a child who has experienced abandonment of any kind to be wary. Your loving parent can create the conditions needed for your inner child to emerge safely and can help you gently restore their ability to trust. This will help them emerge from their protective shell and connect when they ready. Building in your own gentleness breaks and working with a sponsor or fellow traveler can help you adjust the intensity as you make contact with your inner child in this chapter, throughout the rest of the book, and in your everyday life.

It's okay to take a
gentleness break
whenever you need to.

"When I read The Solution, it was like a spark of hope igniting my heart. Could the constant anxiety, loneliness, and lack of peace I felt be related to my inner child? I began talking to myself in a gentle way, 'It's going to be ok,'; 'I won't leave you alone.' I started sleeping better. My anxiety was directly related to a fearful inner child who needed love and attention to be free and whole." -Fellow Traveler

Exercise: *Framing a Picture of Your Inner Child*

"Keeping pictures of myself as a child on my phone helped me build a loving bond with my inner child. I went through the images, observing this beautiful, soft, and curious being. I saw past the flaws I was punished for having. Looking at those pictures allowed me to cultivate loving feelings for this being and, as a result, for myself. That has transformed how I allow myself to be treated and also how I treat others." -Fellow Traveler

This exercise can help you begin to create the conditions for your inner child to safely connect with you. By taking the time to see how vulnerable, courageous, and loving you were as a child, you grow your compassion for your inner child. This picture can serve as a gentleness reminder.

Find a photo of yourself as a young child. Choose one that doesn't hold painful memories and where you look relatively happy, calm, or comfortable. If looking at the photo evokes a pleasant response, that might be a helpful photo to use for this exercise. If not, find one that does or draw or make another representation of yourself as a young child instead. When creating, keep in mind a size that might fit into a standard picture frame.

Take the image and your inner child shopping for a picture frame or use one you have. It's important to let your inner child select the frame. If you hear judgments (e.g., "It's too childish," or "It doesn't match your decor") or feel indecisive, your critical parent might be interfering. Set a boundary: "I get it. We're trying something different, and the inner child gets to choose."

Place the photo or image in the frame and set it where you'll see it regularly. When you look at the image, offer a few kind words to your inner child. You might notice a wide range of emotions, from grief to anger to numbness. Your relationship to the photo might change over time.

"I kept pictures of myself as a child safely tucked away, along with the accompanying emotions. My husband suggested putting one on our family picture wall. I reluctantly agreed.

One day, I rounded the corner and saw my 9-year-old self. I fell to my knees and cried. At nine, I was taken from my alcoholic mother. My grandparents gained custody of me and my three siblings. I touched the picture gently, noticing drooped shoulders, a head tilted downward. I could tell she felt beaten and downtrodden. I took the picture down, sat on the floor, and hugged her tightly. Sobbing, I told her how strong she was, how loving and nurturing toward her siblings, and how proud I was of her. After sitting for quite some time, I kissed her gently, gave her a big hug, and placed her back on the wall. Now, as I walk by, I smile and tell her that I love her no matter what and give her a big thumbs up!" -Fellow Traveler

Guided Practice: *Discovering Your Inner Child*

"My vulnerable children are there, waiting. They have so many stories to tell—joys that they could never express; horrors that were inconceivable, and all they had to "forget" to win enough love and approval to survive." -Fellow Traveler

When connecting to the inner child through guided practices, some people find a pillow or stuffed animal comforting to hold. Others find that closing their eyes and visualizing or feeling the inner child works better. We offer loving parent language examples and imagery that you might wish to use. The most important thing is to find what works for you.

Note: As with all guided practices in this book, please refer to the "Guided Practice Preparation" in Appendix B for suggestions and precautions, and to access the opening script. [Begin recording, read the opening script, and continue reading the script here...]

Allow this time to be present to yourself. Imagine that you and your heart have all the space you need right now. Tune into your body, relaxing your shoulders, your jaw, and your face.

Imagine yourself in a cozy cottage nestled in a lush, safe forest. Picture yourself in a chair near a fireplace under a soft, warm blanket. Another chair faces you with a folded blanket on the arm. A bright orange fire blazes, crackling and warm. Take a moment to feel the warmth of the fire and the safety of the cottage. (Pause)

On the other side of the room a door opens. You see a child and recognize that it's you. Your inner child walks toward you. They stand near you or sit in the chair across from you. Allow yourself to take a deep breath and slowly exhale. Take in their eyes, their face, their hair, their heart. (Pause). See that your inner child is precious and lovable just as they are. This child wants to be nurtured, to be accepted, to be seen, to be loved. You can be the loving parent who protects them, takes care of them, and makes sure they get to play and have fun. Notice how their posture shows you how they've been alone and lacking support for a long time. (Pause)

As you look at them, sadness washes over their face. They look down, and their expression seems to say, "I'm not important." "There's something wrong with me." Tears roll down their cheeks. Gently give the child space to feel their sadness. Your silence and loving attention tell them that it's okay to cry. They've been carrying this grief for a long time. You can honor their tears and their loss. (Pause) Their crying calms, and you reach out your hand. The child hesitates, then places their warm, soft hand in yours. You ask the child if you can share something. The child hesitates; then they nod. You say, "I'm so sorry you believed those things about yourself. They were never true." (Pause) The child stares at the floor and inches closer to you. You continue, "That was your way to stay safe. You needed to believe you were the problem to survive, because no one was there for you. You were never the problem. You are precious and always have been." Your inner child glances up and looks wary, but hopeful. They move toward you and gently climb into your lap. Stay as present as you can for this precious child. (Pause)

When they've had a chance to feel their feelings, tell them, "I am so sorry it was like that for you back then, and I'm so glad you're visiting with me today. I'm your loving parent now, and I'm going to take good care of you. Is there a name you'd like me to call you?" (Pause) Your inner child nestles closer, and you pull the blanket around them. You sit together in silence, and the fire crackles. Your inner child's breathing deepens.

Allow whatever warm feelings you have to flow from you to this precious part of yourself and back, staying as present as you can. If you wish, share some more loving words you know they'd like to hear, unless silence is more supportive.

(Pause to allow your messages to sink in) You ask this precious child, "What do you need?" "What can I do for you?" (Pause) If they answer, let them know you heard them. (Pause)

We don't live there anymore.
Things are different now.
I will take care of you now.
You are a precious treasure to me.
I will not leave you.
Thank you for being so strong.
There were so many hard things.
You never gave up.
I love you just the way you are.

Let them know you will do your best to regularly check in with them to hear their feelings and care for their needs. Let them know you're here now to calm their fears or upsets. (Pause) When you're ready to close this guided practice, let your inner child know, "I'm so glad you've found your way home. Everywhere I go, I carry you with me. You never have to be alone again. I love you, and I will do my best to keep you safe and take good care of you."

Take a few deep breaths and let the experience of the guided practice settle in, feeling the connection, however small or fleeting, between you and your inner child. (Pause) Gently open your eyes or lift your gaze and reconnect with your surroundings. [End recording]

Reflections: *Your Inner Family's Safe Space Guided Practice*

Sometimes it can be emotional to bring up the inner child. At other times, we might not feel much. Your inner child might or might not have been ready to appear in the ways this practice described. Whatever experience you had is okay. You can revisit this guided practice as often as needed.

1. What was the experience of doing this guided practice like for you? What was difficult, easy, or helpful?

2. How did you feel toward your inner child during the guided practice?

3. How do you feel toward your inner child now, after the guided practice?

4. What did you learn about your inner child (e.g., their name, etc.)? What more would you like to know about them?

5. What did your inner child share that they need from you, their loving parent, today to feel loved and safe? Are there other things you can think of now?

"My inner child is about five. He's a very nice person. He's patient. When I asked him what he wants from me, he said he wants to be loved and protected. That's that I try to do now." -Fellow Traveler

The Effects of Having a Wounded Inner Child: Building Compassionate Awareness

"My inner child is afraid of me and all adults because he never got his expectations met. He never got the love. He never got the nurturing that a child should get. He's the child within of different ages saying, 'I didn't get this at ten years old; I didn't get this at 12. I'm angry, and I don't know what to do about it, but I'm going to get everybody for it, because my parents didn't give this to me.'" -Fellow Traveler

Not only is the inner child tender and vulnerable, but their hurts can cause them to react in ways that prevent us from thriving in adulthood. Our wounded inner children walk with us as we go through our lives—they take in the people, sights, sounds, experiences, and interactions. Yet, they see and experience this world through their pain. Our inner children carry a terror of abandonment and rage. Most painful of all, they did not get to learn how inherently lovable they are. To survive our traumatic upbringing, our inner children develop behavioral patterns and strategies that served us then but that no longer allow us to thrive. These patterns were normal reactions to the abnormal situation of being raised in a deeply dysfunctional home. Each was the "right" strategy for the insanity of our childhood environments. We were innocent children who learned to protect ourselves and cope with unmet needs. Our inner children's reactions today—reactions that were once life-saving—are not wrong, just impractical in our adult life. They call for the healing guidance of an inner loving parent.

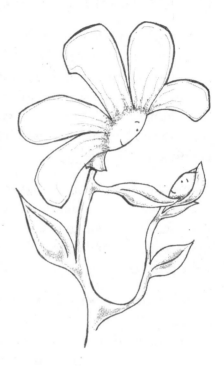

The inner child is our original wholeness who believed in people without effort. Yet, as a result of abuse, their wounds can cause us to behave in passive-aggressive, manipulative, and controlling ways, becoming violent, demanding, dishonest, and even cruel. The distorted thinking of our innocent inner child can keep us in the role of a reactor. These patterns are often ill-suited for the world beyond our families of origin. When we rely on them in our adult lives, they can threaten our health, jobs, and relationships—especially our relationship with ourselves.

We deserve so much more, and we can start by embracing our inner child and helping them heal. The good news is that our wounded inner child will listen, if we take the time to build trust and intimacy from within. Our inner child is most empowered when they have a trusting and loving relationship with our wiser inner loving parent: that's when they can ask for what they want and get it. This allows us to live as actors in the present, rather than as reactors caught in past conditioning. We can live freer, happier lives.

Noticing When our Inner Child's Pain is Driving our Actions

The inner child adopted an array of protective tools. These feelings, behaviors, and tools were necessary to survive the unhealthy family but can lead to great emotional pain today. When our inner child is in the driver's seat or hidden in the shadows, we can act in self-destructive ways, through their fear of abandonment and shame.

We offer some examples below to help you begin to identify when you inner child might be upset by a situation and driving your reaction. These are examples—not cast in stone—and others are possible. These examples serve as a starting point for your own journey of recognizing, working with, and transforming these patterns.

As you read the examples below, it's important to remember that our behavior is an attempt to meet a need. It is not "who we are." Our inner loving parent reminds us to separate our behavior from our essence—our essence is loving, connected, joyful, and innocent. Our essence never strays from this inner form, even as our behaviors and patterns shift over time. We could not have turned out any differently given our childhoods. Now is our opportunity to reparent and grow.

Often inner children learned from their dysfunctional caregivers and difficult circumstances to doubt themselves and their abilities. They can become discouraged or lose their natural confidence. They became dependent on external sources for support and guidance. They fear they cannot survive on their own—a universal childhood fear—but know they will not be taken care of like other children. The traits from The Laundry List tend to be their survival strategies, representing "flight-or-freeze" reactions. In response to the abuse or difficult circumstances around them, they learn to deny their own thoughts, feelings, needs, and intuition for the sake of others. They might often feel ashamed, hurt, sad, helpless, and scared.

They might engage with others in a push-and-pull: being open about their needs and anxiety or dropping hints, hoping others will read their minds because it's just too scary to ask. They might isolate if they experienced their caregivers or authority figures betraying or rejecting them, finding it hard to trust. However, they likely still long for the support they see others getting. When they're most in need of dire care, they might act helpless, get sick, or hurt themselves, since these were often the only moments in which they experienced the care and attention they so sorely lacked in childhood.

Your loving parent can remind your inner child that they're already supported in many ways and that safe people are available today. They need to hear that they're more capable than they think and that it's not their job to handle adult responsibilities today. To help this inner child let go of their debilitating fear and distorted thinking, you can ground your attention in the body and find ways to be present. Doing so can help them relax and feel more secure.

In other cases, inner children might have learned to anticipate the barrage of a caregiver's rejection or betrayal. They might have wisely walled themselves off from their hurt feelings as a result. They can be impatient about having their needs met and act out when they suspect they might get hurt yet again, sometimes becoming demanding, violent, or manipulative. They can act superior out of a fear of not being good enough. They might exhibit traits from The Other Laundry List, representing a "fight" response. Their desperate reactivity is how they adapted to the neglect, abandonment, dysfunction, or abuse they endured.

If you find yourself feeling shame or some other uncomfortable feeling, this would be a very good time to take a

gentleness break

and use the reparenting check-in to help your inner child feel safe.

Your loving parent can help this inner child open their heart again by empathizing with their feelings and letting them know it's safe to be vulnerable with you. Behind their toughness is deep hurt and a need to grieve. Working with a trustworthy sponsor, fellow traveler(s), or therapist can help this inner child trust that it's possible to open up to others. Reassure them that you have their back no matter what and will protect them. Help them recognize their healthy qualities, such as integrity, courage, and seeing strengths in others. Improving your conscious contact with a higher power can help this inner child trust that it's okay to let go of some control.

Sometimes inner children avoid feeling hurt by their neglectful and unsupportive environments by focusing on others. They can knock themselves out for approval, hoping for affirmation and praise, which secretly they don't even believe they deserve. These inner children were likely pressed into a parental role by a caregiver or circumstances. They can come across as controlling, overly-responsible, perfectionistic, and self-sufficient to the point of seemingly having no needs.

This inner child learned to put others' needs ahead of their own, but they might resent others who ask for what they need. They might feel guilty for having to ask for support or be afraid of seeming "needy." It might not even occur to them that they have needs or to trust that others could meet them. They might push away painful feelings and overwhelm by distracting themselves with work or a new relationship. Their super competent external presentation can often be at odds with how they feel internally—hopeless and disheartened from the futile, yet ongoing, effort to save the family and themselves. This might lead them to punish others passive-aggressively and turn on themselves. They tend to exhibit traits from both of The Laundry Lists.

Our loving parent can give this inner child the nurturing and love they've longed for, helping them trust that their needs matter and that they don't need to earn love and approval. We can help them grieve the fact that their needs were so neglected. When this inner child's compulsion to people-please arises, we can remind them, "It's not possible to please everyone all the time. I will lend a hand as long as I can take care of your needs at the same time." We can pause, get still, and find out what this part of us needs. Developing healthy internal and external boundaries (described later in this guide) support our inner child, especially when they struggle with this pattern.

The type of dysfunctional environment[1] we grew up in, as well as our culture, influences the specific ways our inner child has learned to react. Our personality traits, our differences (including the ways we learn and communicate, personal preferences, how we look, etc.), how we were treated for being different, and the ways in which we believed others disliked or misunderstood us, all shaped how we learned to handle situations as children.

Our inner children have wounds because it wasn't safe in our families to grieve and express our pain. By recognizing these feelings clearly as inner child reactions to long unmet needs, we have an opportunity to give ourselves what we've long hoped others would give us. We can notice when our inner child is reacting to a situation and driving our response. We can reparent in these moments and give our inner child the love, approval, and appreciation they seek in others. The reactions we turn to are not who we are but are our false self—how we learned to cope. Reparenting helps our inner child release these behaviors. As inner loving parents, we can choose behaviors that help our inner family thrive.

False beliefs were created by the limiting messages we heard from caregivers and childhood authority figures who told us that our feelings, our needs, and our true self were not okay. Whether the belief is "I'm the best" or "I'm the worst," it comes from feelings of low self-worth. They might not have words to describe these beliefs, but our inner

1 For more on dysfunctional family types, see Big Red Book, Chapter 3.

83

child's low self-worth shows through their feelings and behavior. Our loving parent can create the conditions for more life-affirming beliefs to take hold. We will explore this further, in Chapter 20.

If we ignore our inner child, they'll get our attention in whatever way they can. This could be through physical symptoms, including, but not limited to, gastrointestinal issues, teeth grinding, headaches, backaches, muscle tension, having accidents, racing heart, buzzy anxiety feelings, and the like. Emotions, especially shame, fear, and rage, are ways they speak to us. When we react, we can check to see if our inner child is in pain and reenacting the past. As loving parents, we can get to know, have compassion for, and lovingly address our inner child's various patterns. We learn that, deep down, our inner child just wants to be loved. Their fear of abandonment and rejection can cause them to take over and act out in ways that consume our energy. We can learn to give them the love they need directly, freeing us from the toll of their upset.

"I don't always know how to channel my inner child's energy, but I'm learning." -Fellow Traveler

Reflections: *Getting to Know Your Inner Child*

It can take time to digest the information in the previous section. You might wish to take a gentleness break or connect with a sponsor or fellow traveler(s) before answering the questions below. You can also return to these questions at a later point, if you don't have answers yet.

1. Describe your inner child's voice, body posture, and physical appearance as best you can.

2. What are some of your inner child's likes and dislikes?

3. What core needs weren't met in your early years: love, acceptance, recognition, to matter, support, compassion, being heard? What wounds linger from that time?

4. Did your inner child learn or come to the conclusion that they weren't good enough, or better than others, or some combination? How so?

5. Did your inner child learn to meet others' needs at their own expense, or meet their own needs at others' expense, or some combination? How so?

6.   What physical sensations are present when your inner child has a sense of being safe?

7.   What are some ways to support your inner child to let go of their survival strategies?

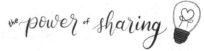

The more we can make space for their feelings and reactions, the more our inner child will be likely to join us in the warm, loving environment we're creating today.

"The first time I pictured my inner child, I saw a child chained in a dank, dark cell. I'd heard other adult children refer to their inner children as wolf-children and felt reassured. After Step work, fellowship, and therapy, I was able to meet with my inner family. I began to show love for all of them. Today my inner child talks to me regularly." -Fellow Traveler

Exercise: *Inner Child Anger List*

Invite your inner child to tell you all the things they feel angry, frustrated, or enraged about and write down their list on a separate piece of paper. Allow them to express their emotions and empathize with them. A simple "I get why you feel mad about that!" shows you understand them. You might want to copy their list here before the next step:

_____

_____

_____

_____

Once you have listened to your inner child for each item on their list, invite them to tear it into pieces if they want to. This gives them a safe outlet for their anger and provides a much needed physical release. They might feel inspired to throw the pieces of paper in the air or find some other way to symbolically release them.

Exercise: *Journaling about Your Early Years*

Another way to connect with your inner child is to journal or use some other way to explore losses, experiences with other children, your feelings, and how you experienced shame as a child (teen years were addressed in Chapter 6). As you reflect on your early years, how did you feel as a child? Did you feel safe, like you belonged in your family, like you could be yourself?

Turn to "Messages We Needed to Hear in Childhood" on page 32 and reflect on the messages you needed to hear and the lessons they represented. What messages did you not receive? What messages do you wish you'd received? How did missing those affect your life? Which behaviors emerged as a result? Were you allowed to be a child going through developmental stages or were you judged as "defiant" or "selfish"? What was your family role—hero, lost child, scapegoat, or mascot?

How did these role(s) become part of your identity and/or change over time? What challenging events happened during those years?

Inner Child Field Notebook

You can learn about your inner child by keeping track of when they appear through emotions, thoughts, bodily sensations, or other cues. Keep a journal, notepad, or note app handy.

- Record any reactive behaviors or thoughts that seem to come from your inner child.
- Track your inner child's tone, posture, volume, and impulses.
- Jot down when and where your inner child gets activated.
- Identify where you feel your inner child in space (e.g., inside or outside your body, close by or far away, in your gut, your chest, etc.).

If you'd rather take an inventory each day, choose from the questions below or use your own:

- Did I notice my inner child react to situations, or influence situations, on my behalf today? If so, how did my inner child feel? What thoughts or triggers led to that reaction?
- Did my inner child view anyone as a threat today? Did they slip into a victim or perpetrator mindset? Did they take things personally? Did they become controlling? What other traits from either of The Laundry Lists did I notice[2]?
- Did my inner child withdraw, deny their needs or demand they be met, isolate, shut down, seek outside validation through people, things, etc.; experience perfectionism, procrastination, or paralysis? Believe they were unworthy?
- What healthy qualities did I notice in my inner child today?

The awareness we gain from observing our inner child helps us be more likely to notice when they get triggered. Rather than allowing them to take the lead in situations that trigger them, our loving parent can tend to the feelings and distorted thinking that are driving their reactions. We might also begin to recognize the inner child in the times we're playful, curious, loving, creative, tender, kind, and full of wonder.

"I try to be sincere with my inner child so he can trust me. If he trusts me, he won't sabotage me." -Fellow Traveler

Exercise: *Letter to Your Inner Child*

"Dear little one,

It happened. We can leave it behind us. I can act when it is needed and set healthy boundaries for us. I'm doing things differently and standing up for us. Now you can be the whole person you are. I will arrange a life that is good for us. You're safe.

I love you, your loving parent." -Fellow Traveler

Build trust with your inner child by writing them a short letter. Let them know you love them, are there for them, and are sorry for how little support they got when they needed it. In the space on the following page or in your journal, write a letter to your inner child. Adapt the language of your letter to reach a particular age or particular inner child.

2 See Appendix F.

Read the letter aloud to yourself, a sponsor, fellow traveler(s), or a therapist. Take your time and allow yourself to feel whatever comes up, setting a boundary if the critical parent appears ("You can relax; I've got this" or "Not now").

Developing a Relationship with Your Inner Child

"When I'm feeling stuck or sad, I ask my little girl what's up. I let her tears fall and give her what she needs— like a hug, affirmations, talking with recovering adult children, reparenting check-in worksheets, breaks from work, or simply being. This program gives me hope for deeper reparenting to come." -Fellow Traveler

Our wounded inner child's behavior—whatever form it takes—is a call for healing and compassion. We were innocent children wounded due to no fault of our own. Our wounded inner child has carried a burden, yet we are more than our past. As this journey unfolds, we begin to recognize and appreciate the qualities, resources, and strengths we developed. The more we connect with our inner child without trying to change them, the more they will trust us and become a source of spontaneity, creativity, and joy.

Setting aside a regular time to check in with your inner child can show them you care, and helps your relationship blossom.

Your Key Chapter Takeaway(s):

Affirmation / Meditation

It's okay if my precious inner child doesn't trust me yet. They're worthy of and deserve my unconditional love, care, and attention. I will keep showing up for them.

Inviting Your Loving Parent into the Driver's Seat

Meditation / Prayer
May I be aware when my inner family members take over so I can lovingly reparent them.

Whenever you want to connect with your inner family members, first make sure your loving parent is in the driver's seat. You'll know your loving parent is in the driver's seat when you feel any of the following toward your inner family members: compassion, curiosity, gentleness, calm, openness, acceptance, and patience. When that's the case, let your loving parent tune in to the inner family member who needs attention. Nurture, love, and guide them. If another inner family member steps in, follow this chapter's suggestions to invite your loving parent back to lead. You can repeat this process as many times a day as needed, using the reparenting check-in process or by connecting in whatever way works for you.

Some of our inner family members might not like the reparenting process or its repetitiveness. They might try to tweak it, intellectualize it, seek new resources, avoid it altogether, or control other inner family members. When we become aware of that, we can invite our loving parent to reparent them. It's the actions coming from love that will heal us.

Over time, as you become your own loving parent, you will feel compassion for what your inner child is feeling. You will understand that your inner teen's angry feelings and reactions come from unmet needs and a sense of responsibility to protect the inner child. You'll be curious about the needs of all your inner family members, including your critical parent. You'll understand their strategies are often a reenactment of pain and trauma. The needs they're trying to meet will become more obvious to you.

You might need to draw on the stillness that comes from practicing mindfulness to be able to listen to your inner children, but over time your connection with them will grow. Speaking to your inner children at first might feel uncomfortable because you have not learned the language. Yet, trying, even if it sounds or feels awkward at first, can help them relax and trust you more.

"At first, workaholism, people-pleasing, and seeking external validation got in the way of regular reparenting. If my inner child felt sad, afraid, or alone, I would often notice, but I would not pay attention to him. I believed things like, "I don't have time for this." "I pay enough attention to myself already." My counselor, my sponsor, and fellow travelers helped me see these behaviors and to make my inner child my priority. The

more my critical parent and inner teenager saw that my loving parent could care for my inner child better than they could, the less they intervened. Today, if I cannot attend to my inner child immediately, I will still acknowledge him and let him know when I'll have time. Because he now trusts me, that's usually enough for him to relax." -Fellow Traveler

Identifying a Takeover

At times, our inner family members can get triggered to the point that we have trouble staying grounded. This is a takeover, and it can happen without our realizing it. We might feel overwhelmed emotionally without understanding why. When this happens, we leave our challenge zone and need to pause and regain our center. The suggestions in Chapter Four, such as the body scan, support us to do so.

At other times, we can be with a triggered inner family member without it becoming a takeover. We can feel their pain, yet be there for them in a healthy, balanced way, giving them a deep sense of empathy and understanding.

Which Inner Family Member Has Taken Over?

Being a loving parent involves knowing when inner family members get triggered so we can reparent them before they take over. This awareness takes time to develop. We might think our loving parent is steering when in fact it's one of our inner family members. For example, when the critical parent is at the wheel, they try to make the inner children behave to give the "right" impression to other people. To achieve this, the critical parent might act reasonable or critical or be so subtle we don't detect them. Yet, what is needed is the love, presence, and guidance of our loving parent who can acknowledge how the inner children feel and address their needs.

Check the takeover signs you've experienced below:

☐ You take on the inner family member's feelings and act out their urges or impulses.

☐ You go into storytelling mode, focusing on what someone else did or said rather than your inner experience.

☐ You over-identify with the inner family member's viewpoint or beliefs.

☐ Your voice sounds different—as if you're speaking like that inner family member.

☐ You notice you're people-pleasing, feeling guilty for saying no, or engaged in traits from The Laundry List or The Other Laundry List.

☐ Panic attacks or tunnel vision.

☐ You lose all sense of time.

☐ Sense of urgency (unless there is an immediate physical danger).

☐ It seems like a feeling has been going on forever and will never end.

After beginning to identify how you experience each inner family member in earlier chapters, you might now be more able to recognize which one of them has taken charge:

- If the inner child takes charge, you're likely to experience feelings such as sadness, shame, fear, worry, disappointment, embarrassment, hurt, despair, and sometimes anger. You might notice physical sensations like heaviness, a racing heart, shakiness, a lump in the throat, or warmth. Other signs are slipping into a victim mindset, pouting, manipulating others through guilt, judgment, and/or acting helpless, and wanting to be rescued.
- If the inner teenager takes control, you might notice feelings of anger, frustration, or resentment and an urgency to resolve a situation. You might also notice a surge of energy, judgment, and impulsiveness. Becoming paralyzed and depressed, wanting to use substances or compulsive behaviors, or wanting to lash out are also signs.
- If the critical parent takes over, you're likely to notice judgments and a sense of sternness, doubt, or a questioning or undermining tone. Criticism, control, and denying feelings are other signs.

Our inner family member's behavior can affect one another in a chain reaction, which is why our loving parent needs to be the one to reparent. If you feel aversion toward the inner family member you're tending, that means another inner family member has slipped into the driver's seat. For example, feeling annoyed with the inner child's fear would mean the critical parent or inner teenager has taken charge. These inner family members can't meet the needs of the inner child in any real or lasting way today, which is why strengthening access to your loving parent is so important.

We are powerless over takeovers happening, though consistently practicing mindfulness, reparenting, and taking other recovery actions reduces their frequency. When we realize what is happening, we have the opportunity to access our loving parent. As adults working an ACA program, we are the only person who can reparent our inner family members in a lasting, loving, and healing way.

It's common to feel emotional discomfort when more than one inner family member comes up at the same time. To reduce any overwhelm you feel in such moments, it can be helpful to picture your inner children sitting in front of your loving parent in a circle or meeting around a table in your internal safe space. You can also let all your inner family members know that you hear and see them and that you will be working with them, one at a time.

Reflections: *Recognizing Takeovers*

Recall a past situation and ask yourself the questions below. This will help you recognize future takeovers more quickly. You can ask yourself these same questions in the midst of a takeover.

1. Describe the inner family member that takes over (what do they look like, sound like, feel like):

2. How did it feel in your body when this inner family member took over, and where in the body did you feel it?

3. What was your breathing like, and what emotions arose?

4. What did this inner family member think; what do they believe? ("I can't do it." "You shouldn't speak up." "Why bother?" "Screw it!")

5. What motivated this inner family member to take over; what were they trying to achieve?

6. What's one action you can take to bring your loving parent into the driver's seat the next time you sense a takeover? (e.g., take a deep breath, do a body scan, etc.)

Managing Takeovers in a Loving Way

"My inner teenager and critical parent are not crazy! They have watched me abandon my inner child for years. That is how I learned to cope in childhood from my overwhelmed caregivers. As an adult, I was run by my little one until I increased my awareness and made a decision to address my inner life differently. Unfortunately, I still sometimes abandon my inner child whenever I choose—consciously or unconsciously—not to use recovery tools." -Fellow Traveler

When inner family members take over, you might or might not be able to feel love and compassion for them right away. Take a deep breath and count to ten. Doing so can make space for your loving parent. Remind yourself that this is an inner family member—not all of you—and invite your loving parent to step in. You can get an image of the inner family member in your mind's eye to create more separation or find some other way to access your loving parent. With gentleness, just notice what inner family member is showing up. Invite them to take a break for now (let them know you won't leave).

If inner family members seem hesitant to take a break, it can help to ask them, "What are you afraid might happen if you were to give me a little space right now?" Often they fear you'll ignore them, leave them, or try to get rid of them. They might worry that if they aren't in charge, the inner child will get triggered or that the inner child's emotions will become overwhelming, resulting in a loss of control. Your inner family members might need you to acknowledge that they've been dismissed and ignored before. Reassure them that you need the space to better care for them and that you won't leave. Invite them to hang out in your inner safe space while you work with the triggered part of you. Asking the inner family member for space, or to take a break, is not about getting rid of them. The goal is to have a relationship with them rather than "become" them.

You might experience lightness or a sense of openness when an inner family member gives you space and takes a break. They might acknowledge your request in your mind—verbally or through images. You might still experience some of the emotion you felt when the inner family member first took over, but it won't be as intense or overwhelming.

The Steps can also support us during a takeover. When we become aware that our loving parent is no longer in the lead, we can "admit," as we do when we take Step 1, that we're powerless over our inner family member's survival mechanisms. Feeling into physical sensations, feelings, and thoughts can help us understand how any unmanageability is affecting our body, heart, and mind. Doing so makes it more possible to come to believe—Step 2—that we can be restored to clarity. Using Step 3, we can make a decision to turn our will and life, and the inner family member that has taken charge, over to the loving care of a power greater than ourselves.

Our inner family members are used to jumping in and trying to push away or rescue the inner child. Accepting that these inner family members are a direct response to our dysfunctional upbringing increases our compassion for them. We begin to recognize they aren't just going to stop their behaviors overnight. We can even come to expect they will return and learn to welcome the opportunity to nurture them and help them heal.

Inner family members need to hear over and over again that we aren't trying to get rid of them. This is especially the case for the critical parent and inner teenager. Their hypervigilance and use of survival mechanisms helped us in the past. We can reassure all our inner family members we won't leave and then follow through by tending to their feelings and needs. Our patience and consistency will help them trust our loving parent to lead.

At any time in this process, a call to a fellow traveler or sponsor can help our loving parent return to the driver's seat. We all need help at times accessing our loving parent.

"When I'm stuck in my inner child, inner teenager, or critical parent, I might need a fellow traveler to help me hear which part of me has taken over. I sometimes can't do it alone. Not expressing my thoughts and feelings to myself, or talking with someone else, can keep me trapped in shame and isolation. Sharing creates new connections in the brain and helps me feel compassion for my inner family members." -Fellow Traveler

Reflections: *Exploring What Nourishes You Spiritually*

We each come to find a spiritual connection with a power greater than ourselves that is uniquely ours and that nourishes and sustains us on our reparenting journey. Some have found this relationship through art, children, animals, music, meditation, prayer, nature, reading, and many other ways.

The Big Red Book states that our actual parent is a higher power of our understanding. Whether this statement is literal or metaphorical for us, improving our conscious contact with a power greater than ourselves can increase our inner family member's trust in our inner loving parent.

Instead of answering the questions below, you might prefer to create a collage or draw.

> *Drawing or writing can be hard for some of us. A **gentleness pause** and **nurturing** can help reduce any pressure your inner family members feel.*

1. What would you like to receive from a power greater than yourself to help you become your own loving parent? You might consider writing a "Help Wanted" ad.

2. What do you do, what have you tried, or what could you try to improve your conscious contact with a higher power and nourish yourself spiritually?

3. With your non-dominant hand, allow your inner child to share what nourishes their spirit and how might or how does a higher power show up in their life.

4. With your non-dominant hand, allow your inner teenager to share what nourishes their spirit and how might or how does a higher power show up in their life.

5. Ask your inner critical parent what it would be like for them to believe you're not alone, that a higher power supports you to lovingly parent your inner family?

It is our hope that, in working the ACA program, we will be guided to find and improve our conscious contact with a higher power of our own understanding. Doing so can increase our inner family member's confidence that they're supported. They can begin to relax and let our loving parent and higher power guide us through life.

Your Key Chapter Takeaway(s):

Affirmation / Meditation

With the support of a higher power, I am freeing myself from childhood reactions as I nurture my inner family members. I am becoming more stable, peaceful, and secure.

The Reparenting Check-In

Meditation / Prayer
Grant me the willingness to check in and make conscious contact with my inner family members. May I tend to them with a gentle, loving heart.

The Solution is to become our own loving parent. Reparenting is a skill that can be learned, and the more we practice the check-in, the more we deepen this skill. Even so, it helps to remember that the reparenting process is not linear. One day we can have a connected, loving check-in, and the next, it might change. This is completely normal, and it's helpful to remember that one day does not define the others.

Initially, we might use the reparenting check-in primarily to work with triggers and address dissociation. While we cannot avoid getting triggered, we can choose to do a check-in to see what part of us needs love and attention. Later, we learn to do check-ins throughout the day. When we check in, we interrupt reactive behavioral patterns and create new healthy ones. These moments are where freedom lies.

Our inner loving parent needs to be in the driver's seat to lead the reparenting check-in process. If we're not feeling curious, compassionate, open, or interested in connecting with our triggered inner family member by the time we reach the last step of the check-in, that's an indication our loving parent is not in the driver's seat. It's best to wait until we're sure our loving parent is fully present.

We increase our ability to protect, nurture, and guide our inner children each time we do a reparenting check-in. In this active practice, we turn the love and care inward that we've directed to, or sought from others, often at our expense.

The check-in helps us return to our bodies. We pay close attention to our present moment experience—physical sensations, emotions, and thoughts. Learning and practicing this tool early in the reparenting process gives us a simple tool we can use in our daily lives and deepen over time. It also helps us engage with the coming chapters in a more experiential way. The reactions it can bring up from our inner family members allow us to help them heal. The more we connect with our inner family through the rest of this guide, the deeper our check-ins can become.

"My loving parent matures by practicing conscious contact with a higher power. Then my loving parent is guided to insight, true perception, and self-love. On this basis, I can hear and nurture my inner child."
-Fellow Traveler

The Reparenting Check-in Tool

These step-by-step instructions will help you do each part of the reparenting check-in. Some find that writing down their answers to the check-in by using the worksheet in Appendix C makes it easier to focus. Others like to do the check-in as a silent meditation. When you notice a need for a check-in, start by acknowledging that an inner family member is triggered and let go of any need to change them or argue with them. Lead with the loving parent's qualities of compassion, calm, curiosity, and kindness.

You might discover you need to adjust the intensity once you've begun a check-in. If this happens, use the tips you learned in Chapter 4.

1. **Ground:** *What are you feeling at this moment?* What is your breathing like—short, rough, fast, constricted? Deep, smooth, slow, or open? What emotions do you feel—sadness, anger, hurt? What physical sensations do you notice— constriction, fluttering, warmth? Let yourself feel all of this without judging. Ground your attention in your body by noticing any other sensations you're aware of, such as the feel of your feet against the floor. Grounding your awareness in your body helps you identify who needs your love and attention. After you identify your physical sensations and emotions, give yourself a chance to experience them before moving on to the next step.

   > *Putting your focus on an outside object or sound can help if you get overwhelmed.*

2. **Who:** *Who (what inner family member) needs your loving parent's attention?* A triggered inner child tends to feel more vulnerable emotions like fear, shame, sadness, or embarrassment. An inner teenager tends to feel anger, resentment, frustration, and rage. Still, all inner family members can feel all emotions. Asking yourself, "How old is this inner family member?" can help you determine who needs attention. If you don't know which inner family member is activated, that's okay. Just being curious helps diffuse the trigger and builds internal trust.

   > *What age does this reaction seem to be?*
   >
   > *What does this **remind me** of?*

3. **What:** *What activated this inner family member?* External causes can trigger us—such as a person, place, or thing. We can also get triggered internally by our critical parent or other distorted thinking. Sometimes it's a combination of internal and external causes, and it's okay if we don't know. Once triggered, we unconsciously think and feel like we did as a triggered child or teenager.

   While the original trigger might be external, the critical parent or another part of us can add blame or shame to the trigger. We can set a boundary by asking that inner family member to take a break and let them know we'll connect with them afterward. "Thank you, I've got this."

   Identifying "what" triggered our inner child or inner teen and reparenting around that helps us not react and instead tend to the original pain as inner loving parents. This knowledge also points us toward actions we can take after we complete the check-in process. For example, we might need to set a boundary or have a conversation with someone. Knowing the cause of a trigger can also help us manage and prepare for similar situations. If you notice yourself trying to figure out the trigger or getting lost in thinking, you can just let it go and move on. Your insight will grow over time.

"Whenever I'm triggered, it helps to ask my inner family, 'What are you believing?' It can be both eye-opening and empowering for them. It keeps them engaged in the process." -Fellow Traveler

What does my loving parent know that my inner child or inner teen might not? What would one of my loving-parent role models do in this situation? How would a power greater than myself respond?

4. **Tend:** *How can you tend to this inner family member?* How do you feel toward this inner family member? Connected? Curious? Compassionate? If not, how can you access these qualities to reparent? Once you sense some connection to these qualities, proceed.

If the teenager is triggered, then listen, empathize, and reassure them. "This was never your responsibility, and you bravely took this on when no one else was there to do it. I will handle this."

If the inner child is triggered, then listen, empathize, nurture, and reassure them by focusing on their feelings and needs. "I see how hurt you feel. You did nothing wrong; it's okay. I love you. You're enough. You're safe with me." Physical soothing helps—a hand on the arm or heart, rocking, a cup of warm tea. Short, simple phrases (rather than lots of detail) seem to be what the inner child needs to hear most.

Tending to your inner child or inner teen's emotional concerns with love is not agreeing or disagreeing with the story they're telling themselves. Engaging with their story or distorted thinking would reinforce brain patterns that keep you in The Problem. Instead, empathize with your inner children's feelings and needs, which helps resolve their distress and puts you in The Solution.

"Once, when I was sad, my sponsor said, 'What would a loving parent say to your inner child?' I had no clue. I was too enmeshed with my critical parent. My sponsor asked me to imagine the best parent I could comforting a crying child. The comforting, loving words came, words I did not know I had in me. I had met my inner loving parent." -Fellow Traveler

Tips for Identifying and Addressing Distorted Thinking and Storytelling

When our inner child and inner teen get caught in distorted thinking they can believe imagined future scenarios are real or certain to happen, take things personally, jump to conclusions, take false beliefs to be true, and the like. They need our loving parent's broader perspective since they tend to interpret reality through the distorted lens of their traumatic past. We can help them ground their attention in the present moment by comforting them with gentle touch or reminding them they're safe in the present. Telling them something like, "I'm so sorry you learned to believe that. It's not the truth, and it never was," communicates that they're not wrong for thinking the way they do, yet their conclusions are not accurate. Over time, this gentle guidance will help them release these old behaviors and painful beliefs.

In general, when we spot distorted thinking patterns during a check-in, we can help our inner children reframe their thought or belief and help them understand what's real. For example, if they take someone's "no" personally, our loving parent can say, "You still matter. Like us, they have the right to say 'no.' Try not to take it personally. You're enough."

> When we're not taken over by our wounded inner family members, **we have wisdom** and perspective to offer them. The **rich potential** of growing our reparenting skills through practice can't be overstated.

We can also use affirmations and The 12 Steps to address distorted thinking. For example, we can remind our inner child that "It's okay not to know everything" to counteract the false belief "I don't know enough." Tending with Step 1 might sound like, "We are so powerless over what others do or say. You don't have to keep thinking about this or trying to fix it, it's okay to let this be."

We can help restructure our inner child and inner teen's distorted thinking little by little. If a triggered inner family member takes over and we lose perspective, we can reach out for support and find a weekly reparenting check-in meeting.

"Sometimes my inner child goes into shame about not 'being perfect.' An affirmation my loving parent uses is, 'It's okay to make mistakes and learn.'" -Fellow Traveler

When to Use the Reparenting Check-in

"I recognized my inner child's fear as clenching in the stomach. I told myself I could be with this a little. I said, 'Okay, thank you so much for trying to protect me. Right this moment I'm okay.' I needed to acknowledge the fear." -Fellow Traveler

You can use the check-in to address a variety of situations:

- When the critical parent is active.
- When the inner child or inner teenager is triggered.
- When you recall a recent trigger.
- When the inner child or inner teenager feels pleasant emotions. This can be a moment to take in and celebrate their met needs or what's working in your life.

You might find it helpful to identify an activity you regularly do and make a point to check in at that time. For instance, at bedtime, when you take a walk, or just before or after you meditate or pray.

When Not to Use the Reparenting Check-in

Signs not to do a check-in or to do a very light check-in are if you:

- Experience a lot of resistance to checking in,
- Feel overwhelmed and ungrounded (a sign of a takeover),
- Have no access to your loving parent, or
- Want to "fix" what's happening.

If you do a check-in these situations, your loving parent isn't in the driver's seat. Inner family members can't reparent in healthy ways, and when they try to do so, it leads to inner conflict.

Leading Your Inner Family with Gentleness, Humor, Love, and Respect

You might find it more useful to do a Step 10 inventory, reach out to a sponsor, fellow traveler, or therapist, or use a supportive resource to help you regain perspective and balance.

At times during a check-in, strong feelings might arise. If the feelings take you out of your challenge zone, try a grounding technique mentioned in Chapter 4 or pause the check-in and return to it when you are more centered.

If your inner family members feel raw but safe enough to continue, adjust the check-in. Rather than going into the pain, focus on your inner family members' willingness to show up and appreciate them for that. "Wow, this is hard for some of you. You want these feelings to go away. That's okay. I'm just going to be here for a moment, and no one has to be any different." Perhaps you stay with the feelings for a few seconds and then need to stop the check-in. Just doing that much is an important start. Rather than expect yourself to nurture, you can offer your inner child or inner teenager a simple message: "I see you. I know you're there, and I care. I will come back again later."

When an inner family member seems unwilling to check in, notice if your loving parent is in the driver's seat and if you feel curious or interested in this part of yourself.[1] If so, you can let this part of you know that you're going to connect with the inner child (or inner teen) for a few minutes. You might then say something like, "You can let me know if you start having concerns." Your loving parent can be curious and negotiate with inner family members but does not turn over decisions or responsibility to them. Your loving parent needs to reparent and be in charge.

Taking Time to Make Conscious Contact

"I made myself a small card with the four check-in steps, writing the key words to help me when I need it the most. Something BIG is changing inside of me, and I am 100% sure that my progress is a direct result of practicing the check-in. I have never felt this connected." -Fellow Traveler

Sometimes after we nurture our inner children in the last step of the check-in, we might feel a little better. Sometimes we feel a lot better. We might even feel a wave of profound inner peace and connection with ourselves, others, and a power greater than ourselves. These moments just after nurturing are precious and healing. Rather than move on to the next thing, we can spend time with the quality of presence that develops from doing a reparenting check-in. It familiarizes us with a much deeper sense of our being. We go beyond our fearful and reactive inner family members to return to—and rest in—our true self. We are, as Promise Two states, "Discovering our real identities by loving and accepting ourselves."

The Reparenting Check-in as a Regular Practice

"I got triggered by something while driving and felt really angry. I decided to use a reparenting check-in worksheet when I got home. I identified that my inner teenager was angry, but underneath that, my 12 year-old felt hurt, scared, and ashamed. I went through the worksheet, taking my time, and felt less charged." -Fellow Traveler

---

1 If you're not feeling curious or interested in connecting with this part of yourself, pause and revisit the previous chapter or find other ways to help yourself reconnect as your inner loving parent.

Eventually, we can learn to do reparenting check-ins regularly throughout our day to help us live in The Solution. A reparenting check-in can be done anytime—while commuting, taking a walk, or as we drift off to sleep, to name a few. Checking in with ourselves becomes a self-reinforcing habit. When we notice our breathing is rapid or choppy, we take a second to feel it. We can ask ourselves, "What emotions am I feeling; What physical sensations are present; What inner family member is activated; What does that inner family member need?" If we are in a meeting or not able to do more than notice that an inner family member is triggered and acknowledge them silently, we return to the check-in when time allows.

We can also do a check-in when the inner child or inner teenager feels pleasant emotions, to affirm them or to celebrate. Making time to celebrate with our inner family allows us to live into The Promises. We can open up to what is working in our lives, breathing, relaxing, and allowing ourselves to enjoy the fruits of our reparenting efforts. We might feel a warm glow in our chest as our pleasant feelings soothe old wounds and fill in the nurturing we needed as children. Perhaps we have a sense of being more connected and serene. By letting ourselves savor pleasant experiences and celebrate, we help our inner family members feel more stable and peaceful. We nourish our whole being.

Reparenting ourselves becomes a spiritual practice—"constant contact"—in our everyday lives. We can learn to trust that a power greater than ourselves is leading us toward the compassion, empathy, and love we didn't consistently receive in our formative years. To experience this, we can take a moment after nurturing to feel our feelings and physical sensations, letting the experience of being our own loving parent integrate. The more we become familiar with this aspect of our true self, the more we internalize it. It is very freeing when that inner shift from being over-identified with our wounded inner family members to being connected to our true self happens. This presence is more the truth of who we are than any story, any trigger, or any one inner family member.

"Checking in with my inner children throughout my day is strengthening my internal sense of trust. Before ACA recovery, I pushed my vulnerable inner children as far from consciousness as possible. Checking in each day communicates to my inner children that they are now a welcome and valued part of my life." -Fellow Traveler

Doing the Reparenting Check-in with Others

"I resisted the idea of reparenting for years because I didn't have access to the inner loving parent and didn't know how to start. As soon as I heard others in check-in meetings, everything changed. I started following their lead, and my recovery accelerated exponentially." -Fellow Traveler

Attending reparenting check-in meetings to hear how other people reparent themselves is a great way to support your efforts. Practicing in a group can create a sense of safety, but that is different for each of us. Reparenting check-in meetings are useful, but they aren't intended as substitutes for private, individual check-ins that you can do throughout each day, nor are they a fit for every adult child.

You might wish to experiment with doing a reparenting check-in one-on-one with a sponsor or fellow traveler(s), as part of a study group, meeting, or through electronic messaging systems and applications. You can also use the check-in as part of focused childhood trauma work with a therapist. Finding ways to do reparenting check-ins with others can help bring your recovery and reparenting practice out of isolation, giving you an opportunity to break the "Don't Talk, Don't Trust, Don't Feel" rule. The point is to make a personal connection with your inner family members and build their trust in whatever way is best for you.

"Since the program stresses not trying to go it alone, I've had to learn that I'm not isolating if I do a check-in by myself. I can do it with others at times, but it's perfectly okay to do it by myself." -Fellow Traveler

Your Key Chapter Takeaway(s):

Affirmation / Meditation

Connection helps my inner family feel safe and secure.
I am doing my best to connect with them regularly throughout the day.

Reparenting
— check-in —

(1) Ground your attention

Tune in to your breathing, where it's comfortable for you, and notice how it feels. What emotions and physical sensations are here?

(2) Who is triggered?

Who or what part of you needs your loving parent's attention?

(3) What was the trigger?

What triggered this part of you? People, places, things? The critical parent or distorted thinking? It's okay if you don't know.

(4) Tend to this part

Notice if you feel compassion, curiosity, or a desire to connect with this part of yourself. Once you do, how can you tend to them?

Feeling is Healing

Meditation / Prayer
May I give myself permission to safely feel all my feelings, even the uncomfortable ones.

Being in The Solution involves taking responsibility for our own life and supplying our own parenting. Our inner child and inner teen will not trust us if we keep abandoning them. We must change our behavior and tend to our inner children's feelings and needs. We gently reunite with the feelings our inner children had to stuff because it hurt so much. Our loving parent allows our inner child's feelings to be felt, heard, seen, grieved, and resolved. This restores our ability to feel and express our feelings.

Claudia B., who wrote the introduction in the Big Red Book, said it this way, "Identifying and feeling our feelings is a part of healing. Where there is loss, there will be tears; where there is loss, there will be anger. But feelings are cues and signals to tell you what you need. It is the repression or distorted expression of them that gets people sick or into personal difficulty."

> "An important part of successful recovery is learning to accurately name the components of our inner life as they come up for us, including our various feelings, and learning to tolerate emotional pain without trying to medicate it away."
> -The Doctor's Opinion, BRB

The repression or distorted expression of our feelings began early. The characteristics common in dysfunctional homes (shown in the image) don't meet emotional needs. We needed empathy, understanding, nurturing, appreciation, acceptance, affection, and love. The emotional abandonment common in dysfunctional homes leads to shame, which the inner child carries today. Accessing and thawing our inner child's frozen feelings require gentleness, love, and patience.

While someone's emotional unavailability today can trigger our inner child's fear of abandonment, their painful feelings stem more from the past. Our loving parent can remind our inner child they are not in the same situation. People will be emotionally unavailable at times in our adult lives. Our inner child has our loving parent now, and they need help understanding they are not being abandoned in these situations.

"After my father called me stupid, I gave up and went into hiding. Later, I dropped out of high school and took any job I could get. A degree and career were only for smart people. I could not see in myself what my dad didn't see. Today I understand that I was powerless over my fear of abandonment, and I nurture my passions." -Fellow Traveler

Giving Yourself Permission to Feel

So then, how do we "feel" our emotions and stop repressing them or expressing them in distorted ways? How do we become more emotionally available to our inner children? As we learned in Chapter 3, healthy families "feel." We can give our inner children permission to break the

*What we can **feel**,*
*we can **heal**.*

"Don't Talk, Don't Trust, Don't Feel" rule. We can tell them, "It's okay to have your own feelings." Helping them distinguish their feelings from another person's feelings helps us be more grounded and responsible for ourselves.

Similarly, we can teach them it's okay for people to have their own feelings.

Building a Feelings Vocabulary

For the exercises in this chapter, it's helpful to refer to, or have handy, a printed copy of the Feelings, Needs, and Physical Sensations in Appendix D.

Dysfunctional homes, as well as many cultures, rarely focus on feelings. Instead we learn to focus on thoughts instead. It is no wonder that feelings might be confusing or hard to name for some of us. Some of us saw caregivers rage but then deny their anger. Others watched parents or relatives use feeling words in ways that did not match the definition of the words. These inconsistencies made identifying feelings difficult.

When our needs are met, we tend to experience pleasant emotions such as glad, peaceful, playful, rested, and thankful. As we feel our feelings more often, nuances get clearer (glad can be happy, excited, hopeful, joyful, delighted, or elated). When our needs are not met, we tend to experience unpleasant emotions, such as sad, scared, mad, confused, tired, and resentful.

Starting with four basic feelings—sad, mad, glad and scared—simplifies building a feeling vocabulary. Try them out as you practice this feeling sentence exercise from the Big Red Book, Step 4:

I feel _____ (emotion) when _____.
Or try switching the order around to: "When_____
__, I feel_____(emotion).

For example, "When you left the room while I was talking to you, I felt [sad, angry, hurt]." We can also add "the story I was telling myself" when we express our feelings and take responsibility for our interpretation. "When you left the room as I was talking to you, the story I was telling myself was that I didn't matter to you, and I felt hurt, mad, and confused."

Exercise: *Identifying Your Feelings*

For the next week, consider writing down a few feelings sentences a day, keeping the Feelings, Needs and Physical Sensations sheet handy. Read your sentences, allowing yourself to feel the effect in your body and heart. You might wish to share any insights with a sponsor, fellow traveler, or in a study group or meeting.

"When I first joined ACA, my sponsor began going through my past to help me get in touch with my feelings. He suggested I log five feelings—mad, glad, lonely, scared, and sad—every hour I was awake for two weeks to identify what I was feeling. I was amazed when I saw the results." -Fellow Traveler

```
c k m u r p g d d b d n o q d
u k a m y v v y e l a a s e v
u h d g r z k l b r m z t r k
r r o y s m m t e d a s e o e
r g j t a y r a r n e c w u p
b f m o m w i y q r o u s h p
e m b a r r a s s e d l d l d
i y y d i m x g t m u w a m a
t h p z q o v t r w d y e p l
i c u t o g u i m a f c g x g
r n m x m a a j g u t j f y t
e z s d y n s x l u d e n w s
d s t w v f u q w a i i f u k
h c g u u m t y j d a s x u t
t i c q u h d y h z r t u v l
```

Feelings Fun Break

Your inner child might enjoy helping you find and circle the 10 feeling words hidden in the puzzle.

scared	tired
mad	playful
rested	sad
embarrassed	lonely
grateful	glad

Distinguishing Judgments from Feelings

As we begin to speak about our feelings more, we might think we're expressing a feeling when we're actually sharing our judgment or interpretation. This can happen easily because the expression "I feel" is not always followed by an emotion. For example, we might say, "I feel ignored," which is our judgment about someone's behavior. We're saying someone is excluding us. It would be more accurate to say, "I *think* you're ignoring me," which is different than saying, "I feel sad because you haven't responded to a text I sent three days ago." When we express judgments to others, it can sound like blame and put them on the defensive; they are then less likely to want to listen.

Our judgments and stories reinforce our tendency to live life from the viewpoint of victims and distract us from tending to our inner family members. We get trapped in the role of "reactor" versus "actor" when we focus on what we think others are "doing to us" rather than on what is happening inside us. Blaming other people prevents us from taking constructive action. While another person's behavior can trigger our emotional response, our feelings come from our needs. Plus, our judgment might not be true, and we miss the opportunity to better understand what happened. Perhaps the person feels overwhelmed with a personal issue and hasn't had a chance to respond to us. This applies to in-person interactions, as well as calls, texts, and emails.

To begin translating judgments into feelings, recall a time when someone seemed to be ignoring you. Tune into your body. You might notice anger, frustration, sadness, fear, loneliness; perhaps you feel warmth in your face, tightness in your chest. Notice any difference you feel between a judgment, such as "I felt ignored by Alex," and expressing a feeling, such as, "I felt hurt and disappointed when Alex didn't return my call."

Next, pay attention to the words you use to express your feelings. If they suggest that someone is doing something to you and imply wrongness or blame, they are most likely judgments, not feelings. Some examples are: abandoned, manipulated, cheated, betrayed, insulted, rejected, attacked, blamed, or pressured. Statements beginning with "I feel that…" or "I feel they…" tend to be judgments, not feelings (e.g., "I feel pathetic as an artist") rather than a feeling, as in: "I feel disappointed in my ability as an artist." Listen for the words "that," "like," "as if," or pronouns or names/nouns after "I feel." For example, "I feel like a failure," "I feel as if it is useless," "I feel they don't like me," or "I feel Pat is inconsiderate." If we think we're a failure, perhaps we're feeling discouraged, sad, scared, or hopeless. If we think someone is being inconsiderate, we might feel hurt or angry.

> "I feel that you don't listen to me," "I felt discarded," "I felt manipulated," or "I felt abandoned" are judgments, not feelings. They are interpretations about what others are doing to us.

It can take some practice to recognize our judgments and translate them into feelings, but doing so moves us into The Solution. Using one emotion word, such as sad, glad, mad, hurt, after the expression "I feel" can increase the likelihood we'll be sharing a feeling. The chart below shows some common judgments translated into feelings and needs. We'll learn more about needs later in the chapter.

Judgment/Interpretation	Could you be feeling…?	Could you be needing…?
I feel *like* a failure	Discouraged, hopeless, sad, scared	To matter, be valued, trust
I felt interrupted	Angry, frustrated, resentful, hurt	Respect, to be heard, consideration
I feel *you* don't listen to me	Frustrated, hurt, sad, angry	To be heard, to matter, caring, connection, shared reality, trust
I felt discarded	Hurt, sad, ashamed, angry	To matter, respect, consideration, caring, belonging, to be seen, to be valued
I felt manipulated	Angry, powerless, frustrated, scared	Autonomy, empowerment, trust, equality, freedom, connection, authenticity, integrity
I felt abandoned	Lonely, hurt, sad, scared	Connection, belonging, support, caring

When parts of us get triggered, we can use any judgments that arise as sign posts to reach our underlying feelings. We can slow down to do a reparenting check-in, do some journaling, or take a mini-mindfulness break. If we're having trouble connecting to our feelings, we can reach out to a sponsor or fellow traveler.

Reflections: *Feelings*

1. What emotions were you allowed to feel and express as a child?

2. What feelings do you allow yourself to feel and express today?

3. What feelings were not welcomed by your caregivers and other family members in childhood?

4. What feelings do parts of you try to ignore, suppress, stuff, or hide?

5. What would those parts of you need in order to be okay with feeling all your feelings?

Emotional pain needs and deserves to be felt and acknowledged, not solved. If we don't feel our emotions when they occur, they will keep coming back until we feel them. By feeling our emotions when they happen, we can avoid acting them out in ways that lead us to feel shame afterward.

"I didn't know at first that when my inner child had severe emotional reactions that he wanted to tell me something, especially how he felt. I learned to ask him what he was feeling, or remembering, or needing to tell me. I let him know I hear him, that his feelings are okay, and that I love him." -Fellow Traveler

Exercise: *Identifying Feelings in Your Body*

"I notice physical feelings first; these are the frozen feelings of an inner child, often in the form of tension I hold in certain muscles or pain." -Fellow Traveler

Learning where our feelings are located in our bodies can help us "feel" our feelings rather than "think" about them. To begin to identify how feelings affect you physically, notice where in your body you feel them when they arise. Get curious and notice their temperature, how they move, their shape, and how they change. Doing so can help you identify and differentiate the emotions you feel.

Color in where you feel the emotions shown. Use different colors to represent temperature, tightness, intensity.

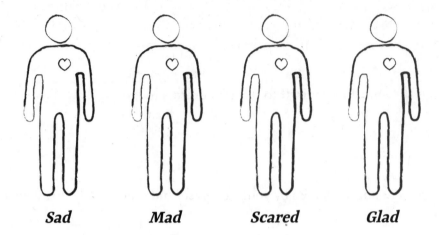

Sad   **Mad**   **Scared**   **Glad**

Your responses to the worksheet below can help you better recognize feeling cues in your daily life.

Worksheet: *Identifying Feelings in Your Body*		
Emotion	**Common or Habitual Thoughts**	**Physical Sensations**
Mad	It's wrong; they shouldn't speak to me that way; it's not fair.	Tight jaw, heat in the hands and arms, racing heart, shallow breathing
Love		
Mad		
Glad		
Sad		
Peaceful		
Fear		
Playful		
Confused		
Rested		
Tired		
Thankful		
Resentful		

With Practice, Feelings Become More Fluid

Young children from healthy homes are given space to feel their feelings. They can go from tears to curiosity to joy in seconds. Our feelings can return to this more fluid nature, no matter our age. It will require us to pause, identify, and be with what our inner children are feeling. This becomes easier the more we practice. Mindfulness can help us remember to pause and check in.

Whenever you notice an inner family member has a strong feeling, try to name the feeling silently to yourself. "This is anger." Naming the feeling can reduce its intensity. Try to also locate where the feeling shows up physically and let yourself feel it. Rating the intensity on a scale of one to ten can be helpful.

Emotions—

energy in motion

Sometimes when our inner children's feelings get stuck, they need to be expressed in safe ways through movement. For example: shake or wiggle your body, sigh out loud, stick your tongue out and shake your head, pound your arm or an object with full force on the bed, stomp, move your body to music that matches your feeling, and the like. When you do this, try to make space for whatever feelings come up, without fixing or censoring them. When you're done, stand and let your head roll down toward your toes, one vertebrae at a time. Stay in this posture of surrender as long as you like and remind your inner family that you see and appreciate how hard they're working.

When we begin becoming more aware of our feelings, parts might find it to be frightening. This makes sense—we're breaking the "Don't Talk, Don't Trust, Don't Feel" rule. Our critical parent and inner teenager might react and try to keep our inner child's vulnerable feelings out of reach. However, our loving parent's patience and love helps our inner family members trust that it's possible, safe, and healing to feel again.

To return to this natural state, stop throughout your day and ask,
"What am I feeling?"
"What physical sensations accompany the feeling?"

"Before ACA, I apologized and felt like something was wrong with me as a man when I cried. One day, while sitting outside, I heard a baby crying. A voice inside said, 'Listen. Babies cry. Human beings cry. It's one of the first things we know how to do.' I realized crying is a part of being human. Thoughts of feeling stupid might still be there, but I allow myself to feel my feelings and cry when I need to. Tears are a blessing for me today." -Fellow Traveler

Feeling Your Feelings with Trusted Others

Allowing ourselves to feel our emotions in the presence of an attuned person can make our feelings more bearable. It's what we needed as kids. Yet, we might feel uncomfortable expressing certain feelings (or feelings generally) in another's presence. We learned how to feel (or not feel) in a social context—in our families—so it makes sense that learning to feel in new ways today might need to happen in a social context too. Feeling our feelings in the presence of a sponsor, fellow traveler(s), or a therapist can make the process easier. Another person's presence and reflective listening can help us stay focused and clear. We can learn to work through feelings with others rather than sit in them alone.

When we begin to feel our feelings and experience compassion from others, we might feel grief about having carried our pain alone. Realizing how long we might have been isolated with our feelings is one way we measure our loss. When we see this, it is important to be gentle with ourselves and know it is part of the journey to a fuller life. As we begin to feel more fully and deeply, others can help us learn to celebrate this blossoming of ourselves. Recognizing our own successes and where we no longer act in dysfunctional ways is an important loving parent task. Acknowledging our fellow travelers' progress is a precious gift we can offer each other.

Connecting to Your Needs

As with feelings, we often learn from our dysfunctional families to ignore, downplay, or feel ashamed about our needs. This leaves us without the skills or vocabulary to talk about them. If our caregivers shamed us for expressing or having needs, this might have led us to deny them for fear of being too "needy." However, there is a big difference between having needs and being "needy." Everyone has needs; they identify what we require to be healthy, safe, and fulfilled. Codependency is rooted in our tendency to avoid our needs and feelings or to expect that another person will meet all of our needs. Being told we're "needy" for having needs is convenient for caregivers and others who aren't willing to meet them. However, sometimes we might, indeed, have an unhealthy level of dependence on others. Becoming aware of this balance is part of our learning. Responding to our own needs in healthy ways is an important part of reparenting and recovery in general. It requires time and practice, but eventually we become skilled in doing so.

All human beings share core needs. For example, all humans have a need for sustenance, safety, and love. Everything we do is an attempt to meet a conscious or unconscious need. Needs point us toward what will make our lives happier and healthier, and help us find strategies to fulfill them. When our needs are met, we tend to have pleasant feelings. Unmet needs tend to trigger unpleasant feelings.

Some Universal Human Needs:
Trust, Compassion, Integrity, Recognition, Connection, Clarity.

Learning that our feelings come from our needs can help us become "actors" who find ways to meet our needs, rather than "reactors" who judge and blame ourselves and others when our needs aren't met. Realizing that others can trigger our feelings but that they can't "make" us feel a certain way can be an empowering revelation. We can identify what need of ours is met or unmet in a situation, rather than attribute the cause of our feelings to others. If we value our needs, it's more likely others will too.

The inner child might not know or trust that it's okay to have wants and needs. They might feel uncomfortable requesting what they need or even acknowledging a need. Asking for what we want is breaking the "Don't Talk, Don't Trust, Don't Feel" rule—it can bring changes, uncertainty, and possible disappointment or embarrassment.

This is why becoming our own loving parent is so crucial. We can help the inner children let go of false beliefs, such as "it's weak to have needs" or "it's selfish to ask for what you need." Our loving parent can help the inner child cope with their feelings and tell them, "Your needs matter. I will find healthy ways to meet your needs." When the inner child has self-worth, honoring our needs, making requests, and not taking someone's "no" personally becomes easier. Ultimately, the more we reparent the more we trust that it's okay to stand up for our needs and set boundaries.

Exercise: *Connecting to Your Needs*

Consider checking in with yourself once a day to notice what need is alive. You could check with both your inner child and inner teen. Emotions and physical sensations that arise when you check in can be pointers to your needs. If a part of you judges your needs in any way, you might need to set a boundary, such as, "We were taught to judge our needs harshly. I'm practicing accepting them and learning how to meet them." You might be able to meet your needs yourself, and at other times you can think of who could help you meet them.

Fun Break

For fun, invite your inner child to help you find the ten need words hidden in the puzzle.

play	connection
respect	belonging
safety	honesty
meaning	care
love	humor

```
t  z  i  h  m  p  v  f  g  o  k  v  n  k  u
r  v  r  g  a  b  l  n  k  q  z  g  o  j  v
e  l  a  h  l  s  i  a  k  l  f  n  i  d  m
s  l  g  o  p  g  o  o  y  h  k  n  t  q  f
p  a  a  q  n  n  d  i  d  v  l  g  c  e  i
e  r  d  o  a  s  u  o  e  q  v  g  e  a  g
c  e  l  c  a  g  n  i  n  a  e  m  n  y  f
t  e  v  f  a  m  j  g  o  o  l  a  n  k  v
b  v  e  o  v  r  h  p  a  x  a  r  o  h  h
b  t  s  v  l  a  e  n  v  d  c  u  c  u  k
y  i  f  h  p  z  h  o  n  e  s  t  y  m  q
c  e  m  t  m  o  r  s  i  a  k  x  c  o  t
g  w  e  b  o  v  i  k  f  b  d  u  w  r  u
b  f  z  u  m  x  o  w  f  z  a  i  y  x  z
k  h  x  j  e  u  l  s  w  n  p  s  p  j  v
```

Distinguishing Strategies from Needs

A strategy is a particular choice for getting our needs met that involves a person, location, action, time, or object. There are many strategies we can use to meet our needs. We can set ourselves up to be disappointed if we get attached to a particular strategy. We might wish that, even now, our parents were responsive and loving, for example. If we hold on to that picture of how our need for love will be met, we deny other possibilities. We might find, for example, that need would be better filled by our inner loving parent, our family of choice, or our fellowship.

Because our basic needs were not consistently met growing up, we developed strategies to meet them that might or might not have been healthy. For example, to meet our need for love, we might have engaged in attention-seeking behavior. If that strategy got our caregiver's attention, we probably kept using it. Even if the attention we got wasn't loving, at least it was something.

Needs are basic; we can't get rid of them. We can, however, adapt and change our strategies. Learning to distinguish needs from strategies helps us realize there might be many ways and options to meet a need beyond our past strategies. When one strategy doesn't work, we can find another that does. For example, when we reach out to fellow travelers to meet our need for support, the first person we call might not answer. We can try calling other people or use a completely different strategy, such as journaling, meditating, praying, taking a walk, attending a meeting, or using another supportive resource.

When we confuse a strategy for a need and that strategy isn't available or doesn't meet our need, we can feel helpless, defeated. Getting attached to how we meet our needs can make us dependent on a strategy and ignore other ways to meet our needs. When we identify and connect to the inner child's feelings and needs and open to new ways of meeting that need, we move from being stuck in The Problem to living in The Solution. We have more choice. This is how our loving parent works with our inner family—gently identifying and acknowledging feelings and patiently addressing the underlying needs, releasing the outcome to a higher power.

Sometimes we can't meet a need, due to time constraints, the setting, or other practical reasons. For example, our inner child might need empathy while we're in a business meeting. In such cases, we can honor the need by telling our inner child that we will listen to them as soon as we're free. We can "connect" with their need as something important, even if we can't meet it right then.

Worksheet: *Identifying the Needs Behind Our Behavior*

When our needs aren't met, some inner family members can become judgmental. We can learn to understand and translate their judgments into identifiable needs. For example, judging someone as "mean" might signal that the person's behavior doesn't meet our need for kindness. Our inner child or inner teenager likely needs empathy but has learned to judge rather than say, "Ouch, that hurt." By translating judgments into needs, we remove the focus from what we're powerless over to what we need. Doing so moves us into The Solution because we are not powerless over being aware of our feelings and meeting our needs.

gentleness break

Adult children developed dysfunctional strategies, such as self-centeredness, judgment, procrastination, perfectionism, and dishonesty, to address our unmet needs. The Big Red Book describes these as "defects of character." When seen as attempts to meet our needs, we recognize such "defects" as coping strategies—they are not who we are.

Imagine an 8-year-old growing up with a parent who criticizes them and demands they get good grades. To avoid the parent's criticism and get their approval, the child's critical inner parent tries to mold them into a perfect child. Perfectionism becomes a childhood strategy to meet needs for safety, acceptance, and self-worth that the person carries into their adult life.

Through reparenting, we uncover more effective strategies for meeting our needs. We can learn to notice when inner family members become judgmental and connect to their needs, so new strategies emerge. We can also learn to make clear requests of others to better meet our needs.

The critical parent can harshly judge some of the "strategies" listed in the worksheet, so it helps to understand how they were born out of attempts to meet childhood needs. Complete the following worksheet to uncover the needs you were attempting to meet in childhood and to discover new strategies for meeting those needs today.

Worksheet: *Identifying the Needs Behind our Behavior*				
Dysfunctional Coping Strategy (or "Defect")	**Example of how you used this strategy in childhood**	**Needs you were trying to meet by using that strategy then**	**Needs you might be trying to meet by using it today**	**New strategy to address the needs today**
Dishonesty	*When my mom asked me if I broke a vase, I said "no" even though I broke it.*	*Safety, connection, and protection from harm*	*Acceptance, belonging, safety*	*Honesty, reparenting for any feelings that arise, making amends*
Self-centeredness				
Judgment				
Procrastination				
Perfectionism				
Envy				
Greed				
Lust				
Dishonesty				
Pettiness				

1. How do you feel when you reflect on the needs you were trying to meet for yourself as a young person growing up in a dysfunctional environment?

2. Is there a "defect" you find troublesome as an adult, that you can now see from the point of view as a child trying to get a need met? How does it feel to see that behavior from this perspective?

3. Think of a recent time an inner family member judged another person. What were they feeling and needing at that time? What might have met their needs better than the strategy of judging?

4. What are some healthier strategies you could experiment with to meet your needs today?

Worksheet: *Translating Judgments into Feelings and Needs*

gentleness break

For every judgment, think of a situation where you confused your judgment for your feeling. Identify what you were feeling and needing in that situation. This isn't easy; it's okay to return to this later.

Worksheet: *Translating Judgments into Feelings and Needs*			
Judgment	**Situation**	**What I felt**	**What I needed**
Example: Rejected	*I asked a fellow traveler for their number, and they said "no"*	*Hurt, scared, angry*	*Belonging, inclusion, closeness, to be seen, acknowledgment, connection*
Example: Abandoned	*My partner left the house during a fight and didn't return until the next morning*	*Lonely, sad, hurt, angry, frightened*	*Connection, caring, nurturing, trust*
Example: Judged	*A friend asked me to go out, but I wanted to rest. When I declined, they said, "You're never available. "*	*Scared, hurt, angry, resentful*	*To be seen, consideration, caring, understanding, acceptance*

Worksheet: *Translating Judgments into Feelings and Needs*			
Judgment	**Situation**	**What I felt**	**What I needed**
Rejected			
Abandoned			
Judged			
Manipulated			
Cheated			
Betrayed			
Insulted			
Misunderstood			
Blamed			
Pressured			

See Appendix E (page 225) for a group/partner exercise for translating judgments into feelings.

Learning to Express Feelings and Needs in Healthy Ways

Listening for our feelings and needs isn't easy, but it's a process that can become gratifying. Adding observations and needs to the Step 4 Feeling Exercise helps us practice. Observations are what a camera sees or hears. A camera can't see "disrespectful," for example, but it can show someone's facial expression and tone of voice.

*Connecting **observations** to feelings and needs can* **diffuse** *the critical parent, making space for the **loving parent** to come in.*

Making an observation helps us move out of judgment and makes it easier for others to hear us, but it doesn't come naturally. We will need patience as we learn a new, healthier way of communicating.

Expanded sentence: "When_____(observation) I felt_____ (emotion) because I _____ (need).

In the following expanded sentence example, what feelings and needs would you have?

Observation: A friend told you they were invited to a mutual friend's party. You did not receive an invitation.

Your feeling(s): _____

Your need(s): _____

Our feelings depend on our needs, so people in the same situation might feel differently. The example below shows how different needs impact our feelings.

Observation: "It was ten minutes past our agreed meeting time, and the person I was scheduled to meet hadn't arrived."

Example 1: "When my friend wasn't there at ten minutes past our agreed time, I felt hurt because my need to matter wasn't met."

Example 2: "When my friend wasn't there at ten minutes past our agreed time, I felt relieved because my need for self-connection (to pause and check in) was met."

Your example: When my friend wasn't there at ten minutes past our agreed time, I felt_____ _____(emotion) because_____(need).

Write a feeling-and-needs sentence after each observation in the imaginary scenario below.

When I left a message for a romantic partner and didn't hear anything back for three days, I felt _____(emotion) because_____ (need).

When someone at a meeting referred to me by name in their share and said, "I, too, grew up with a rageaholic," I felt _____ (emotion) because _____ (need).

When I told a colleague about something they did that didn't work for me, they said, 'Well, that's your issue,' and walked away." I felt _____(emotion) because _____ (need).

The Importance of Empathy

Naming and relating to our inner family's pain with empathy helps us reverse years of stuffing and denying feelings. Empathy is a way of putting yourself in another person's shoes and relating to their pain as if you yourself experienced it. When we empathize, we tap a quality of presence that allows us to hear not just what is said but also the underlying feelings and needs. We can express our empathy through words, but sometimes attentive silence is enough and works better. We can give the gift of being seen and heard, leaving space for the other person to speak. Holding space in this way can remove the pressure to "do empathy" well or to do it to get validation from others. Empathy can create a quality of connection where all needs matter.

As inner loving parents, we can learn to have empathy for all our inner family's feelings. Some feelings might be harder for us to empathize with than others. For example, when our inner teenager feels angry, another inner family member might react and take over, causing us to revert to old behavior. We can learn to notice these reactions and empathize and guide our inner family members.

Empathy is not: analyzing, blaming, fixing, pointing out the bright side, dismissing, minimizing, denying, interrogating, correcting, one-upping, criticizing, or colluding.

You can turn to websites and books to learn more about empathy. It's especially helpful to learn what empathy is not since so many of us have been conditioned to listen in unhealthy ways.

Exercise: *Practicing Mirroring with Others*

True listening is a key element of developing empathy. It's not too late to learn healthy listening skills. A stepping stone to grow our empathy skills is to practice mirroring others. In this practice, we learn to focus less on our viewpoint and more on understanding another person's perspective. Mirroring, or reflective listening, involves reflecting a speaker's words, so they know if "message sent is message received."

Mirroring is not about repeating back everything a person says or recalling every detail they shared. Saying "I get it" or "I hear you" also isn't mirroring because it doesn't offer someone a way to confirm what we heard. Mirroring is listening and reflecting the message the person's words convey without adding our interpretation. We can begin by practicing with other recovering adult children.

Some basic guidelines for mirroring are:

- Listen with your full attention.
- Respond using your words to show you've absorbed what your partner said rather than parroting their words.
- Make space for the person to clarify their message by asking questions. "Am I hearing you say that...?" or "Is what is important to you...?"
- Refrain from sharing your opinion or offering unsolicited advice.

To practice mirroring with a partner, choose a topic about which you'd like to speak. If you're meeting with this partner for the first time, choose something safe and adapt how much to share based on how your partner responds. Do they try to "fix"? Do they pay attention? How do your inner children feel around them? Suggested format:

- Choose someone to be the first speaker and someone to be the listener for a short, set period of time. The speaker shares something they're upset about or would like to celebrate.
- When the time ends, the listener reflects the feelings and needs they heard from the speaker.
- The speaker shares which feelings and needs resonate.
- Switch roles.

You might wish to have a short debrief at the end of your practice session. Some people make "5 & 5" recovery calls. Each person takes up to five minutes to share. When done speaking, some ask for mirroring, as described here, while others ask for the listener's experience, strength, and hope. Some like to share with no feedback. You can vary the length—10x10, 20x20—as you wish. This format provides a structured way to practice healthy listening skills and work the program with other recovering adult children.

Worksheet: *Empathizing with Your Inner Children*

In the next exercise, read each statement as if it were your inner child or inner teen speaking to you. Deny the feeling and notice any feelings or physical sensations that arise. Then practice empathizing with their feelings and needs, letting yourself feel what it must be like for them. Tap into what your heart hears, letting go of getting the words "right." Notice any physical sensations or emotions that arise.

Worksheet: *Empathizing with Your Inner Children*		
Inner Child or Inner Teenager	**Denying**	**Empathizing**
Example: She ignored me.	*She didn't ignore you. You're overreacting.*	*Are you feeling hurt because you need to matter?*
Example: They dropped the ball again. I'm tired of them holding up my work.	*Don't make such a big deal out of it. I'm sure they'll do it.*	*Do you feel frustrated because you value reliability?*
I really messed up.		
I don't have any friends.		
No one listens to me.		
How dare they!		
I can't do this.		
Look what I made!		
I slept well last night.		
They abandoned me.		

The more we feel our feelings, the more we realize they change. Feelings—pleasant and unpleasant—come and go when we don't try to fix them or push them away. Empathy for our inner family members allows happiness, joy, and freedom—feelings that might have been long absent—to return. We live the 12 Step adage, "There is no healing without feeling" and embrace our feelings with a child's sensitivity and simplicity. With this loving acceptance of our feeling and needs, we reclaim our wholeness.

Your Key Chapter Takeaway(s):

Affirmation / Meditation

*I am learning to listen and feel all of my feelings—they are cues
and signals of my precious needs.*

From Distorted Thinking to Clarity

Meditation / Prayer
*May I learn to restructure my distorted thinking one day at a time and
reach out for support when needed. May I have the wisdom to see clearly.*

Most people experience distorted thinking from time to time, but dysfunctional environments reinforce this tendency. Our caregivers operated from distorted thinking that clouded reality, and we learned to do the same, often as a way to cope with the dysfunction around us. Distorted thinking describes thought patterns that cause us to view reality inaccurately and either interpret events through a negative lens or put a rosy outlook on them. The patterns are so familiar that our minds do not recognize them; we have accepted them as fact.

To reparent ourselves, we need to recognize the fear and distorted thoughts coloring our inner family members' reality. The Laundry List and The Other Laundry List Traits are a great gauge of distorted thinking. Freedom from distorted thinking requires that we break the "Don't Talk, Don't Trust, Don't Feel" rule.

Reparenting, The 12 Steps, and working with recovering adult children can help us make a dramatic change in thinking. While the critical parent can be the primary source of distorted thinking, our inner child and inner teenager can also get caught up in a story or think in distorted ways. By helping our inner family members have more perspective, and feel more secure, these patterns gradually fade away, allowing us to live with clarity and serenity.

Our wounded inner family members tend to see the world through **the lens of our trauma.**

Exercise: *Recognizing Distorted Thinking*

Chapter 2 of the Big Red Book covers in depth four modes of internalized behavior (all-or-nothing thinking, judgmental thinking, control, perfectionism) passed on by dysfunctional families. We look additionally at fear, which can cause us to think in distorted ways. We explore some other forms of distorted thinking and control and perfectionism, behaviors driven by fear and distorted thinking.

As loving parents, we can learn to identify distorted thinking as we go through our day and tend to the inner family member engaged in it. We can keep a notepad or note app handy to write down when we had the distorted thought, or the thought itself, what inner family member seems to be involved, and what kind of distorted thought it is from the list below. Check all the types of distorted thinking you've experienced:

☐ **All-or-Nothing Thinking.** All-or-nothing thinking is thinking in extremes. We place experiences, people, and things into rigid categories such as good or bad, right or wrong.

☐ **Over-generalization.** Taking an unpleasant event and drawing broad conclusions. For example, when someone doesn't return our call, we might think, "People never return my call...this always happens to me."

☐ **Mental Filter.** Dwelling on a single negative detail. For example, focusing on one person's critical comment and ignoring everyone else's affirming feedback.

☐ **Discounting the positive.** Rejecting or minimizing our accomplishments or efforts. Telling ourselves our performance wasn't good enough or that anyone could have done as well.

☐ **Magnification.** Exaggerating our problems and shortcomings or minimizing our healthy qualities.

☐ **Projecting into the Future.** Predicting how things will turn out (often badly) in the future. Before a job interview, you might tell yourself, "I'm going to mess this up."

☐ **Catastrophizing.** Assuming that the worst will happen. Involves believing you're in a worse situation than you are or exaggerating the difficulties you face.

☐ **Jumping to Conclusions.** Interpreting things negatively with no evidence. Similar to mind reading, which is concluding that someone is reacting negatively to you.

☐ **Denying Reality or Counterfactual Thinking.** Denying or trying to control reality, not recognizing our powerlessness in certain situations. Telling ourselves "I could have avoided that accident," when the fact is that we got in an accident.

☐ **"Should" statements.** Thinking that things should be the way we hoped or expected them to be. "I shouldn't have made so many mistakes." We can "should" on ourselves by making demands.

☐ **Personalizing.** Taking things personally; taking responsibility for something that is not entirely in our control. "That person said that to hurt me", "They left because of me."

☐ **Blame.** Blaming other people or their circumstances for our problems; overlooking the ways we might be contributing to the problem. "My relationship is terrible because my partner expects too much."

☐ **Bright-siding.** Looking for some kind of positive, rather than being with the feelings of an unpleasant experience; fixing. "Well, at least I/you…." or "It could be worse."

☐ **Worry.** Dwelling on fears and troubles.

☐ **Judgmental Thinking.** Overly-critical thoughts about ourselves, others, situations.

☐ **Rumination.** Overthinking, obsessive thinking, reliving things from the past, rehearsing for the future.

☐ **False Beliefs.** Painful, limiting thoughts we learned to believe as children.

☐ **Delusional Thinking.** Clinging to a belief or altered reality despite evidence to the contrary. Believing we're being spied on, followed, slandered, or cheated on when it is not the case.

When our wounded and reactive inner family members think in these distorted ways, their painful interpretations become their "stories" and shape how they see the world: "I'm unlovable" or "This knee pain means I need surgery." These stories and ways of thinking might have helped us cope with dysfunction, but they feed the inner drugstore of adrenaline and stress. For this reason, letting them go can be hard because they can be so familiar and habitual.

While we can't prevent these thought patterns from arising, we can unlearn them as adults. We can recognize when they happen and ground ourselves in the present moment. The tools of broadening our perspective by making observations, identifying our feelings, and tending to our inner family member's needs help us discern between reality and distorted thinking.

Reflections: *Emotions Fuel Distorted Thinking*

In our emotionally and—for some of us—physically unsafe environments, we struggled to know how to protect ourselves and feel safe. The people who were responsible for keeping us safe in the world were also the source of our greatest fears and hurts. Making up stories about what happened was a way to feel more control and less uncertain about the confusing events in our homes. Thus, distorted thought patterns and stories became survival strategies.

Our hypervigilance, and our critical parent, grew out of our fears. We might have thought, "If I stay fearful and watchful, then I'll be safe. I won't miss anything and can prevent problems." Our fears caused us to become anxious adults. Whether we show it, consciously hide it, or are not even aware of it, we might feel an underlying fear in much of what we do. Learning not to feel this fear (to "stuff" it and "think it away") might be what contributes to the crippling anxiety from which adult children can suffer. The tendency to bury fear under emotions, such as anger, numbness, hurt, and resentment, feeds distorted thought patterns.

Growing up with caregivers who didn't know how to care for themselves, express or honor their own needs, set boundaries, or protect themselves was scary. They could not teach us how to think clearly and manage our feelings in healthy ways. They were probably shamed and, in turn, might have shamed us. Yet, love, play, safety, respect, being seen, being heard, and being valued are all basic human needs.

We can free ourselves from the bonds of our childhood by daring to feel our fears, learning we can survive those feelings, and not shaming ourselves for feeling them. Our childhood fears made sense. They were warning signals that something was not safe. As adults, we can discover what part of the fear comes from growing up with unsafe people and what belongs to the present moment. We can ask for guidance. We can soothe, stretch, and heal our tense, anxious bodies that have carried too many fears for too long. Slowly, we release stored fears with the help of our loving parent and a power greater than ourselves, including our fellowship.

1. What are some of your fears?

2. How might fear and other emotions, such as anger, hurt, resentment, and numbness, fuel distorted thinking patterns?

3. When and where does your inner child or inner teen get scared? What scares them?

4. In what ways has fear affected your life–what have been the costs?

5. What do you think a power greater than yourself or someone who cares deeply for you would say and do when you feel scared or express your fears?

6. What's one thing, however small, that you can do when you feel fear?

Reflections: *Identifying False Beliefs*

False beliefs are often unconscious, limiting beliefs acquired in childhood that our inner child carries until they can be released through reparenting and Step work. To have some sense of control and try to feel safe in dysfunctional environments, we made up "stories" to explain the abuse, abandonment, and/or neglect we experienced and their cause. "Mom never spends any time with me. There must be something wrong with me," or "Dad makes fun of my athletic ability. I must not be good at sports." False beliefs often come in the form of "I" statements.

> *"I'm not good enough,"*
> *"No one cares about me,"*
> *"I am unlovable,"*
> *"I must be perfect,"*
> *"There's something wrong with me."*

When we believe we're not enough, that we don't matter, or that we're unlovable, we experience shame. False beliefs are distorted because they have little basis in reality. The purpose of this exercise is to become aware of false beliefs so you can more readily identify them and tend to your inner child if they arise. We'll explore false beliefs more in Chapter 20.

1. List any false beliefs you're aware of. (e.g., I'm not good enough; I'm a burden; there's something wrong with me.)

2. How can your loving parent tend to your inner child when false beliefs arise?

3. What are some other actions you can take when a false belief arises? (e.g., shift your attention away from the thought, feel the effect in your body, talk about your feelings.)

All-or-Nothing Thinking

All-or-nothing thinking can make it seem like we have little or no choice in our life. "Never," "always," "must," and " have to" become traps. With all-or-nothing thinking, there is no in-between. We are either wonderful or horrible, brilliant or stupid. We learned all-or-nothing thinking early in life so it can take time to recognize it.

When we notice all-or-nothing thinking, we can ask ourselves, "What other options might be available?" We can notice what emotions, interpretations, or inner family members might be driving our thinking. We can question what we're thinking and believing to break the trance of all-or-nothing thinking. "Is it true I'm a bad person because I arrived five minutes late?" "Is it true I'm a loser because I made a mistake?" Get curious about the origin of such thoughts and beliefs. How old do they feel? Does believing them bring serenity or make life unmanageable?

> "*I have to* run at least 5 miles, or it's not worth it."
> "If I eat one cookie, I might as well eat them *all.*"
> "*I can't* meditate on a cushion for 45 minutes, so forget about it."

Our loving parent can help balance our inner family members way of thinking so we can accept ourselves just the way we are, and seriously consider our options.

Reflections: *All-or-Nothing Thinking*

1. How does all-or-nothing thinking affect your life today?

2. What all-or-nothing thought or pattern is familiar to you now or in the past? What inner family member might that be related to?

3. How might a loving parent reframe that all-or-nothing thought or pattern?

Judgmental Thinking

In our dysfunctional homes, many of us were surrounded by judgments and comparisons. We see and hear judgments all around us in the news, on social media, in institutions, at work, and with friends and family.

We can learn to recognize how judgments shape our experience of the world when they arise. We can help our inner family members take judgments—from our critical parent and other people— less personally. We can also notice what causes our inner family members to become judgmental.

*Oh, I'm having **judgmental thoughts**.*

*Who in my inner family is **triggered**?*

*What do they **need**?*

Perhaps we're judgmental because we really wish we could be doing the thing we're criticizing. The reparenting check-in can be a great way to get under the storyline of judgmental thinking. The check-in helps us discover what our inner child or inner teen are feeling and what they need. Sometimes they can act out through us, judging other people when they don't meet our needs. When our inner child feels helpless, our critical parent or inner teen might judge others to feel more powerful. Sadly, the critical parent, and sometimes the inner teenager, use judgment to protect the inner child from abandonment while pushing them further into isolation.

There is a difference between being judgmental and using discernment. We need wisdom and discernment to make responsible decisions in our lives. Judgment involves condemnation and an us-versus-them mindset. Critical thoughts equate a person with their behavior or abilities: "You are bad." Discernment involves seeing differences in people's abilities, experiences, behaviors, and qualities while valuing everyone as being equally worthy. We need discernment to make healthy decisions for ourselves—with whom to work our recovery, share our secrets, and the like. Judgment closes our hearts; discernment allows them to stay open but protected by healthy boundaries. "I care about you and am setting boundaries to limit my contact with you."

Reflections: *Judgmental Thinking*

1. What are your most common judgments toward other people?

2. What judgments or comparisons did you hear in your family of origin? In what ways do you relate or not relate to the judgments and comparisons you heard from adults in your childhood?

3. What are your most common judgments about yourself? Which inner family members seem to do the judging? Which inner family members seem to be the recipients of the judging?

4. How are judgments, shame, and blame related in your experience?

5. How might your consumption of news and social media feed your judgments and critical parent?

6. How can you recognize when you are coming from a place of discernment rather than judgment?

7. How can you practice noticing what is good—those times when people are kind, loving, and gentle?

Worry

Worry is thinking about future events in a way that leaves you feeling anxious or apprehensive. A pervasive sense of worry becomes anxiety and can lead to avoidance, distraction, and numbing behaviors. We tend to worry when we're faced with our powerlessness—not being able to control future outcomes or safeguard our families and personal interests with certainty. Worrying is a reaction to a thought, not a reaction to an immediate danger.

Worrying harms our mental health and takes us out of the present moment where—unless we're in immediate danger—we're okay. Parts of us worry because they think doing so will help us prevent potential threats. Worry (and similarly rumination) is a strategy we use to try to gain a sense of control through thought. Worrying about our powerlessness to change family members, dysfunctional family dynamics, the future, or strong feelings (other peoples' or our own) gave us a sense of control.

Understanding how worry affects our inner child can motivate us to pause and take a program-informed action. Rather than entertain future projections that terrify the inner child, we can set a boundary to disengage from worrying. Instead, we can turn toward the underlying emotional and physical feelings to discover which inner family member needs support. Our loving parent can help that inner family member become grounded in the present moment. "Let's look around. We're okay just now. Let's take a deep breath." We can remind our inner family members that it's okay to be who and where we are and that we don't need to be perfect to be lovable.

*Ask, **"What is happening right now?"** And then **notice** your breath, physical sensations, sights, and sounds to anchor your attention in the here and now.*

*Your body is always in the **present moment**.*

When worries arise, we can ask, "What would my loving parent say or do about this?" We can also ask, "Is this helpful or important to think about right now?" Mindfulness can help us notice worried thoughts and bring our attention to the present moment to feel our feelings.

Worksheet: *Worry Inventory*

List the worries that have preoccupied you in the last six months, whether they happened or not. Put a Y next to worries that actually happened. For example, "I will lose my job if I don't do A, B, and C." If you lost your job, put a Y next to that item. Next, identify the effect worrying had on the inner child, and what your loving parent would say about the worry.

Worksheet: *Worry Inventory*				
Past worry I had:	What might an inner family member be trying to prevent by worrying?	Did what I worry about actually happen? (Y/N)	What was the effect of the worry on my inner child, including feelings and unmet needs?	What can my inner loving parent do or say to help my inner child's worry?
Example: My brother will relapse	*He'll die a horrible death; I'll be left to pick up the pieces. Loss, pain, guilt.*	*N*	*Scared, lost sleep, couldn't relax. Unmet needs: serenity, ease, joy.*	*"You really care about him. We're powerless over what happens; let's turn this over. I've got you."*

Worksheet: *Worry Inventory*				
Past worry I had:	**What might an inner family member be trying to prevent by worrying?**	**Did what I worry about actually happen? (Y/N)**	**What was the effect of the worry on my inner child, including feelings and unmet needs?**	**What can my inner loving parent do or say to help my inner child's worry?**
Example: "If you don't go to work, even though you have a cold, they'll fire you."	*Loss of job; loss of income; destitution for me and my family.*	*N*	*Stress, terror, couldn't rest, probably stayed sick longer. Unmet needs: rest, ease, gentleness, caring, security, safety, serenity.*	*I'm sorry you learned that your needs and health don't matter. It's important to rest when you're sick, and it also protects others.*

Review your completed inventory. What do you notice?

You might wish to add worries to your inventory and review them periodically.

Distorted Thinking Fuels Outdated Coping Strategies
Outdated Coping Strategy: Control

The issue of control is caused by distorted thinking. It is the basis of our dysfunctional behaviors, including perfectionism. Of all the behaviors that adult children develop to survive, control can be the most deeply rooted. We either seek to control, resist being controlled by others, or fear being in control. These are fear-based reactions that are often driven by our inner family members. They might fear that if they don't "take control," our life will be ruined. Letting go of control can feel like an impending death. The Big Red Book describes control as manipulation, passive-aggressiveness, and false kindness (people-pleasing).

Correcting people, needing to have the last word, road rage, being over prepared, and insisting that people see your perspective are all examples of control. They signal takeovers from inner family members whose fear and pain we can act out unconsciously. We learn to recognize control scenarios gradually and to see how they stem from fear and wounding. We start to feel less ashamed and recognize that these parts of us learned to control to survive and cope. Our loving parent can help our inner family members gently let go of control in stages.

Reflection Exercise: *Control*

1. What areas of your life do you (or your inner family members) try to control? (e.g., what others think of you, what people say, what people do, what others feel, how you feel, how things are done, etc.)

2. How does trying to control those things impact your inner child?

3. What might you gain by letting go of control or by helping your inner family members let go?

4. How might reparenting support the letting-go process?

5. How might connecting to a power greater than yourself and the principles of the Steps, particularly Step 3, support the letting-go process?

Outdated Coping Strategy: Perfectionism

"Our perfectionism as adults represents an internalization of our parents' attitudes and discontent with self. For most of us, our parents never said: "You have done enough. Take time to enjoy the accomplishment. Relax." -Big Red Book, page 39

Perfectionism can appear as having excessively high standards, as well as procrastination and paralysis. Perfectionism is a response to a shame-based and controlling home. The child mistakenly believes they can avoid being shamed if they think and act "perfectly," whatever "perfect" means in their family.

Procrastination is a form of perfectionism—not acting until perfect conditions appear. It's a way the inner teenager or critical parent can block the inner child's discomfort by focusing on something other than a triggering task. Yet, when inner family members take over, causing us to procrastinate, we abandon our anxious inner child. Our loving parent can tend to our inner child's feelings and distorted thinking, making it more possible for us to act rather than react. Gratitude and celebration are some antidotes to perfectionism. Our inner loving parent helps our inner child know they're enough and to let "good enough" be enough. When we celebrate our inner children and acknowledge what we're grateful for, perfectionism has less room to invade our thoughts.

> *Perfectionism* leads to *procrastination*, which leads to *paralysis*.

Reflection Exercise: *Perfectionism*

1. In what ways has perfectionism (and its other expressions: procrastination and paralysis) affected your life? What have the consequences been?

2. What inner child feelings cause you to pursue perfection or to procrastinate?

3. What's one recent thing/experience, however small, that you can be grateful about?

4. What do you think a higher power, or someone who cares deeply for you, loves and appreciates about you?

Reparenting Our Distorted Thinking with Gentleness

Attending meetings and applying the techniques you've been learning in this book can help you address distorted thinking. Practicing mindfulness on a regular basis increases the likelihood of noticing distorted thinking in the moment.

> ***Gentle**, gentle,*
> *kind, and **gentle**.*

When we notice an inner family member's distorted thought, we can acknowledge what is happening with a silent mental note such as, *"this is a distorted thought"* or *"this is the critical parent."* Naming our experience helps limit the intensity, creates space to pick up additional program tools, and motivates us to redirect our focus.

> *I am **powerless** over these distorted thoughts, and **life becomes unmanageable** when I listen to them. I can come to believe I can be restored to clarity, and I can make a decision to turn these distorted thoughts over to the care of a power **greater than myself.***

When we lack the capacity to cope with distorted thinking, we can turn to a higher power. That might mean reaching out to a sponsor or fellow traveler or turning to Steps 1, 2, and 3.

We work with our distorted thinking like we do with all our reparenting work—we remember to focus on progress, not the distorted goal of perfection. We won't always notice distorted thinking when it arises in our inner family, and at times we might avoid doing reparenting work. Yet, those times can deepen our compassion for the deeply ingrained nature of the effects of family dysfunction. Rather than listen to the critical parent's messages or distorted thoughts about this, we can use it as a learning opportunity to work through the issue with our loving parent's gentleness and compassion.

Your Key Chapter Takeaway(s):

Affirmation / Meditation

I learned distorted thinking from my dysfunctional family. I can learn clear thinking with the help of my support group, my loving parent, and a power greater than myself.

Tending to Your Inner Children

Meditation / Prayer
May I be sensitive to my inner children's emotional states and care for their needs with gentleness, humor, love, and respect. May my heart fill with compassion for all they've had to defend themselves against.

Children thrive with undivided parental attention. The more we consistently seek out our inner child—and pay attention to them when they show up—the more integrated and whole we become. Learning to be with our inner child's pain keeps their pain from controlling our lives.

Our inner child wants to know if we, as loving parents, can meet their need for unconditional love. Some of their questions are the same ones we grappled with as children:

- Do you accept me? Is it okay to be me?
- Do you see my goodness, even when I make mistakes?
- Can I trust you with my feelings, or do I need to hide the ones you don't like?
- Will you listen to me?
- Will you be in my corner?
- Will you show up even when you prefer to do something else?
- Can I trust you to take action when needed?

When you can, spend time tending to and nurturing your inner child. Even 30 seconds will make a difference. Listening to and being with our inner child, and changing our behavior, is the action and work that helps them heal.

Tending to Your Inner Children

"When I'm feeling stuck or sad, I ask my little girl what's up, let the tears fall, and give her what she needs. That could be a hug, affirmations, talking with fellow travelers, reparenting worksheets, breaks from work, or simply being. ACA gives me hope for deeper, loving reparenting to come." -Fellow Traveler

Your loving parent can tend to your inner child and inner teen in many ways. Here we cover a few tools you can add to your reparenting toolbox. Some also help to regulate your nervous system and rewire your brain.

When you use these tools, if your inner teenager or critical parent are the most vocal, address their concerns first. They might need you to validate their worries before they're willing to take a break.

Tend to: care for, look after, give one's attention to

Exercise: *Nurturing through Touch*

"Putting a hand on my chest and just being with the inner child during his painful experiences is consoling. He gets frightened and needs reassurance." -Fellow Traveler

Gentle, safe touch was often missing in dysfunctional homes. Yet, your loving parent can nurture your inner family through warm, safe touch today. Placing a hand on your body releases the social bonding hormone oxytocin, which reduces levels of the stress hormone cortisol. Oxytocin helps you be with your experience when you're stressed, rather than fight, flee, or freeze. Your own touch is just as powerful as another person's touch and sends a physical message to your inner children. "I've got you; I love you, and it's okay." Making gentle sounds along with physical contact can deepen your inner child's feeling of connection and nurturance.

You can take advantage of this surprisingly simple way of being with your inner children in any setting. During a meeting, placing a hand on your body in a discreet, caring way tells your inner child they're not alone and helps calm them. No one even needs to know you're doing it!

What's nurturing will be different for everyone. You might ask yourself, "What touch does my inner child need to feel safe? Comforted? Seen and heard?" Nurturing touch can create a connection when your inner children are triggered, as well as when you want to make conscious contact with them.

Experiment with the different forms of touch below and add some of your own. Not every suggestion will resonate, but the goal is to find those that work for your inner children. Consider recording the paragraph below to play back when you have a quiet, private place where you will not be interrupted. Pause during your recording so you have time to notice how the touch feels.

Eyes can be open or closed. Try out each option for a few moments. Add soothing sounds (humming, vowel sounds, "there, there"), if you wish. Notice any physical sensations or other signals you get from within. Try gently laying your hand(s) on a part of your body that calls to you. That might be a hand, or both, over your heart or on your face or cheek. It might be a hand or both hands on your belly or a hand on your heart and the other on your belly. You might find it nurturing to sit with both hands together in front of you in "prayer position." Listen deeply to your body. Be patient. Have the patience and courage to give yourself the chance to discover what feels comforting to you. You can try sitting down or lying in different positions, such as the fetal position. Use a blanket or a comforter, if that feels good. Maybe a gentle scalp massage or self-hug would feel nurturing or try rocking or swaying. Listen deeply and gently to your body; it holds all your memories.

Working with your body can unleash strong feelings, such as grief, connecting you to childhood pain and places where you might carry trauma. It's crucial to create a safe space for yourself and to give yourself permission to stop, if you begin to feel overwhelmed.

Some people find it helpful to touch something comforting outside the body. Perhaps holding or focusing on a pet, a tree trunk, a stuffed animal, doll, pillow, or other object will resonate better. Once more trust develops, returning to the body might be possible. Approach this task with gentleness and at a slow pace. The point is to find the touch that resonates for your inner children and to develop the habit of physically comforting them when needed.

"One day I realized that I had been hurt as a baby, before I had words. I had a deep sense of abandonment as my earliest memory. What if my inner child was a baby? What would he need? He wouldn't understand words. That's when I got in touch with Baby Mike. Rather than talk to him, I pick him up and cradle him, hold him, rock him, make soothing sounds. I feel the connection now." -Fellow Traveler

Exercise: *Nurturing through Words*

"I've had to learn to speak 'to' my inner child and inner teen so I am truly in communication with them rather than speak 'at' them or say what I think I 'should' say." -Fellow Traveler

It's okay if I don't know what to say to my inner child or inner teen.

I am **learning**.

*I can start **just by listening**.*

When reparenting, what we say and how we say it matters. Just as we need to lift weights to build muscle, we need to practice speaking as our loving parent to find our voice. This process can feel strange at first. Your inner child, your inner teenager, or critical parent might react or judge the process. This is a natural part of breaking the "Don't Talk, Don't Trust, Don't Feel" rule. Your inner loving parent can take it slowly and focus first on listening.

Questions such as, "What does my inner child or inner teenager need to hear from my loving parent that feels compassionate and supportive?" can guide us. We can tell them all the things we wished our parents would have told us. It can help to listen to their concerns about a particular situation and add personal details so our words resonate more deeply. It's natural if this is difficult. We are learning a new language. We can imagine what we would say to a dear friend or a child who are struggling.

An inner teenager needs a loving parent to match their energy. This is different than the soothing talk offered to the inner child. When your inner teenager has strong feelings, thank them and empathize with their feelings. For example, "Thank you for trying to protect us. You don't have to do that job, I have some different ways to keep us safe today." A loving parent can help talk down a teenager when they get triggered. They appreciate compassion, authenticity, and directness. They watch to see if you, as their loving parent, back up your words with action, like setting boundaries and changing your behavior. The inner teenager's trust needs to be earned.

At times, your inner teenager doesn't need loving words but rather loving attention. You can give them space to vent: "I'll set a timer for two minutes, and you can tell me everything that's bothering you. Then I'll address this for you." At other times, an internal boundary is necessary: "It's okay to stop playing the situation over and over; that seems stressful. I will help you focus on how we can get what we really want in a healthy way."

To practice nurturing through words, think of a current situation that is mildly painful (but not intense) so you can begin to strengthen your compassion little by little. Once you have a situation in mind, ask, "What does my inner child or inner teenager need to hear to feel my loving parent's compassion?" Perhaps they need to hear, "This is hard," or "It makes sense that you feel this way," or "You need kindness like everyone else." Maybe they feel lonely and need to hear, "You will never have to be alone again. I'm here with you." Note how it feels in your body to offer your inner child or inner teen these loving messages.

Experiment with the following messages to see which ones resonate, adapting them and fine-tuning your language to what your inner child or inner teen need to hear.

Example Messages for Your Inner Child

All your feelings are welcome here.	Even though this feels like the past, this is different.
I'm here. I'll keep you safe.	I love you. You are enough, no matter what.
I care about how you feel.	I get that you're angry. I'm on it.
This is an adult job. I've got this.	You seem scared. Would you like to hold my hand?

Example Messages for Your Inner Teenager

Wow, that sounds hard.	You don't have to be strong this time. I'll handle this.
I get that you're angry.	
I've got your back.	How about I do this and, if it doesn't feel good, I'll stop, and we can find another option?
Try not to take this personally; their reaction isn't about you. I see you.	You're feeling a powerful urge. Take a breath, and we'll explore other ways to cope.

Sometimes nurturing through words might seem dry, disconnected, or uncomfortable. Sometimes it lands, and you feel a shift. Whatever the case, keep practicing and noticing what messages resonate. See if it's possible to allow yourself to not be good at this and give yourself time to find your loving parent's voice. Trying to get it right is a sign the critical parent has slipped into the driver's seat.

> *What would a*
> ***loving parent***
> *do or say in this situation?*

Other helpful guidelines for speaking with your inner children include:

- Focus on what your inner children need to hear rather than what you want them to hear.
- Practice deep listening. It's okay if your inner child or inner teen says nothing. Your presence matters.
- Keep your reflections simple and short.

- Show acceptance for your inner children in the here and now, not a future desired state. Rather than affirm qualities like, "you're successful and wealthy," help your inner children see their basic goodness. "I like you just because you're you."
- Use a slow pace, backed up with personal warmth.
- Make requests and ask questions. For example, "Would you like a hug?" rather than "Come sit on my lap."
- Address the inner child and inner teenager directly instead of in the third person; experiment with using "you," or a name with personal meaning, or a term of endearment. If you're not sure what they want to be called, ask them and see what they say.

Loving parent messages aren't meant to "fix" feelings, they're meant to acknowledge and allow them. Your inner children might feel better after you connect, but the main focus is on strengthening the loving parent's unconditional love for the inner children, not changing their feelings or making them "better." A helpful phrase to remind them is, "It's okay to feel this."

Reflections: *Nurturing Touch, Nurturing Words*

"When my inner teenager gets triggered and restless, I give her a hug and say, 'I got you.' It calms her. My breathing goes from fast to normal." -Fellow Traveler

1. What forms of comforting touch resonated with your inner child and inner teenager?

2. What physical sensations and emotions were present when the comforting touch resonated?

3. What are some things your inner child needs to hear?

4. What are some things your inner teenager needs to hear?

5. If your inner teenager is reactive or doesn't seem to trust you or listen to you, ask them what you could do or say to help them trust you more.

6. Are there actions your inner child or inner teenager need the loving parent to take in order to better your life conditions?

7. What are some times, or situations, when offering comforting touch or words to your inner children might be useful? Be as specific as you can, so when those moments arise, you're more likely to remember.

"Waking up each morning is when I experienced the most debilitating anxiety in the past. My living amends to my inner children today involve me pulling up images of my younger selves into my mind's eye when I meditate each morning. My inner children 'speak' to me through felt sensations in my body and emotions that arise." -Fellow Traveler

Worksheet: *Offering Your Inner Children Compassion and Perspective*

With a loving parent in our lives, our inner child can stop assuming they have done something wrong when the critical parent gets activated. A loving parent pauses and listens to the distorted thoughts and false beliefs and tends to the inner children's feelings. A loving parent offers perspective and reminds the inner children they have worth. Below are examples of how we can reframe critical parent messages, with space to add personal examples on the next page.

Worksheet: *Offering Your Inner Children Compassion and Perspective*	
Critical Parent	**Loving Parent**
You won't be able to handle the feelings.	*I won't leave you alone with these feelings. You can feel them a little at a time. I will reach out for support if it becomes too much.*
You're all alone.	*I see you feel scared and lonely. You have me, and I'll never leave you. We have fellow travelers too, and we can meet healthy people.*
You didn't prepare. You're lazy!	*Something must be going on for you. Are you feeling scared? Worried about not being good enough? I will take care of this presentation; it's not your job.*
You really screwed that up.	*Mistakes are chances to learn and grow. You're enough, no matter what.*

Critical Parent	Loving Parent

Reactions to Loving Parent Messages

Loving parent messages can comfort our inner children, but they can also be triggering for more than one reason. Sometimes, no matter how heartfelt these messages are, our inner family members distrust them. They learned early—because of neglect, abuse, abandonment, and mixed messages—not to trust. Moreover, what looked like kindness might have been used to manipulate or abuse us, so our inner family members might perceive loving messages as fake or suspicious.

Sometimes our inner family members react because the loving parent isn't in the driver's seat. The messages might sound like a loving parent, but the critical parent or another part of us has taken over. If our inner child seems hesitant or afraid or if our inner teenager reacts, chances are the critical parent is involved. We can pause and invite our loving parent to take charge.

At other times, our inner child simply needs more time. We can notice how our little one responds when we offer them nurturing words. Are they feeling heard, safe? Are they ready to connect? We can, at last, attune and respond to their needs, which is what they so deeply needed in childhood.

Worksheet: *Reactions to Loving Messages*

Fill out the columns in the following worksheet, allowing your uncensored responses and reactions to the "Loving Parent Message" in column one. The purpose is to reveal any judgments or reactions your inner family members have to the messages. There is nothing you need to do; seeing the pain behind why inner family members can't take in the messages can increase our compassion for them. Record your reaction to how your inner family members react to loving messages in the last column.

Loving Parent Message	Feelings/physical sensations	Thoughts (judgments, responses)	Your reaction/ feelings
Mistakes are chances to learn and grow. I will help you with this.	*Example: tight chest and jaw, heaviness, anger*	No, you won't. Where have you been? You're a phony.	*I understand why my little one doesn't trust. I feel sad they've had to be on guard*
It's okay to feel this.			
I'm here. I'll keep you safe.			
I love you. You're enough.			
Even though this feels familiar, this is different. I'm here to help.			
I get that you're angry. I've got your back.			
You don't have to take care of that. I'll handle that for you.			
What a disappointment for you.			
You seem torn about going.			
That must have been frustrating for you.			
Just because someone had a negative reaction to you doesn't mean you did anything wrong.			
I'm listening.			
I'm sorry you're hurting.			

"My family jokingly referred to me as stupid. When my partners called me names, I felt loved and got attention. Today my favorite representations of love come from how I am accepted by my fellowship. They show me affection, hug me, listen to me, compliment me on my talents, and encourage me when I fall. Thanks to the fellowship's modeling, I began to treat myself in kind, as my loving parent would." -Fellow Traveler

Being With Your Inner Children—Conscious Contact

*"My inner children don't trust words, as words didn't reflect reality. 'Talk's cheap,' and 'Action is louder than words' is their experience. So far my job as a loving parent has primarily been to LISTEN, only asking a question for clarity or speaking to offer subtle encouragement. I hold them. I **am** safety. I **am** not teaching them that I love them so I need no words. I **am** love. I **am** acceptance. I **am** compassion. I **am** empathy." -Fellow Traveler*

There is power in empathetic silence—sometimes the best communication doesn't involve words. Your loving attention meets their need for acceptance as they are—they don't always need to be "worked on." Carve out time to be with your inner child or inner teenager in silence, getting a felt sense of them. Your presence can be as healing to them as words or actions and builds trust. You might find it helpful to set a timer. If your attention wanders, keep bringing it back. Be mindful of your physical sensations and any images that arise from this part of you.

Explore what will best connect you to the innocence of this part of you. Some people spend time with flesh-and-blood children. Others choose to read parenting books, children's books, and watch children's movies. You can do the same with your inner teen.

Your Key Chapter Takeaway(s):

Affirmation / Meditation

I am learning to tend to my inner children with love and gentleness.
Together we are becoming more joyous, happy, and free.

Setting Internal Boundaries:
An Expression of Unconditional Love

Meditation / Prayer
Grant me the clarity and strength to set healthy internal boundaries.
May these boundaries lead to more clarity, kindness, and love toward my inner family and others.

Boundaries represent what does and does not work for us in the form of personal guidelines, rules, or limits. They come in the form of statements, actions, or choices not to do something, and they can evolve over time. Setting boundaries is *action coming from love* because doing so helps us be honest and care for ourselves. For example, saying "no," if we don't feel comfortable receiving a hug or don't want someone to touch us.

We set internal boundaries with our thoughts, emotions, unhelpful impulses and behaviors, and our inner family members. Such invisible "fences" are just as important as the ones we build with other people.

In dysfunctional families, boundaries are typically too rigid, too loose, or a confusing mix of the two. They lead to enmeshment and difficulty with boundaries in adulthood. Permissive or dismissive parenting styles lack healthy consequences or structure and lead to loose boundaries. Authoritarian or hypochondriac parenting styles result in rigid boundaries. In either situation, we reach adulthood not understanding the appropriate and healthy differences between ourselves and others. This misunderstanding can appear in a variety of ways, such as difficulty:

- Keeping promises to change habits around substances, compulsions, and behaviors
- Following through with desired goals
- Being accountable to others, or
- Stopping behaviors that bring adverse health, relationship, work, or financial consequences

Our distorted thinking and lack of healthy internal boundaries perpetuate these difficulties. The result is a chaotic inner life with our inner family members jumping into the driver's seat to cope. They can interpret the lack of boundaries as a sign we don't care or that their ship has no captain.

Healthy internal boundaries help reduce the frequency of takeovers and provide our inner family with structure and safety. Such boundaries help us be honest with others rather than people-please. They also support us to respond in healthy ways when our boundaries get crossed. Our loving parent can help our inner teen not take a boundary violation personally, conserving their energy.

Internal boundaries help your inner family turn over responsibility to your loving parent. At first, though, they might react to these boundaries and could need empathy and support. We can also help them learn to accept and respect others' boundaries. Some examples of creating an internal boundary include:

- Inviting our inner child or inner teen to relax in their safe inner space while we work or handle adult responsibilities: "This is an adult job. I'm in charge of work right now. You get to be a child (or teenager)."

- Letting our loving parent protect the inner child during challenging conversations or situations. In our mind's eye, we can move our inner child behind us (where they can hold on to our leg, hug our back, or whatever they need) where they feel safe and connected to us. They can also hang out in their safe inner space at these times.
- Setting an internal boundary with the critical parent, letting them know they don't get to harshly second-guess mistakes we made in the past. When they project into an imagined scary future, we can tell them "Stop. That's not real. That's scary to the inner child."
- Remembering that our inner children go with us everywhere and setting internal boundaries for those times when we can't tend to them in the moment. We can let them know, "This isn't a good time for me to talk with you. After I leave this meeting, I will be able to give you my full attention."

If you feel scared, anxious, or worried about setting an internal boundary, another part of you is likely reacting. Your loving parent can reassure this reactive part of you: "It's okay to practice a new way. I'm setting the boundary. That's not your job, and I'll handle any consequences."

As your loving parent guides your inner family members with healthy internal boundaries, they don't have to be in charge anymore. They can move out of survival mode, making it more possible to be in conscious contact with a higher power and the present moment. You can begin to sense how you're so much more than your wounded or controlling inner family members.

Boundaries: Thought Patterns

Mindfulness helps us recognize, rather than believe, the distorted thoughts and painful stories our inner family members have internalized. We can set an internal boundary to protect inner family members who get caught in heartbreaking stories or repetitive thought loops. Staying in our heads was one way we learned to have a sense of control and cope. We can remind our inner family members that things are different today. When we recognize distorted thinking, we might tell our inner child, "You're getting scared by an image or thought about the future. This is not the future. Let's stay here. I'm here with you," or "I won't let you hurt yourself with those old ideas that aren't true." We might help our inner teen by saying, "Whoa. Before jumping to conclusions, let's take a breath. Once you feel calmer, I'll check things out."

With practice, we can turn our attention away from the critical parent, label shaming thoughts, and let them go, surrendering them to a higher power. We're powerless over what thoughts come, but we're not powerless over redirecting our attention. Some days we might need to recognize and set internal boundaries with distorted thinking or critical parent messages many times. Doing so helps us notice how powerless we are over our distorted thoughts and how painful it can be to take them personally. Our ability to unhook from distorted thoughts grows stronger each time we are mindful of them and set an internal boundary.

"I learned that my critical parent doesn't have to be scary. I feel empowered and capable when I set a boundary with my critical parent." -Fellow Traveler

Boundaries: Emotional Reactions

Emotional boundaries help us know where we begin and end. Emotional boundaries help us own our feelings while not taking responsibility for other peoples' feelings. Without emotional boundaries, adult children can give unsolicited advice, criticize, blame, accept blame, personalize, and take responsibility for others' moods, feelings, problems, and reactivity.

Internal emotional boundaries are needed to support the inner family. Our loving parent can remind the inner child, "You're not responsible for other people's feelings." The inner teenager, who might feel angry and want to lash out, might need to hear, "I get it. Their reaction is a reflection on them, not you. You don't need to handle this. I'll do it for you." When the inner teenager wants to replay the story and what they could have said, our loving parent can set a boundary. "That's not helpful right now. Let's be with the feelings, and then I'll take action for you, if needed."

Boundaries: Unhelpful Impulses and Behaviors

A lack of healthy internal boundaries with our inner children's thoughts and feelings can lead to unhealthy behaviors, such as numbing our feelings with substances or trying to fix feelings through perfectionism. Internal behavioral boundaries help transform patterns that trap us in childhood reactions.

As loving parents, we can learn to tend to our inner children's feelings and set internal boundaries when their intense feelings get triggered. We begin to sense their impulse to shut down, lash out, or numb themselves in response. Helping them pause and bring down the intensity by breathing or using other grounding techniques gives us the chance to become actors, rather than allowing their urges to drive us into an unhealthy reaction. We can help our inner children trust that it's okay to feel today and that the feelings won't hurt them. Our presence gives them the trust not to stuff or control their emotions. Gradually, they learn it's safe to feel their feelings and that doing so meets their needs better than acting out.

"I let my teenager know, 'Thank you for trying to protect Little Me. Little Me is already feeling afraid. You can't take their feelings away by distracting them, though I know you wish you could. The feelings will still be there when the distraction is over. I will help them through their feelings." -Fellow Traveler

Reflections: *Internal Boundaries*

1. What are some thought patterns, emotional reactions, and unhelpful behaviors that could benefit from internal boundaries?

2. Boundaries for thought patterns, such as rumination and catastrophizing (e.g., "No, I'm not entertaining that thought."):

3. Boundaries for emotional reactions, such as feeling guilty for standing up for ourselves or taking something personally (e.g., "It's okay if someone feels disappointed because I said 'no.' My intention wasn't to hurt them but to care for my inner family."):

4. Boundaries for unhelpful behaviors (e.g., "Thank you for trying to protect the little one from those feelings. It's okay to be with these feelings today rather than numb them."):

5. Imagine that you've just applied one of the internal boundaries above. Notice any emotions and physical sensations that arise and note them here.

Internal boundaries are a form of unconditional love that allow the inner teenager and inner child to gradually relax and trust us as loving parents. It takes time, support, and courage to create internal boundaries, but it can be done.

Internal Boundaries with Your Inner Children

"I have to know my adult limitations and only make promises to my inner child that I can keep. I need to follow through on my commitments and meet her needs as well as my adult needs. If I don't give her the attention she needs or wants, she takes over completely, and neither of us gets what we want. I firmly guide her by explaining and negotiating. I have to set and maintain reasonable boundaries with her. I keep her safe from abuse, and every time someone violates my boundaries, I stand up, make my truth known, and hold my ground." -Fellow Traveler

In Chapter 5, we practiced setting boundaries with the critical parent. Here we learn to set gentle, firm boundaries with our inner children to protect, support, and guide them. This helps us regain the driver's seat and avoid the unwanted consequences that can come when their wounds drive our behavior. We can do a reparenting check-in to identify who's triggered in order to tend to them and then set an internal and external boundary, if needed. We acknowledge their feelings and needs. "I get that you're mad. You'd like more accountability. I'm here, and I'll address this with that person. It's not your responsibility."

Mindfulness can help us recognize when we might need to set boundaries with our inner teen around overthinking, compulsive behavior, substances, lashing out, and judgmental thinking. We might say, "Something isn't working for you. Would you be willing to tell me what you need so I can better support you?" or "I'll set a two-minute timer, and you can let all your thoughts and feelings out. Then I'll help resolve this for you."

If our inner child's distorted thinking is active, we can set a boundary with their false belief: "You don't need to believe that. It's not the truth. You are enough, no matter what." After setting an internal boundary with the inner child's distorted thinking, nurture them and tend to the underlying fear and shame.

These are some examples of gentle internal boundaries:

- "There will be times when you won't feel like doing something. It's okay that you don't want to do it. I'll do it because I want to uphold commitments." "I understand you're not enjoying this. What would make it less awful for you?"
- "Avoiding that project sounds really tempting, doesn't it? You don't have to do it. I'll take care of it while you kick back and relax."
- "This isn't your job, little one. I was hired for the job, and I have the skills. You get to be little."

As loving parents, we can learn to allow and accept all our inner children's feelings while setting loving boundaries at the same time. An internal boundary is most effective once we've first tended to the inner child and inner teen's feelings and needs. Suppose we just set an internal boundary. They might experience it as the "Don't Talk, Don't Trust, Don't feel" rule. Our inner teenager, for example, needs to be seen for their efforts. They need to trust that if something needs to happen to protect the inner child—such as speaking up—we'll make that happen.

Let's imagine, for example, that a fellow traveler makes passive-aggressive comments in a study group. Our triggered inner teenager might want to say something like, "Making passive-aggressive comments is dysfunctional. You should know better and stop." If we jump straight to guidance by telling our inner teen, "We're powerless over other people," this might upset them. It removes their means of protecting the hurt inner child and doesn't address their concern. Instead, we need to first thank our inner teen, tend to them, tend to our inner child, and meet their needs in an adult way appropriate to the situation.

Other gentle but firm boundaries:

- "I can see how mad you are with that person. I will go to another room so things don't get worse."
- "Feeling angry is okay. Lashing out is not. You can express these feelings to me, and I'll address it with that person if needed."
- "Dad told you you were stupid. It wasn't true then, and it isn't true now. Let's let that thought go, it's hurting you."
- "I'm turning the TV off for now. We can watch more another time."

- "Just because we're taking some time to rest doesn't mean you're lazy. It's okay to relax and let those judgments go."
- "You feel so angry at my boss because you're mistaking them for _____ (childhood authority figure) and believe you have no choice here. This is not that same situation. You can express that anger to me, and I'll handle things with my boss."

Our inner family members might react to boundaries based on what they learned, or didn't learn, about boundaries in our dysfunctional families.

Loose or No Boundaries
can lead to...

Trouble distinguishing between wants and needs

Difficulty tolerating discomfort, disappointment

Struggle with discipline, entitlement, impatience, or disregard for rules

Rigid Boundaries
can lead to...

Resisting or ignoring other people's boundaries

Resisting healthy changes or structure

As loving parents
we can help inner family members...

Have more realistic expectations and respect inner and outer limits	Realize current situations are not past situations	Cope with discomfort and disappointment	Discover what will help them trust the proposed changes

Your inner children might have feelings when you set loving boundaries with them. You can honor their feelings without complying with their requests (or demands!). When they don't want to do something, get curious about what's driving their reaction. Are they putting you in touch with your intuition or reacting from shame and fear? When they want to do something, check to see if your loving parent is in the driver's seat. We can gain clarity and lovingly address their concerns, as well as those of the critical parent. Are the concerns based on reality or distorted thinking? As inner loving parents, we can put healthy boundaries in place that meet our whole selves' needs.

"My inner child and I have an agreement that if someone crosses our boundary-lines, she gives me a tiny tap from inside to alert me. It is then my adult job to resolve the situation amicably, if possible. If not, I decide what healthy action to take about this situation. That might mean deciding if the fight is worth fighting at all. If not, I walk away with the full understanding there are some things that are not worth dying for; there is a time to stand and a time to walk away." -Fellow Traveler

Building Trust By Setting Boundaries and Expressing Our Needs

As we learn how to love and nurture ourselves as our own loving parent, we come to know and appreciate the importance of our needs. We remember to honor them and develop the courage to express them to others. Doing so gives others a chance to be there for us and show us the respect and care we're learning to show ourselves.

Expressing our needs in healthy ways can lessen the urge to set reactive boundaries. Honesty, rather than rigidity, can inform our decisions about how we take care of ourselves. As we become healthier adults, we learn to respect and love ourselves by standing up for our inner children and values. Setting and maintaining healthy boundaries is a form of living amends we can make to our inner children.

We are no longer dependent children who need our caregivers' approval to survive. We learn to set our boundaries with clarity, grace, kindness, and firmness. We maintain them, too, since establishing a boundary is only a first step. While our boundaries are a gift to ourselves, they're also a gift to the person on the receiving end, providing clarity about what we need in order to have a reciprocal relationship or situation.

Withholding this gift out of fear of another person's reaction erodes our inner children's trust and compromises the health of the relationship. Sharing our needs and making requests gives another person the chance to meet our needs or teaches us that they cannot or will not.

The more we set boundaries and express our needs, the more our inner children will trust and respect us to lead and guide our inner family. Our courage to model safe communication and healthy behavior helps them heal and trust. Growing up, we often couldn't do that because the consequences were too brutal, but today we can.

Once our inner family members trust us to protect them, regardless of how others react, healthy external boundaries become easier to set. We become *actors*, not *reactors*. Our new skills and inner intimacy benefits all areas of our life—friendships, work, family, and romantic partnerships. We learn to expect the best and get it.

Your Key Chapter Takeaway(s):

Affirmation / Meditation

With the help of my support group, I am learning the skills to protect my inner child and inner teenager from unhealthy situations and messages. Healthy boundaries are becoming easier for me to set.

Building Trust – Loving Parent Tools & Techniques

Meditation / Prayer
Grant me the courage to try out new activities to strengthen my bond with my inner family members.

When we take action as our own loving parent, we deepen our commitment to reparenting and build our inner family members' trust. With practice, it feels more natural to make time for our inner children, to tell them how we love them, and to show up for them. We remember what gave them joy in our past and take time to help them play again. We invest time and effort to build a healthy relationship with them, just as we do with all the people we care about.

There are many ways to build trust with our inner family members. The important thing to remember is to establish a connection, show up regularly for them, and care for their needs. The following activities offer an opportunity to give our inner family members the precious gift of our attention. Building trust requires consistency and patience. Our inner family members learned to distrust others as a way to protect themselves. They will watch for signs that we are giving them attention out of obligation, frustration, or a desire to quiet them. If that's the case, we'll need to get our loving parent back in the driver's seat.

"I see and develop my loving parent the most at bedtime, when my inner child is more likely to feel lonely and vulnerable. Sometimes I catch myself reading compulsively before bed and can have trouble stopping. My loving parent can help me recognize why I'm doing that, and what I can do about it." -Fellow Traveler

Exercise: *Observing Children at Play*

Visit a playground or watch family-friendly online kid videos where you can see children at play. Notice the qualities they embody and how they engage with the world. This exercise helps you reconnect with qualities such as fun, play, and spontaneity that live in your inner child today but that might be repressed.

This exercise might bring up grief or a mix of emotions. You might realize you were never taken to playgrounds. You might witness parents who play with their children in loving ways and who set boundaries with kindness. You might notice parents who do not. The sadness or longing you might feel helps pinpoint your loss. This exercise might also connect you to happy childhood memories of times you were allowed to play and have fun.

Reflections: *Observing Children at Play*

After you observe children at play, note on the next page what thoughts, emotions, and physical sensations you noticed while doing so. Consider drawing any images that reflect this experience for you.

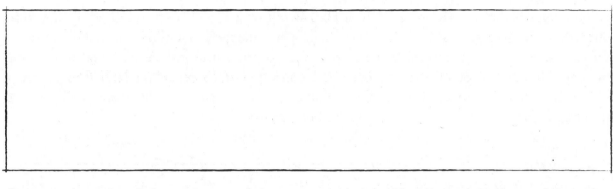

"I went to the park and observed parents being present with their kids. I listened. They were patient. They didn't criticize. They allowed the child to express themselves. They treated the child like a person."
-Fellow Traveler

Building Healthier Beliefs

"I wanted to make myself a Valentine's card for my first Valentine's Day in the program. One of the new ideas that had made it into my mind was to listen to what I needed and be the loving parent who would meet those needs. I wrote down the things I needed to hear on a big piece of paper. I drew a big heart around the words and put it next to my calendar. Every time I saw it, I noticed that I was there for myself." -Fellow Traveler

After decades of hearing harsh or undermining messages, it's important to come up with new, gentle, loving messages: affirmations. Affirmations help your inner children release critical parent messages, internalize truths, and discover their true identity. Affirmations help lay healthier tracks in the brain.

When you first say affirmations to your inner children, it can seem foreign, empty, awkward, or hokey to some inner family members. That's okay; give it time. You will need to experiment to find the affirmations that work. Ask yourself: "What wasn't said in my childhood that would have helped me?"

Simple, heartfelt phrases beginning with "It's okay to..." have helped adult children to counterbalance critical parent messages and distorted thinking. "It's okay" affirmations help our inner children talk, trust, and feel.

The **simplest affirmations** come from asking

"What does my inner child or inner teenager ***need to hear*** *from the loving parent?*

Focus on affirmations that address your inner child's false beliefs and wounds in a healthy way. Affirmations with a comparison or value judgment, like "You are the best," are not healthy, as they create comparisons and encourage striving. Affirmations like, "You're enough" and "I like you just the way you are," don't create this dilemma for the inner child.

Rather than force an affirmation, offer it and see what arises inside. Different affirmations might work better at different times. Your body can help you know which affirmations resonate with your inner children. Take note of your physical responses to help you choose supportive words and phrases.

Choose some of the affirmations from the list below, or from page 329 of the Big Red Book, to read out loud daily. Keep the list handy in your phone, planner, taped to a mirror, or in a desk drawer for easy access. Consider recording the affirmations so you can play them back and hear loving messages directed to you in your own voice. You can listen on a regular basis and also use it as a supportive resource in times of stress. Some adult children fill a jar with affirmations and pick one to say each day.

It's okay to...
- *feel this.*
- *trust, talk, and feel.*
- *be you.*
- *not take care of others' feelings or thoughts.*
- *have fun and celebrate.*

It's natural and human to have needs.
I am here to protect you.
You never have to be alone again. I'm here now.
You're not responsible for other people.
You...
- *are enough no matter what.*
- *are wanted.*
- *matter.*

I like you just because you're you.
There's nothing wrong with you; you're just right.
You don't have to do anything to get my love and appreciation.
May you...
- *be safe and protected.*
- *be happy.*
- *be healthy.*
- *be at ease.*
- *heal.*
- *feel loved.*

It can be helpful to create affirmations that address your unique struggles, beliefs, and fears. For example, if your inner child believes they're not good enough, an affirmation such as "It's okay to be who and where you are" can address that false belief.

You might want to revisit these affirmations at different points because what works can change with time. Once you've made contact with the inner children, they will let you know what affirmations work best through feedback in your body.

Exercise: *Speaking to a Photo of Your Younger Self*

To help you connect emotionally with your inner child, gather a childhood photo and make time to listen to and be with the child looking back at you. Connect with what they might be feeling and what they might have experienced at that time in life. Use affirmations to begin speaking to them in gentle, loving ways. Share what the experience was like for you in your journal and with safe and trusted others. You can repeat this exercise often, choosing new photos or revisiting ones you've worked with before.

Reparenting Dialogues: *Connecting through Writing*

Reparenting dialogues offer us an opportunity to connect with our inner child and other inner family members. As with all exercises that put us in touch with our inner family members, we want to proceed once our inner loving parent is in the driver's seat.

Non-dominant handwriting is a popular reparenting technique. It helps us bypass the logical part of the brain, helping us access our inner child's feelings, intuition, spirituality, and creativity. We describe this technique in terms of the inner child, but we can use it to communicate with any inner family member. When we put a pen in one hand, take a breath, and let our inner family speak to us, each voice becomes distinct and recognizable. This might happen as a felt sense, as voices we hear, or as images we see. The handwriting of each inner family member might be recognizable too.

In non-dominant handwriting, you write out a question to your inner child with your dominant hand (the hand you use to write). Then you write the response to the question by placing the pen, pencil, or crayon in the opposite hand (your non-dominant hand), giving your inner child a chance to answer. If you're ambidextrous, you can assign one hand to speak for the loving parent and the other as the inner child. As odd as it might seem, this technique can yield illuminating responses.

With your dominant hand, you might write: "Hello, little one. I would like to get to know you better. How are you feeling today?" Respond with your non-dominant hand. It's okay if the writing isn't legible and takes longer than with your dominant hand. Imagine how it must have been for you to first learn to write and how meaningful it was (or would have been) when parents and teachers were patient and gentle. As a loving parent, you can give your inner child the time they need to form their letters in whatever way they can.

The thoughts might be random or incomplete sentences but write down whatever arises. Accept whatever responses your inner child or teen shares. If you notice judgments or impatience, or if another inner family member hops in the driver's seat, step in with an internal boundary, (example responses would be "Not now" or "It's okay if we try something new; you can take a break").

The goal isn't to fix but to feel and open up communication channels. Keep an open mind and avoid trying to force solutions or results. You will be more likely to make a connection if you are patient and consistent with the exercise.

It's helpful to dialogue when you have privacy and quiet to better hear the inner child. Some who use this technique find that if they set a certain length of time, it's best to stick to that limit. This consistency creates predictability for the inner child, helping them trust. You might find it helpful to write an opening that you read aloud at the beginning of each session. Here is an example:

> *Dear little one,*
>
> *I care about you and how you feel, and I want to know you better. I'll be asking you some questions. It's okay to give whatever answer you feel like giving, and it's okay not to answer at all. I want to hear what you have to say. Thank you for trying this with me.*
>
> *Love, your loving parent*

Consider drawing your answers with your non-dominant hand to explore if that works for you. Dialogues can also be done with voice-to-text technology, by starting off the dialogue with a phrase to identify who's speaking, such as "Inner teenager says" and "Loving parent says." You can talk to other adult children about how they connected with their inner child using this technique, while being mindful to be true to your connection. You do not have to impress anyone or embellish any response. This exercise can literally speak for itself when you practice it often.

"In the beginning I was unsure which part of me was replying, but as I kept doing it, it became clear. The answers from my inner children/teenagers were more intuitive and sincere." -Fellow Traveler

Reparenting Dialogue Exercise 1: *Asking Questions*

"When I started using non-dominant handwriting, I used one pen and passed it back and forth. Later I used two different colored pens to make it easier to see when speakers switched. Eventually, I bought a special pen for my inner child as a gift. At the end, I write a few notes on the right top corner to indicate what the session covered." -Fellow Traveler

This exercise helps you establish and strengthen a bond between your loving parent and your inner child. Some inner family members might feel nervous about what your inner child wants to share, so it helps to start with easy-to-answer questions. Ask open-ended questions that require more than a yes-or-no answer, and let your curiosity drive your conversations. What would you like to know about your inner child? You can get to know them one session at a time and build up to deeper questions about specific memories, family members, and big hurts.

Let yourself feel whatever arises as you do this exercise and focus on the connection with your inner child. Accept whatever responses your inner child shares and step in with a boundary if another inner family member hops into the driver's seat. The goal isn't to "fix" your inner child or inner teenager's feelings but to open up communication.

The following list of questions can get you started:

- How old are you? (You might encounter different ages of your inner child)
- How are you feeling today?
- What do you need from me today?
- What are two of your favorite things to do (or eat)?
- What are two of your least favorite things to do (or eat)?
- What is your favorite movie? What is it that you like about that movie?
- What bothers you?
- What's something you recently enjoyed?
- What would you like to do for fun today?
- Would you like to _____ (for example, watch a movie) or _____ (for example, read a book)? (Limiting choices to two options makes it easier for the inner child to answer.)

Some additional questions to ask your inner teenager:

- What would help you trust that I have your back?
- What needs would you like met more often? Can you imagine ways to meet those needs (See "Appendix D: Feelings, Needs & Physical Sensations Sheet" on page 224)
- How do you feel about me?
- What are you afraid would happen if you didn't try to distract from or numb painful feelings?
- What would you like the critical parent to know?
- What would you like the inner child to know?
- What do you need most from me, your loving parent?

After each dialogue session, thank the inner family member you worked with for spending this time with you.

"I set aside about 30 minutes to write almost daily using my dominant hand, which works better for me than using my non-dominant hand. After a short introduction, I make a line down the center of the page. I ask a question out loud as I write it on the left side as my loving parent. I pause and feel my emotional response without judging it. I write the response on the right side of the page as my inner child. Topics of conversation can range from what my inner child is excited to do that day, to current problems, to deeper patterns of relationships. These sessions are a valuable way to access thoughts, feelings, opinions, and plans that I am not clearly aware of." -Fellow Traveler

Reparenting Dialogue Exercise 2: *Inner Child's Letter to a Higher Power*

Take the picture (or image) of your younger self that you framed in Chapter 7. Find a safe place inside or in nature to visit with your framed picture. Allow yourself to get still and be present with the image of you at this innocent stage in life. With your non-dominant hand, allow your inner child to express what they wanted and needed from a higher power in childhood. Address the letter in whatever way feels true to your inner child (*Spirit, Universe, God, To Whom it May Concern, and the like*).

Your inner child's letter:

As a follow-up, what physical sensations and emotions did you feel while writing this letter?

Reparenting Dialogue Exercise 3: *Letter from the Inner Child*

Invite your inner child to write a letter to your loving parent. What do they want you to know as their loving parent? It might involve a thought they want to share, a feeling, an image, a memory, or a present concern. This might seem strange, or it might feel uncomfortable. Consider this letter an exploration. Your inner child's letter:

> *Dear loving parent,*

As a follow-up, what physical sensations and emotions did you feel while writing this letter?

Reparenting Dialogue Exercise 4: *Building Healthier Beliefs with Affirmations*

You can focus your dialogue sessions on an affirmation to help your inner child internalize a new, healthy belief. Pick one affirmation per dialogue session. Write down the affirmation with your non-dominant hand or on the left side of the paper, if you're using your dominant hand. You might notice physical sensations or thoughts in response. Write down what you notice with the hand you've assigned to speak for your inner child. Allow and acknowledge any response in writing from your loving parent with a message, such as, "Thank you for telling me that."

Repeat the affirmation in writing a few more times, pausing each time to allow your inner child's response to be just as it is. It's okay if their response doesn't change. When working with deep conditioning, it takes time for new truths to take root. It's okay to spend several days or even weeks on one affirmation.

Reparenting Dialogue Exercise 5: *Resolving Conflicts*

Reparenting dialogues can help you explore internal and external conflicts. As you bring a conflict to mind, use your loving parent hand to ask your inner child what they need from you regarding the situation. If it's a conflict with another person, invite your inner child to share their feelings and unmet needs about that past conflict. Empathize and explore how to meet those needs now. Sometimes the inner child simply wants to be heard and have space to grieve. At other times, it's important that you voice their feelings and needs to the person involved.

If it's a conflict with an inner family member, support the inner child to share their feelings with you. In writing, empathize with them by using your dominant hand. Then ask the other inner family member how they feel hearing what the inner child shared, using your non-dominant hand to write their answer. You can continue like this to help reach a mutually satisfying resolution.

Creating an Ongoing Reparenting Dialogue Practice

In childhood, we longed for consistency, love, and the sense we mattered. We can fulfill those needs for ourselves today by making time to regularly communicate with our inner children. Consistency can show your inner family they matter; even a few minutes a day helps you build a connection.

As our reparenting practice strengthens, we can use dialogues to proactively deepen our relationship with our inner family members, including helping them see and relate to each other. We can work with them one at a time, starting with simple questions and introducing more complex ones over time, letting our curiosity guide us. If we begin to argue with an inner family member or notice a critical tone or extra tension, it's a sign to invite our loving parent back in the driver's seat.

Locating Healthy Sources of Nurturing and Support

We can support our inner child by selecting new sources of nurturing. However, the loving parent must make this choice because the inner child can seek out people who exhibit our parents' behaviors (which can happen without our awareness). The inner child believes such "substitute" parents will love us the way we needed to be loved in childhood. The Big Red Book refers to this tendency as trying to "heal or fix our family of origin."

Our inner child's unmet needs are dependency needs. External sources of love and nurturing can't meet them in a complete way today. We can help our inner child grieve and release false hopes. We can locate healthy sources of nurturing to help us meet our inner child's needs, such as fellow travelers, a sponsor, helping professionals, and whatever helps us make conscious contact with a higher power of our understanding.

Over time, we can help our inner child trust that we are the one person who can meet their needs most consistently. This helps us choose to love people who can love and be responsible for themselves. Our inner child will learn what healthy love is and be able to surrender their unrealistic expectations of parents or "substitutes." Our loving parent becomes the reliable source to nurture the inner family and meet their needs.

Reflections: *Locating Healthy Sources of Nurturing and Support*

1. As an adult, how have you tried to fill your inner children's unmet childhood need for love, appreciation, security, and acceptance with parents, caretakers, relatives, or others?

2. With whom have you formed relationships that you now realize exhibited behaviors similar to your parents or caretakers? What was your inner child or inner teen seeking from them?

3. If you had to name your inner child's deepest unmet need, what would it be? What are some ways you could begin to meet that need for them? (For example, if their deepest unmet need is to be seen, what are some specific ways your loving parent can see them more often?)

4. List some healthy sources of nurturing you can call on to help you be an inner loving parent.

Taking Care of Ourselves is a Loving Parent Act

Becoming our own loving parent means we protect, nurture, support, and guide our inner family. This is *action coming from love*. It also involves consistently caring for our physical, mental, emotional, and spiritual health. It's a positive feedback loop. Practicing self-care makes our loving parent more available to us, which makes self-care more possible.

Self-care is unique for every individual. By being a loving parent to yourself, a beautiful exploration unfolds, and you uncover your inner family's true needs. For example, you might need alone time to recharge while another adult child feels energized being with other people. Include your inner children in self-care decisions and activities so your choices are fun for them too. If you don't know what they'd like to do, you can ask them. Their answers might surprise you. If they don't respond, explore different types of self-care such as yoga, movement classes, artistic activities, etc. and see what connects. Perhaps you'll take up a new sport or hobby.

Your loving parent can remind your inner family members of basic truths, such as "It's okay to explore and say 'I like this or I like that'" and "It's okay to change your mind." For inspiration, talk with other adult children about how they care for their well-being.

"If my inner child is hungry, tired, cold, needs to go to the bathroom, or doesn't have the energy to do one more errand, I try to listen and change my adult plans. I feel so at ease when I can do that. Often whatever I had planned can wait until tomorrow or some other time." -Fellow Traveler

Exercise: *Building Trust*

"My counselor suggested I tell my inner child I would have his back no matter what. Telling was less important, though, than showing it was true. If I didn't follow through or ignored his feelings, my inner child was sad, and my inner teenager was mad. When I fell short, rather than listen to my critical parent, I made amends to my inner child and told him I was still learning. That started to build trust. Gradually, I was able to match my actions to my words. My inner child started to trust me more. My inner teenager was able to trust and relax. My critical parent, seeing they were fine, started to relax, too. My whole life became more enjoyable, peaceful, and serene." -Fellow Traveler

Our inner children don't really want to be in the driver's seat, but they want to know if it's okay to let go of the wheel. If we say nurturing words but don't change our behavior, they have reason not to trust us. If we make promises but don't follow through on our commitments to them, trust will be weakened not strengthened. What commitments and actions will help you connect with and integrate your inner children more actively throughout your day?

The actions on the next page are examples of ways you can meet your inner children's needs and build their trust. Consider choosing one concrete action to meet their needs for each category and focus on it for a period of time before moving on to another action. You can also refer back to Chapter 3 to take actions that healthy families model.

As a result of using these tools and continuing to practice, you are becoming more and more your own loving parent. What you practice grows stronger. Reparenting can become second nature the more you do it.

As you move into the next chapters that involve deeper connection, notice how you feel toward these inner family members. If you're not feeling curious about, compassionate toward, or connected to them, ask yourself what program tools could help your loving parent return to the driver's seat. You might find it supportive to read through previous chapters, journal about what's coming up for you, or find other ways to replenish yourself for this next leg of the journey.

"The Serenity Prayer is a favorite tool that my loving parent uses at bedtime when my thoughts and feelings often become unmanageable. With the unmanageable thing in mind, we pray the Serenity Prayer. Once we recognize the difference between what we can and cannot change, it becomes clearer what to do and easier to let go of the worries of the day." -Fellow Traveler

Your Key Chapter Takeaway(s):

Affirmation / Meditation

Even if I can't see it, I am making progress in becoming my own loving parent.

ACTIONS THAT BUILD TRUST

NURTURE

- Make conscious contact with your inner children and inner teen regularly. Get to know their likes, dislikes, feelings, and needs.
- Give your inner child and inner teen approval every day. Practice affirmations.
- Make time for play.
- Physically comfort and nurture your inner children with your loving words and attentive silence, especially when they're triggered.
- Make time to nourish your emotional well-being.
- Revisit painful situations to help your inner children grieve.

Specific actions I can take to meet the need:

_____

_____

_____

Specific actions I can take to meet the need:

_____

_____

_____

PROTECT

- Set internal and external boundaries with your critical parent and people in your life, a form of living amends to yourself.
- Bring your loving parent in the driver's seat.
- Speak for your inner children, advocate for their needs.
- Exit unhealthy situations.
- Take space from dysfunctional people/situations and set internal boundaries when needed.
- Follow through on promises and commitments.

SUPPORT and GUIDE

- Break the "Don't Talk, Don't Trust, Don't Feel" rule at meetings and with trusted others.
- Identify what triggers your inner children and be ready to support them in those situations.
- Make time for prayer, meditation and to simply "be" to become more aware and accepting of feelings and reality.
- Work with a fellow traveler, sponsor, therapist, and/or private study group.
- Use a supportive resource.
- Practice the Steps, especially in times of distress.
- Offer perspective for distorted thinking.

Specific actions I can take to meet the need:

_____

_____

_____

Tuning In to Your Inner Child

Meditation / Prayer
Grant me the courage to truly see my precious inner child.
Help me regard my inner child with gentleness, humor, love, and respect.

We can learn to see and hear our inner child with the compassion, empathy, and love we longed for as children. Mirror work—taking time to gently look into our own eyes—is one way to "see" and tune in to our inner child in ways caregivers and parents didn't. If we are visually impaired, we can adapt the mirror work exercises by gently cradling our face in our hands. We could also picture our inner child in our mind's eye. We can use these same exercises to connect with our inner teenager.

Learning to See Who We Truly Are

Attunement is an important part of healthy childhood development and involves helping children be seen, heard, and accepted for who they are. As children, we needed to feel like we were treasure waiting to be discovered, not clay waiting to be molded. In dysfunctional families, parents don't often reflect a child accurately. For example, if a child feels sad, a parent might deny the feeling or tell them to cheer up. If a child is disappointed, a parent might reflect the child's feeling as "angry" or judge them as "difficult." This lack of attunement from caregivers caused us to doubt our perception and lose touch with our hearts.

An attuned parent "tunes in" to and responds in healthy ways to a child's feelings, needs, and behavior, both verbally and non-verbally. When this happens, the child has a sense of "being known." When a child is sad, an attuned parent might say something like, "You look like you're feeling sad about something." This attunement helps the child trust the world as a safe place where they can form healthy relationships, take risks, and trust their perceptions. We can learn to attune to our inner child today in the ways we needed our caregivers to attune to us.

Reflections: *Getting in Touch with Childhood Attunement*

1. In what ways did your parents or caregivers attune to you (see, hear, feel, know you) and not attune to you?

2. Imagine yourself as a child looking up into your caregivers' faces. Are they looking at you or away? What are their facial expressions? How do you feel?

3. Growing up, what feelings were you allowed to have and express? How did your primary caregivers react when you had or expressed those feelings in their presence?

4. Growing up, what feelings were you NOT allowed to have and express? How did your primary caregivers react when you had or expressed those feelings in their presence?

5. Picture yourself as a child in your mind's eye. How do you feel toward that child?

6. What would you like to say to your inner child about who they are and what you see in them?

Mirror Work

If someone lit up with genuine affection every time they saw you, you'd likely feel comfortable and trust that person. As loving parents, we want our inner child to feel that same comfort. Over time, mirror work helps us to create that foundation and leads to self-acceptance.

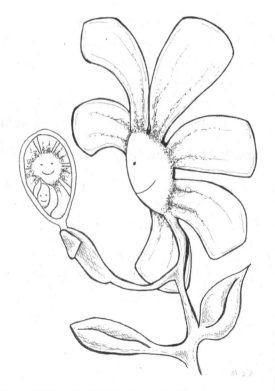

It is said the eyes are the reflection of the heart. A powerful way to get to know someone is to look them in the eyes. What we see—joy, sadness, mistrust—can help us connect to what's happening inside them. The same is true for ourselves. You can set aside time in your day to truly "see" and connect with the inner child. Mirror work gives your inner child the chance to receive your inner loving parent's attention, care, and love. Consider beginning each day by gently looking into your eyes in the mirror while saying a simple affirmation or greeting, such as, "I love you" or "Good morning, little one."

We learned a lot about who we were through eye contact with our parents and caregivers. Harsh facial expressions, shaming statements, and abuse taught us to avoid eye contact with them and then ourselves. It's not unexpected then, that when we first look into our eyes when doing mirror work, our critical parent might judge our appearance or judge the process. If this happens, it can be a powerful opportunity to set a boundary and ask a higher power for help. "Help me see with my loving parent's eyes and heart."

Mirror work can soften our hearts, allowing us to see ourselves and our innocent inner child in a more loving light. If we feel uncomfortable looking in the mirror, we can pause and remind ourselves we're not alone. We can reach out to a sponsor or fellow traveler to talk about our feelings.

Respect your inner child's pace and rely on gentleness to guide your next steps. If you keep tuning in, you will eventually see your younger self as the precious being you hoped your parents would cherish. The following exercises will guide you in doing mirror work. Note that the exercises become progressively more intimate.

Instructions for Reflection/Mirror-Work Preparation

"I live with a visual impairment and need to modify most of my activities. Through my higher power's guidance, I have learned alternative ways to benefit from mirror work. I get quiet and focus on my breathing. Then I bring up a screen in my mind's eye and think of myself as a little child. Sometimes I think of an event to help connect with the feelings. I place my hand on my heart to deepen the connection. I let her know I am present for her, and she can let me know anything she wants or needs. I affirm that she is safe and allow her to engage as she is comfortable. I keep her image on my inner screen, and most of the communication is verbal as I feel the emotions in my body. " -Fellow Traveler

Mirror work is an intimate exercise that requires our undivided attention. We recommend taking a few moments to center yourself through prayer, meditation, or whatever else will help you be present. You might want to record the questions in each exercise so you can keep your focus on the mirror versus reading.

General Instructions:

- Find a quiet place with privacy. Prepare your space to make it less likely the process will be interrupted after you begin. Mute your phone or turn it off. Inform your family or friends that you will be taking some private time, to please refrain from knocking or interrupting. Our inner child needs our undivided attention in this process.
- Use a mirror large enough to show your face. Compact mirrors, a cell phone's selfie camera, or a car mirror can be creative ways to practice when away from home.
- Stare gently into your eyes/heart. This exercise isn't about scrutinizing your appearance but making eye contact. Check that you feel curious about, compassionate or calm toward, or connected to your inner child. If you feel otherwise, set a boundary with the intervening inner family member. "I need you to step aside right now as I practice something new" or "Not now." Stop when it feels right to you. Give yourself time to integrate the experience by taking a gentleness break afterward.
- You might find it helpful to keep a journal nearby when doing mirror work, but journaling doesn't resonate with everyone. You might prefer to process your experience with a sponsor or fellow traveler or quietly sit with your inner child as a way to process what comes up, reaching out if needed.

Mirror Work—Working with Challenges

Some inner family members might balk at doing mirror work before we give it a try. For those inner family members, we can follow the instructions in Chapter 8 to connect with them and create some space. At other times, inner family members will react during or after mirror work, and we might experience a shame attack. This might go unrecognized as we can dissociate or numb out. If this happens, take a gentleness break so you can get your loving parent back in the driver's seat. Tend to the inner family members who are reacting before trying mirror work again.

Exercise 1: *Loving Parent—The "First Glance"*

The purpose of this exercise is to show up for your inner child as their loving parent. It's okay if the inner child doesn't appear. The goal is to show them you are there for them, with no expectation. Take note of any feelings and memories that arise during the exercise.

First, review the mirror-work preparation instructions above. Then, when you're ready, proceed:

1. Gaze into your eyes/heart, noting your feelings, thoughts, and physical sensations. Let yourself feel whatever you feel.

2. How connected do you feel?

3. Do you want to get to know your inner child?

4. Let a few moments pass as you gaze into your eyes/heart. Close the exercise with a simple phrase like "Thank you" or "I want to get to know you," whether your inner child came out this time or not. What was this experience like for you?

It would probably be good to spend a few days on this mirror exercise before moving to the next.

"I sat in a chair and looked into a floor-length mirror. My counselor stood behind me and asked me what I wanted to say to my little girl. As I looked in my eyes, I caught a glimpse of my innocent little girl. I saw her pain. My chin trembled. 'I'm sorry,' I said. Tears welled. I felt the loss of all the years I'd abandoned her. That moment made my inner child real to me." -Fellow Traveler

Exercise 2: *Giving Ourselves Approval*

The first of ACA's 12 Promises tells us that our self-esteem will increase as we give ourselves approval on a daily basis. One way to practice this is to try to find at least one thing you appreciate about your inner child each day and write it down. Be as specific as you can and note any physical sensations that might arise. If this is hard, imagine what friends of yours or beloved pets appreciate in you.

Sit with what you wrote. In front of a mirror, look into your eyes or heart with a gentle gaze and share your appreciation. For example, "I appreciate your _____," or "I appreciate you because_____."

The goal in this exercise is to begin to see or reflect on yourself with more balance and to appreciate your inner child's qualities and strengths. If you find it to be a struggle, invite your loving parent back into the driver's seat, setting a boundary with the critical parent if needed. At times you might need to ask for support from a power greater than yourself. Consider trying this exercise for a week and journal about any effects you notice or share with a sponsor, fellow traveler, or in a meeting. See if your experience changes over the week.

"When I stand in front of the mirror or the reflection glass of a window or door, I say, 'You are so welcome. I love you just the way you are.'" -Fellow Traveler

Exercise 3: *Speaking from Your Heart*

Follow the mirror-work preparation instructions. Then, softly look into your eyes or heart. Ask yourself, "What do I, as the loving parent, need to say to my inner child?" Perhaps you want to say you're sorry for not being there for them. You might want to tell them you want to get to know them. Say this out loud while looking into your eyes.

1. Can your inner child hear you or receive your message?

2. How connected do you feel to your inner child?

3. Can your inner child receive your loving parent's care and attention?

You can continue to dialogue with your inner child, if you wish and if the pace feels comfortable to them. When you end the exercise, thank your inner child for spending this time with you. Remind them it's okay if they don't want to be seen yet. You'll give them the time they need. Let them know if you'll be checking in with them in this way again soon.

Consider repeating this mirror exercise daily over the next week. Share your discoveries with a fellow traveler, sponsor, therapist, in a study group, or through journaling.

Exercise 4: *Mirror Work with Affirmations*

Affirmations help us counteract distorted thinking. These loving messages can re-teach our inner child how to believe in their worth and help them release shame. We combine affirmations with mirror work to make them even more powerful.

Develop a list of personalized affirmations you can draw upon regularly. Choose affirmations from this book or affirmations of your own that resonate with your inner child and that address false beliefs. State your affirmation with a gentle and loving tone, while looking into your eyes or heart. Pay attention to what arises, noticing any physical sensations and emotions. Your inner child might speak back. They might say "no" or the opposite. Perhaps they will receive your words. Perhaps you will experience a sense of lightness in the body. Note this without judgment.

If you notice the critical parent in the form of skepticism or judgment, you can acknowledge them and help them relax ("Not now." "Let's just try this."). Then repeat the affirmation while looking in the mirror, noting your thoughts and feelings each time. Your inner child might not believe you or might react; that's okay. Seeing their reactions is a helpful part of reclaiming your inner child. Keep returning to this affirmation with gentleness, until the inner child can begin to receive it. You might spend a day, or many days, on one affirmation.

Consider making this a twice-daily habit for the next week. Begin each morning with a loving message to the inner child. You could put a hand on your heart, or wherever feels soothing, as you greet them in the mirror with: "Hello, little one. I love you." You can say good night in the same manner. You can also choose a time when you will naturally be in front of a mirror such as while brushing your teeth or washing your face. For a moment, pause and gently look into your eyes/ heart. Silently or aloud, offer a simple acknowledgment that feels comfortable to you. "I see you," or "I want to get to know you." You might consider taping an affirmation to your mirror.

Suggestions for Mirror Work in Everyday Life

You can get creative about how you incorporate mirror work into your day. Seeing your reflection in a shop window, or glancing into your rear-view mirror while waiting at a stoplight, can make for a sweet moment of connection with your inner child or can reassure them when they get triggered. Every glance in a mirror can become a moment of connection with this precious part of yourself.

Some adult children practice mirror work for 21 days or more to help it become a healthy habit. You could also do the mirror exercises in this guide until you feel a sense of calm, gentleness, care, love, or warmth towards your inner child when you look in the mirror. Some people use mirror work as an ongoing way to connect with their inner child and inner teenager.

Your Key Chapter Takeaway(s):

Affirmation / Meditation

*I will gradually become more comfortable looking into the mirror or
in my mind's eye and telling my inner child, "I love you."*

Reparenting Your Inner Family

Meditation / Prayer
May reparenting become the natural way for me to respond to life and its challenges.

Making Conscious Contact with an Inner Family Member

We can choose to set time aside to connect with our inner family members so we're not only with them when they're triggered. We can ask whether there is a part of ourselves we'd like to get to know better and proactively plan time to do that. Cues from our body, emotions, or thoughts (including images or movies in your mind's eye) can help us know who is present. We can invite an inner family member to visit by asking about a past situation. "What can you tell me about the time _____?"

When attempting to connect with an inner family member, check to see if you feel a heart connection or curiosity about the inner family member. If not, you might need to ask another inner family member to give you space so your loving parent can regain the driver's seat. Some inner family members might lack trust; they might feel angry that a loving parent hasn't been present. See if it's possible to let this be okay. By continuing to be there for all your inner family members, they will relax.

Once you've made a connection and your loving parent is present, you can ask questions or wait for what this inner family member wants to show or tell you. Here are some topics you might want to explore:

- How they feel about a past incident,
- Their role in the inner family and how they feel about their role,
- Their fears and hopes, their feelings and needs.

Your loving parent can ask the inner family member, "If you could trust that I would take on your responsibility, what would you like to do instead?"

You might encounter adult-aged inner family members as you reparent. They can have unprocessed trauma, just like the inner child and inner teen. The loving parent's responsibility stays the same— to relate to all inner family members with love, care, curiosity, and compassion.

Reflections: *Giving Your Inner Family Permission to Break Dysfunctional Rules*

The more we practice new behaviors and make healthy changes, the more our inner child might feel anxious about breaking the "Don't Talk, Don't Trust, Don't Feel" rule. They might still believe they're at risk of being punished or abandoned by our family of origin and that no one will protect them when others react to these changes. They might not realize they have you as their inner loving parent to protect them today.

Your loving parent can give your inner child and inner teen explicit permission to talk, trust, feel, and be who they are. Your answers to the following questions can help them understand that you, their loving parent, have the ability and power to disobey old rules.

1. What can you say to help your inner child know it's okay to break dysfunctional family rules?

2. If there are consequences for breaking "the rules" and trying new behavior, how will you, as the loving parent, protect them—both in the outside (people might not be pleased when we stop people-pleasing) and inside worlds (with the critical parent or distorted thinking)?

3. What affirmations could support them to break dysfunctional rules?

4. What choices do you have in your life that you did not have as a child? For example, "I can choose where to live, how to earn money, when to leave a gathering; I can reach out to trusted others." List as many examples as you can below:

5. Once you have your list, connect with your inner child (and then your inner teenager) in whatever way is comfortable. Once you sense them, tell them about the items on your list. How are they responding?

Meeting Your Inner Child's and Inner Teenager's Needs

Emotional presence is giving ourselves what we need. Whenever a part of us is triggered, we can explore as we do in the reparenting check-in: "How old do I feel right now? I feel about 5 years old. What inner family member of me is activated? What do they feel? My 5-year-old feels scared. What need of theirs isn't being met? My 5-year-old needs some structure and consistency right now."

A loving parent can help remind the inner child that no matter what they're feeling, they are still worthy and lovable: "I know this feels so real and like it won't change, but this feeling isn't who you are, and it won't last forever. This is shame, and it's something you learned. It's not the truth. You are enough just the way you are."

Focus on empathizing with your inner child or inner teen's feelings before reassuring them. They need to be seen and heard. Listening to them—simply listening—is an act of love. You can say things like, "I'm so sorry you don't think you matter. I see you; you matter. If others can't see you, that's not about you. It's about their inability to see you." When stumped, we can ask an inner family member what they need. They can become wonderful guides to what they need in the moment.

It might not always be practical or possible to satisfy all your inner children's needs or meet those needs with their preferred strategies. You can, however, empathize with their feelings with statements such as, "I wish I had that here for you now," "I hear how much you want that," or "You would have so much fun with that." Show that you understand what specifically matters to them. For instance, if they want to go to the beach, what part of that experience do they like? "You love to play in the sand and build castles. That would be so fun."

"I have lots of ways to be a loving parent to my inner child. Some are simple: rewarding her after a hard day or a difficult task by giving her a treat—feeding her a snack, reading her a bedtime story, working on a jigsaw puzzle, letting her pick out a new notebook for non-dominant handwriting practice, watching something funny on TV—along with telling her what a great job she did! Most of all, I try to check in with my little kid before I make any decision, big or small, so she knows how important she is." -Fellow Traveler

Encouraging Cooperation Through Choice

Think about what would have encouraged you to cooperate as a child. Often our parents made demands and didn't offer us choices. When you need to take care of adult responsibilities today, you can enlist your inner children's help by offering them choices. The goal is cooperation, not manipulation. Manipulation is a form of control, and they will detect "false" choices quickly.

Offering a couple of simple choices seems to work best:

- Would you like me to work on the project before or after dinner?
- Would you rather I read with you for an hour before or after exercise?
- Would you like me to send the email now or spend three minutes with you first?

Sometimes neither choice works for your inner child or inner teenager. You can then either repeat the choices or offer other options.

The inner family doesn't always know what's in their best interest, such as recovery practices and behaviors. When you plan for these necessary activities you can include your inner children by asking them to help you problem-solve. "I need to meditate. What would make it easier for you?" or "Can you think of something that will help a little as I work on my *Steps Workbook*?"

Relieving Your Inner Children of Adult Tasks

Your inner children are not responsible for adult tasks or to care for one another, but they might try to do those things until they trust your loving parent to do them. It will take time to build this trust, but, as this trust strengthens, your inner children will feel less pressure to fend for themselves.

You can be honest with your inner children and let them know you're learning to be their loving parent. "I won't be perfect, but my intention is to take really good care of you and ask for support to do that when I need it." When you struggle to access your loving parent, you can still access other resources. This can mean making conscious contact with a higher power, with nature, with trusted fellow travelers or a sponsor, with program materials, and more.

One thing you can do to help take the pressure off your inner children is to notice how you speak to them. Are you using "we" when it's not their job? For example, "We will handle this problem at work." Or perhaps "you" as in, "It's okay for you to set a boundary with that person" or "Your roommate is being difficult, and you have a right to speak up to them."

When you use "you" and "we" in this way, it is a sign your loving parent is not fully in the driver's seat. In this case, remind yourself that the feelings belong to your inner child or teenager. This will give you more space to respond to their needs and guide them. "I hear that you feel scared. It's okay to feel scared about going somewhere new. I'll be there to hold your hand," or "I know you think this is your responsibility, and you're feeling really overwhelmed. You're not alone anymore. This is an adult responsibility, and I'll take care of it."

While our inner family members are with us in whatever we do, they are not equipped to handle adult situations. Your loving parent can take care of the inner family while you, the adult, interact in the outer world.

Sometimes your loving parent can use "we" or "us" to build connection, but it's important even then that the inner children know you will be in charge. "Ouch. Sometimes things happen that we're powerless over. It's not easy to be with the uncomfortable feelings that come with that. It's okay to feel it now. I won't leave you alone with these strong feelings," or "I've got you; a higher power has you. I'll get us through this." These are examples of what removes pressure.

It helps your inner children relax when you remind them they're not responsible today and that they have a loving parent and a support network to lead them through life. It also helps you connect more regularly with who you are when you're not taken over by your inner family members. This presence goes beyond any one inner family member and can be a way of experiencing your true self.

Exercise: *Distinguishing Between the Inner Teenager and Critical Parent*

"At first, I thought all the anger and criticism came from my critical parent. But the more I listened to my inner voices, the more I could hear that the tone and content of the messages were different. My critical parent rarely used a mean or angry tone. It would undermine and doubt my motives and actions in a soft, questioning tone, like my parents. My teenager would rebel and get mad at me for not standing up to the critical parent, for procrastinating, or for people-pleasing." -Fellow Traveler

Being able to distinguish between the inner teen from the critical parent will help you intervene more effectively, since they each need different guidance. The best way to tell them apart is to get curious and observe them in your own experience since everyone's inner world differs. The following pointers about what each does and about what each needs might help your exploration.

Critical Parent	Inner Teenager
• Tries to manage our behavior and inner life to prevent the inner child's pain from arising. Tries to get us to achieve goals and to make our lives orderly because it believes that will keep the inner child safe.	• Reacts quickly after the inner child is triggered to distract from and numb feelings. Can try to meet the inner child's needs by lashing out protectively of the inner child. Does this to get outside validation/attention but in a teenage way, which doesn't usually work.
• Proactive—cares about potential consequences in the outside world.	• Reactive—ignores potential consequences in the outside world.
• Rational, organized.	• Not rational, reactive, impulsive.
• Tries to help us function in daily life.	• Tries to protect the inner child from experiencing what it sees as intolerable pain.
• Responds to reason—if you explain how your loving parent will protect the inner child, it might be willing to negotiate.	• Responds to hope—once you connect with the inner teen and show them you'll care for the inner child, they might feel hope about letting go of their role.
• Needs the loving parent to guide the inner child and inner teen so they can relax. Needs loving parent to set a boundary and drive the bus.	• Needs the loving parent to make behavioral changes to protect the inner child. Needs to trust that the loving parent won't abandon the inner child.

What are other differences you notice between your critical parent and inner teenager?

Reactions Between Inner Family Members

The inner teenager and critical parent try to protect the inner child in different ways and might engage in power struggles. They can interact in painful cycles that lead to reactive behaviors and emotional distress without resolving the inner child's pain. The tools in Chapter 8 help you manage takeovers, so your loving parent leads the reparenting process.

As loving parents, we can pause and identify which inner family members are in conflict. You can connect with them, one at a time, to listen to them and address their concerns. The more you can be curious about and understand your inner family members and what they're trying to achieve for you, the more you can negotiate between them.

These patterns can be hard to detect and can be unconscious. They are so ingrained, quick, and fleeting that we might not notice them. The more we build our ability to be mindful, the more we'll spot them.

It helps to work with

one inner family member at a time.

Journaling can also help. Give them each a voice—one at a time—by dividing a paper in two. This gives you a chance to see the thoughts and determine what each inner family member needs. These inner family members are fighting because the inner child doesn't feel safe and secure. The more you tend to the inner child, the less the critical parent and inner teen need to battle. You might recognize some of these patterns in your inner family and see opportunities for the loving parent to step in:

When the inner child...	The inner teenager can...	The critical parent can...	The loving parent can...
Has strong feelings	Numb or distract from the inner child's feelings.	Shame, criticize, try to control the inner child.	Tend to the inner child's feelings and needs.
	Lash out to "defend" inner child.	Judge inner teen for trying to soothe or distract from inner child's feelings.	Set boundaries with the critical parent and inner teenager as needed.
	Use reactive behaviors.		
	Rebel against critical parent.		
Gets caught in False beliefs such as "There's something wrong with me"	React to make the feelings go away.	Push the inner child to perfection, hoping shame will motivate them.	Set a boundary with the critical parent.
		Affirm the false belief so the inner child won't take risks and be visible (and therefore won't be abandoned).	Help the inner teen turn over responsibility for the inner child's feelings to the loving parent.

When the inner child...	The inner teenager can...	The critical parent can...	The loving parent can...
Is criticized or compared to others by the critical parent	Rebel against the critical parent. Defend the inner child to the critical parent. Distract or numb inner child's feelings.	N/A	Acknowledge the critical parent and set a boundary. Nurture and reassure the inner child.
Takes over, causing you to people-please (which, ironically, abandons the inner child)	Judge or become resentful toward the loving parent or others for not protecting the inner child. Battle (and berate) the critical parent.	Shame the inner child. Try to manage with demands of what "should" be done to "fix" the situation.	Empathize, make amends if needed, and be willing to spend more time listening and connecting with the inner child.
Gets triggered by something someone says or does (feels hurt)	Get angry, ruminate. React rather than respond.	Deny or dismiss the inner child's feelings and judge the inner teen.	Tend to the inner child. Offer support and guidance (perspective).
Has strong feelings	Reach for substances, behaviors. Feel frustrated and view the inner child as a burden. Feel alone and resentful.	Minimize or dismiss the inner child's feelings. Threaten the inner child by warning them of potential consequences in the outside world.	Set a boundary with the critical parent. Tend to the inner teen and set a boundary. Tend to the inner child.

Reflections: *Reactions between Inner Family Members*

After reviewing the chart, reflect on your own experience.

1. When your critical parent takes over, how do your inner child and inner teenager feel? What are their reactions?

2. When your inner child takes over, how do your inner teenager and critical parent feel? What are their reactions?

3. When your inner teenager takes over, how do your inner child and critical parent feel? What are their reactions?

4. Think about a time when your inner child felt sad, ashamed, disappointed or some other feeling the inner teen wanted to distract from or numb. Be sure your loving parent is in the driver's seat and then ask your inner teenager if they're willing to give space for the inner child to feel and talk about their feelings, so your loving parent can help them heal the pain. If they're willing, see 4a. If not, skip to 4b.

4a. Ask your inner child to share their feelings with you and the inner teen. Your inner child might need reassurance that you'll protect them if the inner teenager reacts. As your inner child shares, note your inner teen's response below.

4b. Ask them what they're afraid will happen if the inner child feels and talks about their feelings. Record your inner teen's answer, if any, below. You can empathize with their answer and return to the above question when they have more trust.

When the critical parent shames the inner child, the inner teen can react in self-destructive ways, which creates more shame, causing the cycle to repeat. Being aware of this cycle can help your loving parent support your inner teenager more effectively.

> *Mindfulness helps us recognize when we're using a survival trait out of fear **to shield pain** or when we're picking up a recovery tool out of love **to work through the pain.** We can remember to be gentle with ourselves either way, since we're practicing new habits.*

Exercise: *Reparenting Commitments*

Consider the reparenting commitment(s) you're willing to make for the next month to a year and write them below. While we are powerless over how fast we heal, we can take concrete actions coming from love.

Perhaps you're willing to work through this guide one-on-one or in a private study group, do a reparenting check-in at least once a week, or greet your inner child every morning. Our commitments help us work in partnership with a power greater than ourselves.

Honoring your commitment builds trust with your inner child and inner teenager, so be sure you can honor any commitment you make. If you can't make a commitment right now, revisit this later. It's better to make no commitment than one you can't uphold.

Commitment(s):

Exercise: *Daily Reparenting Inventory*

You might find it helpful to have a daily reparenting inventory. You can make a list of actions that healthy families take by referring back to Chapter 3 and drawing on what you've learned so far in the guide. Then do those for your inner family and reflect each day on the actions you took.

Some people add reparenting questions to their Step 10 inventory, such as: Have I been loving to myself today? Did I connect with my inner child and inner teen?

"I try to work on the second promise and give myself approval on a daily basis. Did I accomplish something today? Did I do something to make my life more manageable? Did I take care of myself? Did I connect with another person? As I think through the day, I need my loving parent's help to recognize the good moments and let them sink in. I try to be specific: "That email was kind and clear," or "I handled that confrontation without giving up or blowing up. That's progress." -Fellow Traveler

Your Key Chapter Takeaway(s):

Affirmation / Meditation

*My loving parent is emerging more fully, working together with a higher power
to make decisions that take all inner family members into account.*

From the Traits to Freedom

Meditation / Prayer
*May my loving parent's compassion and care allow my inner family members to
release their survival traits so we can move toward a new way of living, grounded in trust.*

The Laundry List and The Other Laundry List describe how we were affected by alcoholism and family dysfunction, and the behavioral traits we developed in response. These traits might have hindered our emotional and spiritual lives, but they also protected us as children. Even though they create the internal pain and isolation that has driven us to ACA, they are not easy for our inner family members to leave behind. When we attempt to meet life's demands through the traits today, life becomes unmanageable.

As loving parents, we can help our inner family members understand they no longer need to rely on these survival mechanisms. The Flip Side of the Laundry List and The Flip Side of The Other Laundry List (found in Appendix F) reveal what it's like to be free of these unhealthy patterns. Reparenting and practicing the 12 Steps help our inner family members move beyond surviving to thriving, and we discover healthier, more satisfying ways of being in the world.

An example from Chapter 2 of the Big Red Book illustrates how reparenting can help us find more effective strategies to care for ourselves than the survival traits. We use Pat, an imaginary adult child, to show the traits in action.

Meeting Life's Demands with the Traits

Pat's inner child fears Pat's boss (Trait 1), which leads Pat to engage in approval-seeking behavior while accepting a high level of abuse on the job (Trait 2). Pat's inner child feels scared, while Pat's inner teenager wants to leave the position (Trait 7).

Caught in a victim mindset (Trait 5), Pat calls a friend and vents about the boss's behavior, without discussing their own feelings. Pat ends the call in a state of negative excitement (Trait 8). Pat goes home to their alcoholic partner (Trait 4) and stuffs their feelings by not speaking up, since Pat knows their partner won't be responsive (Trait 10). Pat takes on an inordinate amount of house chores by being overly responsible (Trait 6). They want to leave their partner, but have confused love and pity and fear facing the abandonment that will come from walking away (Traits 9 and 12).

Notably lacking in this scenario: a loving parent and a power greater than oneself.

Meeting Life's Demands with Reparenting

Pat recognizes their inner child fears Pat's boss (Trait 1), and tends to Little Pat's fears, which helps Pat stop engaging in approval seeking behavior (Trait 2). Pat protects their inner child by saying "no" to abuse on the job. When their inner child feels guilty and scared (Trait 7), Pat practices Steps 1, 2, and 3, making space for support from a higher power. Pausing to surrender and make conscious contact with that support gives Pat renewed resolve.

Pat reminds little Pat that it's okay to leave unmanageable situations and that little Pat isn't doing anything wrong. "I see you're really scared. Let's take a breath. You're safe today. I won't tolerate abuse. I'll handle the boss." To the inner teenager Pat says, "We don't need to rebel against the boss or prove anything. I will say no and set limits with others. It's also okay to say we can't do everything, and ask for help, even from the boss." Pat reminds the little one, who still feels a bit anxious (Trait 5), "It's going to be okay. I'm here to keep you safe."

Pat notices the inner child's victim mindset (Trait 5) and tends to their feelings. "You feel scared when you think you have no choice. You didn't have a choice with your family and this is not that situation. This is my job. I'll handle this. I see other options. Talking to the boss is one of them. If that doesn't work, I'll speak to my boss's manager or find work somewhere else. I will also call my sponsor to get perspective on this."

Pat notices their inner child's compulsion to re-enact childhood abandonment when they want to run to Pat's alcoholic partner to share their day (Trait 4). Also, they see the inner teen's impulse to stuff feelings (Trait 10) by not feeling or talking about the inner child's feelings. In the parking lot before heading home, Pat calls a fellow traveler to talk about the inner family's feelings and explore some options. After hanging up, they reassure little Pat. "I'm sorry you feel scared. Big Pat is here to handle this." Pat takes Steps 1, 2, and 3, and realizes their inner loving parent can love and nurture Little Pat better than their emotionally unavailable partner. They speak tenderly to their inner child and comfort them with a hug. Pat returns home with more inner strength and clarity.

At home, Pat can tell that their inner child feels overwhelmed and responsible for completing all the undone chores (Trait 6) and is believing the critical parent's messages. Pat thanks the critical parent for worrying about Little Pat, and sets a boundary. Pat reminds Little Pat that they're not responsible for their partner's chores. They know taking on too much leads to resentment. Pat does their share of house chores and avoids enabling their partner. Pat validates their inner child and inner teenager's feelings, and reassures them that it's okay to practice a new way.

Both the inner child and teenager fear abandonment but show it in different ways. The inner child has confused love and pity and feels abandonment terror (Traits 9 and 12) when Pat contemplates leaving their partner. The inner teenager wants to defend the inner child by lashing out at Pat's partner (Trait 8). While not a satisfying form of connection, arguing gives the illusion of connection and distracts from the inner child's abandonment fears. Sometimes Pat's inner teenager takes over, causing Pat to threaten to leave the partner without intending to follow through. Pat can talk the inner teenager down by saying, "Thanks for trying to protect the little one. I have a different way to handle this. It's okay to set a boundary without becoming abusive. I'll help work this out or I will leave if needed."

Pat also lets their inner child know that love is different than pity. "I know you feel sorry for this person, but our well-being matters, too. If someone isn't responsible for themselves, it's not mean to leave, it's actually healthier. It's okay to take care of ourselves."

Like Pat, when our loving parent is present, we have a healthier perspective and see other options. Our inner children are reassured, knowing that their loving parent will never leave them. Rather than be pulled into codependency, and feel responsible for someone else's feelings, our loving parent can remind our inner child that it's okay to feel sad when a relationship ends, but another adult is not their parent; ending an adult relationship or being left is not abandonment.

"I have come to realize that my inner children are attached to my laundry lists. When I feel an emotional charge about a situation or person, I ask myself, "Where am I in The Laundry Lists?" Then I ask, "How old is this part of me?" I validate my inner child's truth and needs. We "heart-storm" a collaborative solution with our loving parent and higher power. We are building a strong and trusting relationship. I have never felt so free and whole." -Fellow Traveler

Consider taking a
gentleness break
to let the information above settle.

Exercise: *Reparenting Helps Us Become Actors*

Take each trait from The Laundry List and The Other Laundry List and reflect on what your loving parent could do or say that would help you move to its "flip side," or integrated and healthy side. (See "Appendix F: Framework for The Laundry Lists Traits" on page 226). We provide an example for Trait 1 of The Laundry List below. This might seem like an advanced exercise if you are not familiar with *The Laundry List Workbook*. Just do what you can given your own understanding—and you can always return to it later.

> **Trait 1 of The Laundry List.** We became isolated and afraid of people and authority figures. --> **Flip Side of The Laundry List.** *We move out of isolation and are not unrealistically afraid of other people, even authority figures.*

Example of what your loving parent could do or say to help you move to the flip side: I can help my inner child and inner teenager understand that authority figures in the outside world are not their authority figures from the past. "This feels similar, but this is not the same as what happened back then." I can tend to my inner child's fear and my inner teenager's anger.

Continue the exercise for each trait you identify with in The Laundry List and The Other Laundry List, using a notebook or journal for your answers.

Your Key Chapter Takeaway(s):

Affirmation / Meditation

I appreciate myself for the active steps I am taking to create a nurturing inner home for my inner family.
I trust that a power greater than myself will take care of the rest.

Connecting with Your Inner Teenager

Meditation / Prayer

May I have compassion for my inner teenager and come to understand how they developed their armor due to family dysfunction.

In Chapter 5, we discovered our inner teen, reflected on the situations that commonly trigger them, and understood how their survival mechanisms are their sincere, well-meaning attempts at responding to these triggers. We began nurturing our cooperative relationship with them. In this chapter, we deepen this cooperative relationship by supporting them in some of the most challenging situations they encounter.

Working through these challenges will help you build trust with your inner teen and facilitate better cooperation between all your inner family members.

Working with Your Inner Teenager's Emotional Reactivity

Our inner teenager's overt or buried anger can serve as a shield, protecting the younger, more vulnerable inner child. Like any emotion, it's okay to feel anger and, like any emotion, anger needs to be witnessed, felt, and addressed in a healthy way. If our inner teenager's anger is not met with empathy and support, they may act on their reactive survival mechanisms. While these survival mechanisms can provide our inner teen with a sense of power, this is a fragile partnership: left unchecked these mechanisms become destructive in and of themselves.

Our inner teenager might resist the idea of setting these behaviors down or giving up their false sense of power. We need our loving parent in the driver's seat to protect, nurture, support, and guide our inner teenager.

The inner teenager's anger can be challenging, and can trigger another inner family member's fear of angry people. When our inner teen's anger arises, the inner child may feel shame or panic about overreacting or being "out of control" in the past, or fear "losing control" in the future. They may believe there is something wrong with them for feeling angry. If the inner child's fear or false belief takes over often, we may start keeping people at a distance to avoid conflicts or situations that could provoke our inner teen's anger. In other situations, our parentified inner teen can be so preoccupied with fixing situations that our inner child gets neglected entirely. Learning to work with our inner teenager's anger can free us from this self-imposed isolation.

To work with your inner teenager's anger:

> When the inner teenager tries to defend the inner child, your loving parent can thank them and help them take a break. "Thank you for watching out for the little one. **I'll handle this now.**"

Be mindful of it. Feel it in your body, and empathize with your inner teen.

Provide a safe outlet for your inner teen's anger. Then help them let their feelings be. Safe outlets for anger include:

- Pounding the mattress (with clenched fists, a tennis racket, etc.), shouting into a pillow
- Movement such as dancing, shaking, stomping, or strenuous exercise
- Listening to music
- Wrapping your arms tightly around yourself; pressing your palms together and then releasing; fast and deep breathing; letting a growl come from your belly
- Ripping up paper; popping bubble wrap; writing down what's bothering you and crumpling the paper; scribbling hard on paper; journaling; squeezing a stress ball
- Calling a fellow traveler or sponsor to "vent" for a couple minutes to help access your underlying feelings

Sometimes our inner teen's anger can arrive with an intensity that is challenging. This can sometimes be because their anger is fueled by distorted thinking and judgments masquerading as feelings. It can be helpful to begin with a few breaths to ground yourself. Then:

Observe your thoughts. What is your inner teen thinking and believing? Write it down. "What a rude jerk!"

Compare your inner teenager's thoughts with what happened. Write down an observation (the facts). "I said hello to that person, and they passed by in silence."

Focus your inner teen on their feelings to be in The Solution. Your loving parent might ask, "How did you feel and what did you need then?"

Help your inner teen have more perspective. "Thank you for trying to protect the little one. I see you and I see the little one, too. I'm sorry your needs weren't met. I know it seems personal but this isn't about you. It's okay to feel the anger and then let it be."

Your loving parent may need to tend to and guide other inner family members who react to your inner teenager's anger.

When the inner teenager...	The inner child...	The critical parent...	The loving parent can...
Feels angry and gets reactive	May feel afraid, alone, hopeless.	May try to shut down your inner teen's anger.	Reassure the inner child. "I'm here now, you're safe. I'll support the inner teen. You can hang out in the safe space if you'd like, while I do that." Set a boundary with the critical parent. "Thanks for trying to help. It's okay for the inner teen to feel angry. I'll be with them."

When anger is an alarm signal of boundary violations and unmet needs, you might turn to the suggestions below for assistance.

Acknowledge your inner teenager. "You're angry. I get that. Not only are current needs not being met, but this situation also brings up past painful experiences."

Empathize with your inner teenager's feelings and needs. "Are you feeling angry because that person's judgment didn't meet your need for respect?"

Evaluate when it's important to take action when people violate your boundaries. Your loving parent must do this, not the inner teenager. "We are powerless over this person, but I will do what's needed to keep us safe." Making healthy changes is paramount–the inner children won't trust you if you stay in unhealthy situations or accept abuse.

In the early stages of building trust with your inner teen, it might be helpful for your loving parent to make explicit commitments to your teen: for example, "If our co-worker is still treating us this way in two weeks, you can trust me to take further action," or, "I know that our roommate is unkind to us—I am working on finding us a new living situation. You can trust me to take care of that."

Set internal boundaries. Ask the critical parent to give your inner teen space for their anger, or ask your inner teen not to personalize another person's words or behaviors.

Practice self-care. Take a walk, make a cup of your favorite tea, whatever nourishes you.

Talk it out with a sponsor or fellow traveler. Trusted others can help you access the feelings and identify your inner teen's needs. Consider seeking professional help if anger is a consistent issue, present in extremes, or contributes to harmful patterns.

When the loving parent listens to the inner teen's concerns, and makes choices and changes to benefit the inner family, the inner teen can relax. A protected inner child and inner teenager learn an important lesson: "I'm worthy of protection."

Worksheet: *Boundary Violations*

Inventory the times from age 20 onward that you acted out traits from either of The Laundry Lists and later realized you didn't honor your boundaries or inner truth. Your intuition told you to say "no" but you went ahead and said "yes." It's likely that your inner child's fear of abandonment took over, causing you to say "yes" against your better instincts.

Note: The inner teenager can also act out through our behavior which leads to violating other people's boundaries. This exercise focuses on boundary violations that trigger the inner teenager, not those they cause.

Worksheet: *Boundary Violations*				
Describe the event and the boundary violation. List your age	**How did your inner teen feel after the violation?** (feeling words)	**What trait(s) drove your behavior? Which part of you was in the driver's seat?**	**What does your inner teenager need to say to your inner loving parent?**	**What can your inner loving parent say to your inner teenager to acknowledge the boundary violation?**
Example. At 32, I let someone take over my project because my mentor asked me to.	*Angry, resentful, outraged*	*Traits 1, 2, 4 . My inner child's fear of abandonment took over. My critical parent then told me I "should" share the spotlight.*	*You didn't stand up for us. You abandoned us. We gave up something important and I'm mad at you.*	*I'm sorry I wasn't there to step in when the little one's fear of abandonment took over. I am working on protecting you all better.*

Reflections: *Inner Teenager Rebellion*

Inner teen strategies of rebelling against others and the critical parent can bring unwanted consequences in adulthood. Record your answers to the following questions.

1. What were boundaries like in your home—rigid, loose, inconsistent, or absent?

2. As a teenager, did you rebel against authority, comply with it, or both? How did these survival techniques help you? In what ways did they work against you?

3. In what ways does your inner teenager's rebellion and/or compliance play out in your adult life today?

4. What consequences have you experienced due to rebellion or compliance (e.g., lost relationships, jobs, friends, integrity, abandonment of own values)?

Exercise: *Identifying What Angers Your Inner Teenager*

What angers, frustrates or leads to resentment for your inner teenager? Make a list below. Write as much as you can without censoring the list. It's okay to be petty. Allow your inner teen to express their emotions about each item on the list and empathize with them.

_____

_____

_____

_____

_____

Transfer your list to a separate piece of paper. Next, invite your inner teenager to rip the list into pieces or ask them what they'd like to do to express their anger. Feel your feelings as you do, and find a meaningful way to close the exercise.

Reflections: *Working with Your Inner Teenager's Anger*

Think of a recent time when you felt angry and wanted to react. Then, record your answers to the following questions.

1. Describe the situation in a couple of sentences. (e.g., where you were, who you were with, what happened.)

2. What happened inside you? Note the physical sensations in your body and emotions you felt.

3. What needs of your inner teen weren't met in that situation?

4. When did you feel the same reaction to these unmet needs as a child or teen? Describe a childhood event that triggered the same feelings if you can remember one.

5. How might unresolved feelings from childhood events have been contributing to your reaction in the present-day situation?

6. How can your loving parent tend to the inner child, both addressing pain from the past and pain from the present-day situation?

Guided Practice: *Honoring Your Inner Teenager's Anger*

This guided practice can help bring your inner teen reparenting work more into your body to be felt and released.

Note: As with all guided practices in this book, please refer to the "Guided Practice Preparation" in Appendix B for suggestions and precautions, and to access the opening script. [Begin recording, read the opening script, and continue reading the script here...]

Think of a person who easily triggers your anger or around whom you tend to get reactive, even if you're able to hide your reactivity. This could be a family member, someone at work, someone in your community with whom you tend to argue, get judgmental, use sarcasm, or try to prove yourself. This may be someone who seems unable to see you or respect you, or who doesn't follow through when they say they will. (Pause) In your mind's eye, recall a specific time with this person when you got triggered. (Pause) Where were you, what were you wearing, how were you feeling? Notice any physical sensations that arise as you remember this situation. Tune in to your breathing. What feelings are present? (Pause)

Notice any desire to lash out or defend, even if only in your mind. Connect with this part of yourself who feels angry and resentful, perhaps even enraged. Try to stay open and let them feel what they feel. (Pause)

Invite your inner teen to speak to you directly, letting them know you're there to listen. What bugs your inner teen about this person and that situation? How do they feel about interacting with this person? (Pause) How do they want to react to this person? What do they wish they could say to this person? Let them get it all out. (Pause)

Empathize with their feelings and thank them for their honesty and vulnerability. (Pause) You might ask them what the situation reminds them of from childhood. How far back have they felt this way? (Pause) Give yourself a moment to be with the feelings, not to change them, but just to be with them. (Pause)

What does your inner teenager need to hear or need you to do? Pause and let any answer come. You don't have to search for an answer. (Pause) Maybe they need to hear you understand how alone they've felt. How they survived the best they knew how. How angry they are about the adults in their life who didn't hear, see, protect, or support them or your little one. (Pause)

Perhaps the way to connect is to just be with them in silence, making space for their complicated feelings. Let them know that they won't always feel such strong emotions. (Pause) They don't need to take it personally when others don't respect boundaries. People won't always get or respect boundaries, but there's an adult inside who can set and maintain boundaries with people.

Let your inner teen know it's okay for them to be exactly where they are and exactly who they are. It's not their responsibility, and it never was, to take care of the inner child or situations like the one with this person. Your loving parent is there now. You're going to take excellent care of this inner teenager, and you understand it will take time to build their trust.

Let your inner teen know that you hope they can relax and just be a teenager—as they feel comfortable and trust you more. You will find ways for them to let off steam, maybe through movement, art, being in nature, sports, trying out a new style of clothing or haircut, laughing with friends — whatever feels right. Taking safe risks, such as having a voice and advocating for your inner family's needs are ways to let their beautiful qualities like authenticity and courage shine.

Take a moment to let this guided practice settle. (Pause) When you're ready, open your eyes or lift your gaze and reconnect with the world around you. [End recording]

Reflections: *Honoring Your Inner Teenager's Anger Guided Practice*

1. What was this guided practice like for you?

2. What did you learn about your inner teenager's anger and needs?

3. What was difficult? What was easy?

4. What did your inner teenager respond when you asked them what they needed your loving parent to say or do? Note how you felt hearing their response, or hearing no response.

5. What are some ways you could build your inner teen's trust?

Exercise: *Helping Your Inner Teenager Express their Anger Safely*

While we could not always safely express anger to parents, caretakers, or other childhood authority figures, we can give our inner teenager a voice today. Provide your inner teenager the opportunity to pile their anger into a note (sometimes called a "hot letter") that you'll later destroy or set aside until emotions calm. Allow their uncensored thoughts and feelings to come to life on the page. Your inner teen might want to address the letter to a parent, caretaker, or childhood authority figure. Writing a letter like this provides a safe outlet for angry thoughts and feelings, and can be cathartic and clarifying. Some prompts to consider are, "What I need you to know..." "I feel so angry about..." Your inner teen's "hot" letter:

Allow yourself to experience your feelings as you read the letter out loud to yourself. It's vital to let your inner teenager understand that you know how they feel.

Later, you might wish to read the letter aloud to a fellow traveler(s), sponsor, in a study group, meeting, or to a therapist. Sharing anger can push us out of our comfort zone, but if we can do so from our challenge zone, it can be deeply healing. Our loving parent can guide this process by protecting our inner family members and finding trusted others with whom to share. Some adult children create a ritual of composting or ripping up the letter at the end of the exercise.

Worksheet: *Inner Teenager Grief Work*

Under anger, we often find grief. The following worksheet can help you to measure your inner teen's losses for painful situations. In column four, invite your inner teenager to speak directly (in your imagination) to the person from that time. Let them know you'll have their back. For the last column, focus on how you would have responded if you had been standing next to your inner teenager in that situation.

Worksheet: *Inner Teenager Grief Work*				
Event, my age (from 13-19)	What I received (abandonment, denial, shame, abuse, codependency, criticism)	What I would have received from healthy caregivers in the same situation, what I needed	What my inner teenager wants to say to the person at that time	What my inner loving parent would have done
Example: Dad promised not to move my last school year if I helped Mom with my younger siblings. He moved the family anyway. Age 18	*Manipulation, parentification, emotional abandonment, disregard for my needs, unreliability*	*Care for my needs, honesty, autonomy, respect, caring, consistency, accountability*	*I trusted you and you lied. It was awful to move every school year. You only care about yourself. I'm not helping you anymore.*	*Whew. You're outraged. You wanted to trust him and to know you mattered. I'm sorry he wasn't reliable. I will take care of you and prioritize your needs.*

Record any insights or feelings you have about doing the exercise in your journal or share them with trusted others.

The Inner Teenager and Sexuality

Sexuality is a sensitive area of healing for adult children and for the inner teenager. Some adult children were sexually abused, and as adult children, we can all have a complicated relationship with sexuality. We may not have learned to nurture or value our sexuality. We may feel shame about things we have done or not done sexually. We may have used sex and romance to feel safe or connected, or believed that every relationship needed to lead to romantic or sexual involvement to last.

We may compulsively seek sex, relationships, or romance to medicate painful feelings. We may be in relationship after relationship with the same predictable patterns and chaos, or we may avoid relationships or sex altogether, and feel isolated and lonely. Sex may be present, but lacking intimacy or love. Or we may deal with sex addiction, or be stuck in a romantic fantasy that isn't real to avoid the pain and grief of our own lives.

If the inner teenager chooses our relationships, we can become involved with compulsive, dangerous, or emotionally unavailable people. We can equate sex with intimacy and settle for unfulfilling relationships where we are not seen, heard, or valued. The inner teenager could lead us to seek out relationships with people we can see as "rescuers" to resolve our inner child's unmet needs for love, protection, and support. Or we could get lost in dissociative "happily ever after" fantasies about others, and how good our life would be with them.

To end this destructive pattern, our loving parent needs to fulfill the inner child from within and support the inner teenager. As we reconnect with our sexuality, our loving parent can set internal behavioral boundaries around romantic fantasy, love addiction, sexual compulsion, flirtation, emotional affairs, infidelity, promiscuity, addiction to excitement (loving falling in love), or jumping into relationships without thinking. An internal thought boundary can help limit the inner teenager's obsessive fantasy thinking about romance, sex, or another person. "No, that's not real. Let's ground back in the here and now" or "There is a lot of thinking going on. What are you feeling? What are you needing?" When your inner teenager feels safe and can relax, you more naturally make choices about relationships and sex from a place of wholeness.

> **Healthy sexuality** means being able to comfortably talk about your feelings and needs, initiate sex or say no to sex, and enjoy sex without fear, guilt or shame. It involves mutual respect and a commitment to trust and honesty.

1. What are some ways your inner teenager has led you into problematic romantic and/or sexual situations?

2. What signs tell you that your inner teenager is in the driver's seat for sex, love, or relationships?

3. What are some boundaries your loving parent might need to set around the inner teenager and sexuality?

4. How can you tend to your inner teen's pain around missing out on healthy sexual expression and intimacy in adulthood due to your dysfunctional upbringing and abuse? (e.g., if you've practiced relationship "anorexia" (which means avoiding social, sexual or emotional intimacy to avoid being hurt), what might your inner teen need to hear?)

Reflections: *Making Living Amends to Your Inner Teenager*

You can make amends to your inner teenager about your actions or inaction in adulthood that affected them and your inner child. You might want to focus on losses from:

- Your boundary violation worksheet (earlier in this chapter).
- Unmet needs, including being seen and heard, mattering, autonomy, choice, support, guidance, structure, and safety.
- Sexuality and relationships during your adult years.
- Losses due to using survival mechanisms.

Make amends to your inner teenager and let your inner teenager know how you plan to change your behavior so you and they feel better. This is known as making "living amends." You may choose to write a letter or poem in your journal, telling them how you plan to do things differently. Speak to your teenager from your heart. Keep in mind the pain and loss they experienced in adolescence and how hard they've been working to protect the inner child.

Part of a living amends is showing appreciation for our inner teenager. As stated in Promise 2, "Our self-esteem will increase as we give ourselves approval on a daily basis." We can take time to appreciate our inner teenager on a regular basis. Reflecting regularly on the qualities we admire in our inner teenager helps them heal and shows them that they matter to us.

Your Key Chapter Takeaway(s):

Affirmation / Meditation

I am developing a trusting relationship with my inner teenager and helping them set down their survival tools so we can move beyond surviving, and into thriving.

Transforming Your Relationship to Your Critical Parent

Meditation / Prayer
May I have curiosity and courage as I explore my critical parent's positive intent.
May the insight I gain help me integrate my critical parent with love, wisdom, and discernment.

When you transform your relationship to your critical parent, you will trust yourself more and grow your inner love and peace. To begin this transformation, it helps to understand the critical parent's positive intention. We began to understand this positive intent in Chapter 5 and continue that work here.

The examples below are meant to help understand the reasoning of the critical parent. The "I" speaking is the critical parent:

Criticism motivates and protects. *If I criticize you, you'll be careful, and others will want you around. If I judge you as selfish, you'll focus on meeting others' needs more than your own. You'll be "needed" by others and safe from abandonment. If I criticize others and make them seem "less than" to you, you'll stay safe in your isolated bubble. No one will be able to hurt you or take away what is yours.*

Self-judgment protects. *If I judge you, it won't hurt as much when others judge you. Using judgment, I will try to control and prevent your pain.*

Judging others protects. *"If I judge others, it will keep you from getting close to them. It'll also make sure that they don't try to get too close to you. If you get too close, you will inevitably get hurt, be abandoned, or be taken advantage of. If I judge others, it will keep your behavior aligned with your family of origin; it's how you will feel "normal" and stay safe."*

Approval-seeking keeps you safe. *Disapproval and disappointment are to be avoided. You cannot do anything that might cause rejection. I help you to make sure you're not more visible and thus more vulnerable.*

Being visible or strong is risky. *If you act in self-deprecating ways, others might not get angry or be threatened by you for being good or better at something than them. They might also see you as a victim and want to rescue you or protect you. This helps you fit in with the family, circle, group, and community.*

It's possible to fix you. *I can fix it, but you must follow my rules. Home is chaotic and dangerous, but I can fix you. I can make you smarter, more polite, and/or perfect so your family will take better care of you. If I make you feel guilty and wrong, you'll avoid future mistakes and be more lovable.*

Comparing helps you. *If I point out someone else's flaws, you can feel superior. If I point out someone else's strengths, you'll work harder to be "good enough."*

Some critical parents can be more destructive than others and might have been attacking you since before you could speak. They might intentionally inflict pain on the inner child in an attempt to prevent external abandonment or greater harm through debilitating images, words, or shame. Working with a therapist—in addition to a supportive sponsor, fellow traveler(s), or a study group—might support you in effectively setting boundaries with this type of critical parent.

Identifying a positive intent might seem impossible or even dangerous with this kind of critical parent. It can, however, be helpful for you to understand what they're trying to achieve:

- The destructive critical parent is anticipating others' attacks on you. If it strikes first, you will have your guard up.
- If your parents punished, mocked, or stifled you, your critical parent might decide it is safer to lock up your energy. Some people express this unconsciously when they say, "I'm just too much," or "I have too many feelings."
- If you experienced relentless abuse and neglect, or had a strong sense of being unwanted, your critical parent might feel angry about that. The critical parent turned the anger inward because it wasn't safe to express anger to authority figures.
- The critical parent might have decided to blame you for the abuse and neglect you experienced so you would work on yourself. They thought you'd hurt less if you changed yourself. This was preferable to you feeling utterly helpless in an intolerable situation.

"When my inner child wrote messages of encouragement and support (non-dominant handwriting), I noticed she was playing loving parent to my adult self, instead of vice versa. On an ACA retreat, I realized my inner child stayed hidden because she didn't trust me. I habitually thought about suicide because it seemed like an escape. No wonder she kept her true feelings hidden and tried to encourage me—she thought I was going to kill us! From that moment, every time I had a suicidal thought, I made amends to my inner child. Eventually, my non-dominant hand wrote about fear, sadness, anger, and joy—my little kid finally felt safe enough to share her true feelings." -Fellow Traveler

Recognizing the Critical Parent's Efforts To Keep You Safe

You can have compassion for your critical parent's protective efforts to keep you safe while setting boundaries with them at the same time. The focus is on what your critical parent is attempting to do—their positive intent—not on their behavior or words.

Sometimes it's hard to appreciate a critical parent who has inflicted pain. The loving parent can see past the behavior to the needs the critical parent is trying to meet. "I see how hard you've been working and how desperate you've been to keep us safe." This doesn't condone the behavior but honors the critical parent's efforts, however misguided. This can go a long way toward creating a more cooperative relationship. At some point, you might notice that the critical parent is no longer active, takes more breaks, has integrated, or has even become more of an ally.

"One night I heard my critical parent demanding perfection. For the first time I listened. I expected to find a monster but instead found a scared, tiny version of myself who had tried to keep us safe in childhood by finding mistakes before my raging parent did. She thought of herself as a protector and cried. The little critic hadn't attacked me; I'd attacked her. She'd been trying to keep us safe by being amazing and perfect." -Fellow Traveler

Worksheet: *Identifying the Need Your Critical Parent Is Trying to Meet*

"It was enlightening to feel compassion for my critical parent. It has always been a cruel energy. It's been freeing, healing, and empowering to meet it with compassion." -Fellow Traveler

The critical parent is not simply a parrot of past authority figures and caregivers. They're attempting to meet a need when they shame, question, judge, and doubt you or others. The purpose of this exercise is to understand the needs the critical parent is trying to meet. We can help the critical parent trust that we have more effective ways to meet those needs today. By understanding the underlying need, we become able to set a boundary from a loving place rather than from the rebellious anger of our inner teenager.

For each inner critical parent message below, think about a situation in your life where this message came up or could come up. Feel free to add to the second and third columns in the examples provided to make them more relevant to your life. You might find it helpful to refer to the Feelings, Needs, and Physical Sensations sheet in Appendix D on page 224. Then complete the remaining rows with your own critical parent messages.

Worksheet: *Identifying the Need Your Critical Parent Is Trying to Meet*		
Critical parent Message	**What is your critical parent's positive intent? What needs are they attempting to meet?**	**Impact on inner child; Feelings, unmet needs**
You're not pretty/ handsome if you don't smile, build muscle, dress well, etc.	*Wants people to like you, prevent "abandonment." Needs: Belonging, inclusion, acceptance*	*"Smiling when I'm sad is fake."* *Feels uncomfortable, frustrated, sad, scared, etc. Unmet needs: affirmation, acceptance, love, support, emotional safety, self-worth, to be seen, authenticity, honesty, integrity*
You're not so special	*Prevent you from taking risks that might end in failure, avoid rejection. Needs: safety, belonging, acceptance, inclusion*	*Believes, "I don't matter."* *Feels shame, hurt, lonely, sad. Unmet needs: Love, to matter, to be seen for unique self, contribute, recognition, reassurance, support*
You need to get more done	*Encourage accomplishment, success, motivate you. Needs: self-worth, belonging, safety*	*"I'm not good enough."* *Feels ashamed, distressed, discouraged, angry.* *Unmet needs: unconditional love, acceptance, to be seen, to have value, self-worth*
You're bad and selfish, if you say "no"	*Wants you to keep people's approval. Needs: Acceptance, belonging, safety, connection, to have value*	*Guilt, shame, fear.* *Unmet needs: guidance, understanding, support, authenticity, integrity, honesty, clarity*

Worksheet: *Identifying the Need Your Critical Parent Is Trying to Meet*		
Critical parent Message	**What is your critical parent's positive intent? What needs are they attempting to meet?**	**Impact on inner child; Feelings, unmet needs**

"I realized my critical parent really did love me all along and was just trying to protect me 'out of love' with primitive family skills. Thanking my critical parent melted its heart." -Fellow Traveler

Reflections: *Identifying Your Critical Parent's Positive Intent*

1. How did your inner critical parent help you in childhood (even if its method also hurt you)?

2. What is your critical parent trying to accomplish by judging, doubting, questioning, undermining, and/or scrutinizing you today?

3. What does your critical parent fear would happen if they didn't judge, doubt, question, undermine, control, and/or scrutinize you?

4. What kind of feelings or experiences is your critical parent trying to protect you from?

5. Ask your critical parent to show you their childhood origins. When did they need to start controlling and managing your life? Why did they need to do that?

6. What could you say to show your critical parent you understand what they're trying to achieve, even if their approach is counterproductive today? Note down any response your critical parent has to what you say.

It is much harder to view someone as an enemy once we learn their story. The same is true for our critical parent. Transforming our relationship to our inner critical parent can take time, and it's not uncommon to experience resistance to doing so. If you feel no change, consider revisiting this exercise at a later time.

How are you feeling after answering these questions? Would a gentleness break be supportive?

"The critical parent, whom I have often called 'C.' has transformed over time and become allied with other, more compassionate parts of me." -Fellow Traveler

Reflections: *Showing Your Critical Parent the Pain*

"I have learned to ask the critical parent what it is afraid of when I notice it is active and shaming or judging. Often it is trying to look out for my best interests and see to it that I don't set myself up for abandonment. I can now say: 'Yes, that is important, and so I will address the situation with my loving parent.'" -Fellow Traveler

Like an outdated software program, our critical parent's operating system needs an update. They might not realize your inner child is already experiencing childhood pain and that their efforts are making it worse. Sometimes explaining this to the critical parent can help them adjust their behavior.

The following questions are intended to help your critical parent understand the pain they can cause the inner child. You'll refer to the situation you list in question #1 below for all the questions that follow. You could also record the questions to play back as a guided practice.

Think of a time or situation when your critical parent became activated—they criticized, doubted, undermined, questioned, shamed, controlled, or scrutinized you. This can be a general situation or a specific moment in time.

1. Describe the situation that activates/activated your critical parent. (e.g., whenever I speak in a meeting, my critical parent critiques my share afterward.)

2. What does your critical parent say, do, or show you in that situation? (e.g., my critical parent tells me what I "should" have said. They show me images of others shunning me.)

3. How does the critical parent affect your inner child in that situation? How does your inner child feel, and what false beliefs arise? (e.g., my inner child feels shame and wants to isolate. The critical parent's judgments make it hard for me to listen to people who speak after me.)

4. Share with your critical parent how they affect your inner child. (e.g., "My inner child hears your messages. They feel hurt and ashamed. Are you aware of how your words harm the little one?")

5. What is your inner critical parent's response? They might say something, show an image, give a felt sense, etc.

6. Ask your critical parent how they feel hearing the impact of their words on your inner child (e.g., what do they say or show you, or what feelings are present)?

7. If the critical parent recognizes their effect on the inner child and seems sorry, ask if they're willing to relax and decrease their judgments. Record your critical parent's response here.

8. If your critical parent doesn't recognize their effect or doesn't seem sorry, ask: "What are you afraid will happen if you stop judging the inner child so much?" Whatever their answer, try to identify the need(s) they're trying to meet.

The critical parent might not be ready to take a break or soften their controlling behaviors. We can acknowledge our critical parent's concerns and tell them something like, "As the loving parent, I will continue to try to understand your concerns. At the same time, I will protect the inner child and set boundaries with you when needed."

Worksheet: *Loving Strategies to Address the Needs the Critical Parent Is Trying to Meet*

As we've discussed in Chapter 5, the critical parent relaxes most when they trust we have more effective ways to meet our needs today. This worksheet can help us demonstrate to our critical parent that our loving parent will be there to protect, love, support, and guide the inner family.

Refer to the previous worksheet on page 188, in which you identified critical parent messages and the underlying needs motivating the critical parent. In the first column below, list the critical parent needs you identified, one need per row. In the second column, write out some loving strategies that can address these same needs without harming your inner children.

Worksheet: *Loving Strategies to Address the Needs the Critical Parent Is Trying to Meet*	
Needs your Critical Parent is attempting to meet	**Loving strategies to address these same needs**
Example: Belonging	*Nurture them when shame arises, and they don't believe they belong. Give them inner belonging by affirming and protecting them, by reminding them that by being their true self, they will always belong, no matter what others say or do.*

Integration is a process and requires different things for each of us. For some, our critical parent might fade away as we become our own loving parent. For others, the critical parent uses their discerning qualities to kindly alert us to a possible amends. Some people report that their critical parent takes on a new role, becoming a champion, cheerleader, or ally to our loving parent, alerting the loving parent when the inner child is in need of protection and attention. No matter how, or if, our critical parent integrates, our loving parent, supported by a higher power, is the one to protect and guide our inner family.

Your Key Chapter Takeaway(s):

Affirmation / Meditation

I can experience freedom in spite of my inner critical parent's judgments.
As I reparent myself, my critical parent's role in my life will be revealed to me.
I deserve to experience—and will experience—the joys of integration and clarity.

20

Helping Your Inner Child Grieve

Meditation / Prayer
Guide me to be gentle and compassionate with what my inner child reveals to me.

In this program, we break the "don't remember" rule and instead seek full remembrance. Grief work helps us understand our past, explaining where we came from and how the past has shaped us. We learn that we are not what happened to us, which frees the inner child from emotional bondage. Grief gives us freedom from the past so that we can live more fully in the present.

We begin our grief work in earnest when our critical parent softens, our inner teenager relaxes, and a loving parent creates a safe space for our inner child. Our inner child remembers the neglect, abandonment, and abuse of the past. When this happens, you will feel the pain of your buried feelings and memories. You may experience shock, anger, depression, hurt, sadness, remorse, despair, or shame. Grief work, which is associated with the shame and abandonment work we do in Step 4 and 5, makes space for all of these feelings. Reparenting has a deepening effect on Step work, especially the work we do in Step 4 and Step 5.

> *Grief* is the loss of what was and will never be again.
> *Grief* is also the loss of what never was and will never be.

Adult children can be afraid that grief will overwhelm and consume them. Doing this work alone magnifies this fear, connecting us to our abandonment wound. Today, we have the support of a power greater than ourselves, including the love of our fellow travelers and tools for getting our loving parent back in the driver's seat. We are not alone.

Creating Space to Connect with Your Inner Child's Grief

At times, your inner child's grief may take over and it can seem like you're feeling all of their feelings all at once. The inner child has taken over the driver's seat. This makes accessing your loving parent more difficult and leaves the inner child alone in their pain. If this happens, you can create space so that your loving parent can be present to their grief. You can reassure your inner child and use the suggestions in Chapter 4. "I want to know how you feel. I won't leave. I can be more present if you breathe with me and you can feel a little calmer." You can also ask them to look in your direction so you can see them better, breathe together, or do whatever would help them feel calmer.

If they are not willing to look at you, that's okay; they might be feeling too afraid, ashamed, or angry to do so. You could ask them what they're worried would happen if they met your eyes, or wait until they're ready. They might not trust that you'll understand how they feel if they don't take over. Help them understand you want to know how they feel, and help ease the pain they carry. At times you might need to let them know that you need to take a break and return to this issue when you can be more fully present.

Beyond nurturing words, they may need a hug, to be rocked, or need your loving parent to hum or sing to them. They may need you to help ground them in the present moment and use the techniques discussed in earlier chapters, especially Chapter 4.

Pinpointing and Measuring the Loss

Exercise: *Loss Inventory*

Inventorying your losses can help you validate and accept what happened in the past. Our inner child needs empathy for what happened, or didn't happen in childhood. If any inner family members minimize or make justifications for the abuse or neglect you experienced, let them know that it's okay to break the "Don't talk, Don't trust, Don't feel" rule. Your loving parent will keep them safe.

"Significant" losses include the death of loved ones, traumatic experiences, physical or emotional abandonment, neglect, abuse, or stressful life changes, such as moving homes or schools. A lack of "significant" losses, may lead us to minimize or discount our losses. Yet, accumulated losses, such as a parent not showing up for events, questioning our choices, and/or acknowledging us only when we did exceptionally well, can affect us in profound ways. Some recovering adult children describe this as "death by a thousand paper cuts."

Check the losses you've experienced below:

Some "significant" losses include, but aren't limited to:

- ☐ Loss of close relatives, friends, or pets through death or other circumstances
- ☐ The loss of something important including missed opportunities
- ☐ A move or instability of where is "home"
- ☐ A parent's job loss that impacted the family
- ☐ Divorce
- ☐ Illness, yours or someone in the family
- ☐ Loss of safety, integrity, wholeness, and healthy sexuality due to child sexual abuse

the power of sharing

Examples of "accumulated" losses include, but aren't limited to:

- ☐ Having no parent or caregiver present for sporting events, plays, award ceremonies, graduations, or birthdays, as well as not following through on other promises or commitments
- ☐ A parent or caregiver criticizing your clothing, interests, preferences, or performance
- ☐ Being forgotten or picked up late from school, left regularly at others' homes or for long periods of time
- ☐ Not being read a bedtime story or tucked in

- ☐ Needing to make your own meals, getting yourself off to school at a young age
- ☐ Not being asked about how you feel, what you like to do, your interests, your opinion
- ☐ Exposure to adult problems, fighting, and triangulation (i.e., when a parent talks about another parent or sibling to you)
- ☐ Having a codependent parent who cyclically packs up the kids and leaves (or threatens to leave) the rageaholic/alcoholic/abuser only to later return
- ☐ Being yelled at consistently
- ☐ A lack of limits; a caregiver seemingly not caring what you did or being largely absent
- ☐ Exposure to adult/violent books, movies, magazines, and/or conversations
- ☐ Being punished when you expressed emotions; having your feelings minimized, denied, mocked; being yelled at when you hurt yourself, fell ill, or made a mistake

Doing a loss inventory may trigger inner family members since we stuffed our feelings about these losses to protect ourselves as children. We can honor any resistance inner family members feel and respect their pace. Some find it helpful to write down a loss or two at a time followed by a gentleness break. Others schedule time with a fellow traveler or sponsor to talk about their feelings before, during, or after their inventory work. Others like to quietly sit with their inner child or inner teen as a way to process what comes up and reach out if needed.

Honoring our losses is an intimate process and our inner child deserves our full attention. We recommend taking a few moments to center yourself through prayer, meditation, or whatever else will help you be present before beginning this type of inner work.

On a blank piece of paper, record your significant and small losses from early life up to age eighteen. Next to each loss, list a few feeling words that capture how you felt at the time. For each loss, reflect on:

- Who was there to empathize with the loss.
- How others in your family dealt with their feelings.
- Did others understand your needs and give you the necessary time to grieve?
- What did others tell you about your loss?

Written life stories, drawings, or collages are other ways to do a loss inventory.

It's okay to cry, feel sad, angry, or numb while doing this exercise. No one will judge your work, and you don't need anyone's approval. Aim for honesty and to honor your inner family's true feelings. Take your time. Let your thoughts and feelings flow without censoring.

You may wish to give yourself time to be with the feelings this exercise brings up before proceeding to the next exercises.

gentleness break

Worksheet: *Witnessing the Origins of False Beliefs*

The critical parent's attacks harm your inner child, but much of the inner child's pain comes from childhood abandonment, neglect, and abuse. Those circumstances gave rise to their false beliefs. As loving parents we can help our inner child release these limiting messages.

> *Work with false beliefs one at a time, taking **gentleness breaks** as needed.*

Some false beliefs:

I am unlovable

There's something wrong with me

Others' feelings are more important than mine

I failed my family; it's my fault

I am not enough

I don't matter

I am responsible for others' feelings

It's not okay to ask for help

As you complete the worksheet below, check to see that your loving parent is in charge. Please use additional paper as needed for these worksheets.

Worksheet: *Witnessing and Releasing False Beliefs*				
False Belief	**Situation / Loss** (age and any details you remember)	**Your inner child's thoughts and feelings about that situation** (their pain)	**Empathy from your loving parent to your inner child**	**Supportive loving parent message (new belief) to your inner child**
I don't matter	*Age 3+ My parents rarely played with me or asked me about my thoughts or feelings.*	*It hurt. I felt very lonely. It was as if I didn't exist. I'm a burden, they don't love me.*	*That was so painful and hurtful. I'm so sorry you weren't seen and heard.*	*You do matter. Your thoughts and feelings matter. You are a precious child of the universe. You are worthy.*

You will probably want to allow a few days to pass between the previous exercise and the next. Consider sharing these beliefs with a sponsor or fellow traveler(s) and creating a ritual to release them. Some people write the false beliefs on scraps of paper and burn them, compost them, create art with them, or find another way to release them symbolically.

Processing grief and releasing false beliefs is a long-term practice. When false beliefs arise, we counterbalance them with supportive, loving parent messages.

Worksheet: *Setting Down the Bundle*

The following worksheet helps your inner child revisit past losses and set down their burdens with your loving parent's support. You will have done a similar worksheet for the inner teen in Chapter 18.

Focus on painful situations from childhood. In column four, invite your inner child to speak directly (in your imagination) to the person from that time. Reassure them that they can say whatever is in their heart and that you'll keep them safe. For the last column, focus on how you would have responded if you, as the loving parent, had been standing next to your inner child in that situation.

Worksheet: *Setting Down the Bundle*				
Event (up to and including age 12), **my age**	**What I received** (abandonment, denial, shame, abuse, codependency, criticism)	**What I would have received from healthy caregivers in the same situation, what I needed at the time**	**What my inner child wants to say to the adult in charge**	**What I would have done as the inner loving parent**
Example: When I skinned my knee while playing, my father scolded me. He lashed out in anger instead of with affection	*Punishment, emotional abandonment, shame*	*Empathy, affection, caring, model of how to be kind to oneself, self-care. "That looks like it hurts. Are you okay?"*	*I feel scared when you yell. I'm hurting. I want to be held and comforted.*	*I would have pulled him close and said, "Ouch! You scraped your knee. Are you okay?" I'd ask him what he needed. I'd say, "Just because your dad got mad doesn't mean you did anything wrong. Accidents happen."*

When you're done, you may wish to create a ritual with your inner family members, helping them hand back the bundle to your family of origin or releasing it into the safekeeping of a power greater than yourself. Give yourself time to make space for your feelings.

Exercise: *Expressing Anger*

Anger is as valid for the inner child as pain, and is a natural part of completing the grieving process. Your inner child needs your loving parent to witness their anger, which they've often had to bottle inside. You may want to visit this exercise periodically, and do a little at a time.

Pick a situation that your inner child still feels angry about (from worksheets in this chapter or your anger list in Chapter 7); perhaps situations where a caregiver or other authority figure shamed, criticized, or attacked you as a child. Once your loving parent is in the driver's seat, support the inner child in whichever way below feels comfortable to your inner child:

Option A: Inner Child Taking the Lead

1. Revisit the situation in your imagination with your inner child and support them to stand up to the caregiver if they want to.

2. Support them in whatever way feels comfortable to them. That may be a hand on their shoulder or standing in between them and the authority figure.

3. Support them to express their feelings and thoughts to this person and reassure them that you have their back. They may wish to say something such as, "You were not kind! I was just a kid and that hurt, Mommy. I needed you to speak nicer to me."

4. Once your inner child has had a chance to let their anger out, invite them to tell you anything else they need to say about this situation.

Option B: Loving Parent Taking the Lead

1. Revisit the situation in your imagination with your inner child.

2. As you visit the original scene, speak up for your inner child to the caregiver as the child watches.

3. They may wish to stand behind you as you face the caregiver or hold your hand to feel comfortable and have safety. Or they may wish to observe from their safe inner space.

4. Let the caregiver know that their behavior is not okay and that you won't allow the child to

be mistreated. Help them understand how their words and actions are harmful.

5. If the caregiver responds, allow your loving parent to dialogue as long as the conversation seems productive. Maybe the caregiver makes amends, or wishes to change their behavior. If they become reactive or unkind, set a boundary with the caregiver and end the exercise.

Option C: Loving Parent Do-Over

1. Visualize the interaction about which your inner child is still angry.

2. Connect with that memory and replace that caregiver, authority figure, or sibling with yourself, as the loving parent.

3. Replay that situation or memory as the loving parent. Tell your inner child or inner teen all the things they wanted and needed to hear in this situation. Only you know what this inner child or inner teen needs. You have the opportunity now to address that need and help them let go of the anger they have been carrying for so long.

When your inner child or inner teen feels complete with the exercise, nurture and comfort them. Affirm that it's okay to talk, trust, and feel. Affirm them for their courage and vulnerability. Address any concerns they have about having interacted with the caregiver in these ways.

Record any insights or feelings you have about doing the exercise in your journal. Doing grief work in these ways can be a corrective emotional experience with transformative results. You can use this same exercise to express sadness, hurt, grief, or disappointment.

gentleness break

Notice your breathing. If it's tight, take a few breaths, releasing any tension as you exhale.

Additional Grief Work to Deepen Your Healing
Exercise: *Birthdays*

Birthdays can be complicated for adult children. Some of our parents forgot our birthdays while others made a big deal out of them. Perhaps we didn't receive any gifts or expressions of love. Maybe we got everything we wanted, but still felt empty inside. In either case it may have seemed that something important was missing—that sense that we mattered, that our parents were happy that we were born and happy we were who we were. The following questions may reveal areas where you can help your inner child and inner teen grieve and create new ways of celebrating your birthday.

1. What were birthdays like for you as a child? How did you feel about them? What birthdays stand out to you in particular?

2. How do you relate to birthdays today?

3. If birthdays are hard for you, which inner family member(s) needs your loving parent's attention on your birthday?

4. How might your inner loving parent help you celebrate your birthday?

5. What is your Adult Children of Alcoholics and Dysfunctional Families birthday/anniversary (i.e., the date you began this program)? If you don't know, ask yourself if you'd like to choose one.

6. Do you celebrate your program birthday/anniversary? If not, would you want to, and if so, how could you do so?

If your parents never gave you a birthday party, you may want to throw one for your inner child. You can invite fellow travelers and friends and tell them you're making up for your childhood. Our birthdays can become powerful reparenting moments to honor our inner child and let others celebrate our life with us.

Exercise: *Goodbye Letters*

In childhood, confronting the effects of dysfunction was too painful, so we may have dissociated by creating stories or fantasies to help us cope. Our inner child can still cling to these fantasies today, such as being a famous movie star, finding a fairy tale prince or princess, or becoming a millionaire. While these fantasies provided a sense of relief to us as children, they can keep us lost in "happily ever after" stories, and inhibit us from taking healthy action in our lives today. For example, we may fantasize about our "recovered" life but take little action to heal ourselves.

Once we peel back the layers of our denial and reparent ourselves through our grief and loss, our childhood survival fantasies begin to crumble away. In their place, we find new strategies for meeting our needs and a renewed vitality for pursuing our interests.

The questions below help you prepare your goodbye letter to those old fantasies:

1. Reflect on and list any unrealized childhood fantasies you hold onto today.

2. What needs did your younger self imagine would be met if your fantasies came true?

3. What needs aren't being met by holding onto these fantasies or stories? For example, ease, trust, peace, acceptance, self-worth.

4. What are some more effective strategies for meeting those same needs today?

5. What could your loving parent do or say to encourage your inner child and/or inner teen to be open to the strategies you listed above? (e.g., they might need space to mourn the pain behind those fantasies or stories, or reassurance you won't abandon those needs.)

6. In the space below or your journal, write a goodbye letter. Address it to yourself, saying farewell to childhood fantasies as you welcome new ways to meet your needs.

While you may not feel grief the first time you do this, return to the letter later to see if new feelings arise. We can let our inner child and inner teen know that we understand they may need to hold on to some stories or fantasies. They can let them go in their own time, and in the meantime, we will find new ways to meet their needs. Reading this letter to a sponsor, fellow traveler, therapist, or private study group can help you access your emotions more deeply.

Saying goodbye to fantasies allows for new energy, changed behaviors, and new ways of being. The fantasy may arise again in the future, but you'll be able to comfort your inner child and inner teen. You'll be able to help them understand how the strategies you're pursuing in the present will better meet their needs and the needs of your whole inner family.

gentleness break

After you write the letter and your inner family members have grieved enough, consider creating a ritual. You may wish to bury the letter, tear it into small pieces, or compost it.

Reflections: *Honoring Your Journey*

By working through this book, we've taken the courageous step of revisiting and grieving our childhood. Taking time to reflect on the strengths we've developed and the lessons we've learned on our journey is part of the healing process. We understand our past, but we live in the present, which allows a brighter future to emerge.

1. How do you feel when you reflect on your childhood and what you know now?

2. If you could go back in time, what would you tell your younger self?

3. What personal qualities, resources, and strengths helped you navigate your childhood challenges?

4. Where can you see these personal qualities, resources, and strengths at work in your adult life?

You might feel moved to write your inner child (and other inner family members) a letter to share this perspective.

Your Key Chapter Takeaway(s):

Affirmation / Meditation

Grant me the patience to let my inner child grieve.
Allow all feelings to be present for healing.

Reclaiming Your Inner Child's Joy and Playfulness

Meditation / Prayer

Grant me the freedom to play today and encourage me to explore my inner child's interests and talents. Help me remember it is safe and that play fuels my creativity, tickles my inner child, and nurtures my spirit.

Our inner child's natural state is playful and joyful, like a baby who delights in being alive. Yet, fun and play can be hard for adult children, particularly when going through deep grief work. Even in the midst of challenging times, however, moments of joy are possible. Reconnecting with the tender parts of ourselves from whom we've been distant and measuring our losses can give rise to sweet sorrow—a joy in rediscovering our true identities and our innate wholeness.

We each relate to joy and playfulness in different ways. Joy might come naturally to us, or we might feel anxious about the concept of joy. Perhaps we pressure ourselves to feel the kind of happiness we see in advertisements, TV, and social media. We might have "put on a happy face" as children to avoid further abuse, neglect, and abandonment. Perhaps our caregiver's pursuit of "happiness" resulted in our neglect, and so we're suspicious of it. These are only a few examples, and we want to be careful not to pursue fun, play, and happiness to avoid the pain that comes with doing grief work and reparenting ourselves. Our loving parent can help us find balance.

Unlike happiness, which tends to depend on circumstances, joy comes from within and naturally arises when we become more comfortable with who we are. The more we grieve and come to terms with our past with compassion and understanding, the more joy is available to us. Being in nature, sitting in silence, improving our conscious contact with a power greater than ourselves, and our connection with our inner child all can give us joy. Joy is not dependent on the conditions in our lives. Even people in devastating circumstances have found ways to appreciate the joy of being.

"When I think of celebrating, I think of joy, frivolity, or silliness. I am not outwardly like that. My humor is more intellectual than silly. It may be that being able to celebrate my little girl is more of an acknowledgment of her gifts, her value in my life, her value of having acquired the skills or the perseverance to get through a difficult childhood." -Fellow Traveler

Joy and Gratitude

The more our inner child feels secure, the more we experience joy inside and an overall sense of gratitude. We find ourselves seeking external sources of happiness less and feeling more grateful for what we have in our life now. We experience the simple pleasures in little things. Gratitude practice and reparenting reinforce each other. To begin to cultivate joy, consider beginning a gratitude practice.

A gratitude practice can be as simple as taking a few moments each day to reflect on a few things for which you're thankful. You might choose to practice with a fellow traveler, sponsor or study group, sharing your gratitude list by phone, email, or text each day. To deepen the experience, use the feelings and needs sentence from Chapter 10 for each item on your gratitude list, sharing how you feel now recalling the needs that were met. Add an observation, by describing what the other person/situation/thing did that enriched your life. You can also reflect on how you feel now recalling the situation.

For example, imagine a friend brought you a home-cooked meal when you were recovering from surgery. Your observation might be, "When I recall that Pat brought me a home-cooked meal (observation), I feel grateful (feeling), because it met my need for support (need)."

You can also be mindful of times that you thank others during the day. Commit to pausing one of those times to notice what specifically you're grateful for (identifying your met needs) and allow yourself to savor the feeling of gratitude. Routinely practicing gratitude can help us feel more joy.

"Celebrating my ability or willingness is something I do when I make up gratitude lists. When I look back on a period of time, I remember what made me smile or feel good by writing it down and reliving it by thinking it through. These are some of the ways I try to celebrate who I am, who I have been, and how I got here."
-Fellow Traveler

Exercise: *Express Your Gratitude to Your Inner Child*

It is meaningful to know what others appreciate about us and how we've contributed to their lives. In this same way, we can tell our inner child what we cherish in them. One way to do this is to write them a gratitude note celebrating their qualities and their willingness to share with us and trust us.

You can do this exercise in a journal, or consider taking this one step further and write a letter since many children love to receive mail:

- Prepare an envelope and write your inner child's name above your address.
- Add a stamp and mail the letter.
- When it arrives, make a date with your inner child to open it and read it together.

You can do this more than once, sending a note or postcard to your inner child on a regular or spontaneous basis. When you travel, send a postcard to your inner child, letting them know how you appreciated being together with them on that trip.

Consider creating a ritual of sending your inner child and inner teen a birthday card.

Learning to Play and Have Fun

A promise of reparenting and working our program is that "We will learn how to play and have fun in our lives." There are many ways to have fun, and they don't need to be over-the-top exuberant. Children enjoy simple pleasures: running in a yard or on a beach, playing with a pet, hiking in the woods, hanging out with a favorite pal, eating a juicy piece of fruit, playing games, or singing. Playfulness is as natural to healthy children as breathing. They find any excuse to play or to turn any activity into fun.

When you allow yourself to try out the activities in this chapter, you make space to connect with the inner child's curiosity, wonder, and awe. The following ideas and exercises tend to access the subconscious mind and are offered in the spirit of exploration. They are not meant to be exhaustive; your connection with your inner child will be your best guide to how to spend time together. You can also use some of these same exercises to connect with your inner teenager. Some of us choose to do these activities with a sponsor or fellow travelers.

"I picked up children's stickers and I stuck them on my wall calendar when I did something nurturing. Different stickers represented different activities such as going to a meeting, doing Step work, getting exercise, playing guitar, socializing with friends. Every night, my little one and I put up the stickers." -Fellow Traveler

Reflections: *Identifying What's Fun*

One way to cultivate play and fun is to think about things you liked or wished to do as a child. Be curious about what makes your inner child feel alive, which may be different from what caregivers taught you to believe or encouraged you to do or not do. Work toward letting go of perfectionism by keeping it simple. It need not be costly, either.

1. As an adult, how do you relate to fun and play? Joy?

2. As a child, how did you relate to fun and play? Joy?

3. If fun, play, and joy seem challenging or inaccessible, what could your loving parent do or say to support those inner family members for whom it's difficult?

4. What were some of your favorite activities as a child?

5. What were some of your favorite activities as a teenager?

6. Play can be defined as doing something with no defined purpose or goal, just for the fun of it. What forms of fun and play would you like to try?

7. If you could choose, what fun or playful thing would you do more often? What prevents you from doing that?

8. What activity would you do if you could let go of false beliefs such as, "It's too late" or "I'm not good at this," or "People will judge me"? (e.g., sing in front of others, paint, dance).

"Play and fun can be as simple as putting on the clothes I want to wear in the morning. As a trans person, I wasn't allowed to do that as a child. Now I can wear whatever I want. I know that others may form negative opinions about me based on these clothes, but I'm comfortable enough without their approval these days."
-Fellow Traveler

the *power* of *sharing*

Exploring What's Fun

Inner Child Playground Date. Visit a playground on your own or with another recovering adult child, and let your inner child play. Try out the monkey bars, the swings, the sandbox. Let yourself have fun. You may feel uncomfortable doing this while other children are around. In that case, find a time where you and your fellow traveler will have the playground to yourselves. Alternatively, visit your old school or a favorite spot: Sketch the playground, or draw or doodle. Ask your inner child what they liked to do there.

Revisit Childhood Hangouts. Visit places you enjoyed in childhood - or wished to visit when you were young. Some possibilities include fairs, the circus, amusement parks, mini-golf courses, arcades, go-kart tracks, water parks, skating rinks, open spaces, parks, beaches, woods, and mountains.

Make your Space Inviting for Your Inner Child. Ask your inner child to help you redecorate or rearrange your living space in a playful and fun way. Create a spot for board games or clear floor space for dancing or lying on your stomach as you did as a child. The space we live in impacts how we feel, and you can invite the playfulness, creativity, and freedom of your inner child into your living space.

-Fellow Traveler

Art. Art helps your mind rest so your feelings can be expressed through your hands. Finger-painting, drawing, and coloring can help you tap into childhood creativity. Drawing helps express your inner child's emotions as well. Try free-writing or free-drawing, letting your conscious mind rest while your inner child expresses themselves. Such exercises can be a powerful source of creativity and fun. Consider setting an intention to let your inner child express themselves as they see fit and set a boundary if any judgments arise.

Join Groups that Share Your Interests. The inner child loves to create and share with others. Adult children lose their identities in childhood, but we can rediscover our interests and preferences as adults. You can explore activities by joining book clubs, movie clubs, craft associations, writing groups, meet-ups, sport leagues or outdoor recreation organizations.

Ride a Bike. Children discover newfound freedom when they learn to ride a bike. On wheels, they can explore, visit friends, or wander under their own power. Riding for fun is something you may no longer do, so this could be a great time to break out your bike—or rent or borrow one—and head out for an adventure.

Enjoy "Recess." As kids, we took scheduled breaks to play and get some exercise. Now that we're adults, many of us forget to give ourselves a break. Taking breaks benefits our relationship with our inner child and helps us be more refreshed for our adult responsibilities.

Be Silly—Whatever That Might Be for You and Your Little One. Here are just a few ideas: scribble, try a Hula-Hoop, skip, wear a funny hat (or wig), wear wild sunglasses or bright-colored shoes, play with a dog or cat, wear a nose and glasses, make up words that make you giggle...the possibilities are endless.

Exercise 1: *Writing Poetry*

The Sanskrit word for poet is kavi, which also means "seer." To write poetry is to see more deeply, and it can be a way to connect emotionally and "see" your inner child. You can explore poetry books for prompts, or just go with what feels right to your inner child. Some prompts like "What I don't remember is..." and "What I've forgotten is..." help sidestep the rational mind to access feelings and memories.

The poetry you create may also be sprinkled with delightful humor and doodles, which could be an expression of your inner teenager. It doesn't need to rhyme, or even make sense. Let it flow from your mind and heart. Some of your poetry may reveal buried feelings and memories your inner child and inner teen have been longing to share.

If you notice critical thoughts about your ability as a poet, invite your critical parent to step aside. Let the words come from your inner child and inner teen as free association or a stream of consciousness. Using your dominant hand, begin to write a poem, imagining holding your inner child's hand, the child's hand on yours, within yours, writing together, seamlessly. Some topics:

- About the day.
- The way you feel or felt at another time.
- What you see in front of you.
- A funny image or story.

Once the poem is complete, set out a variety of colorful art supplies for your inner child to use as they add to the poem, either with drawings or more words. Using your non-dominant hand, allow your inner child to choose which supplies to use. After they've decorated the poem, ask your inner child about what they added. Keep the questions simple and listen for their response or use a non-dominant handwriting technique.

Hang the poem on the refrigerator or in another visible place in your home. This will help your inner child feel seen and heard. Repeat this exercise as often as you like.

Exercise 2: *Dancing, Music, Bouncing*

As children we were naturally expressive, free to move our bodies without concern. Moving our bodies to music (or without music) can stir memories and feelings. Listening to various forms of music can help us tap into memories and feelings as well. Nursery rhymes, or songs our parents listened to can help us remember our childhood and our child within.

Parts of you may feel awkward dancing because of messages received in childhood and adolescence. That's okay. Your loving parent can set boundaries as needed, tending to whatever comes up with reparenting.

Throw a dance party for yourself. Make sure to include songs from your childhood and teen years in your playlist. Dancing can help you burn off stress, and allows you to express yourself creatively and connect with the present moment.

Bouncing on trampolines is a similar way to be free. Small trampolines can help us reconnect with the body in safe and gentle ways and can be stored easily within the house, under a bed or couch. Adult children who suffer from PTSD can experience the body as a stressful place. Using a trampoline can gently bring us back into the body in a gradual way. Trampolines that use elastics rather than jarring springs are said to be more supportive for those who've experienced trauma.

You could also rent a bounce house, or reserve space at a trampoline park, and invite fellow travelers to a bounce party.

"I dance a little bit every day to my favorite music. It always changes my mood, builds my self-esteem, and connects me to my true self, however I am feeling. If I am tired or emotionally worn out, even one minute is enough. It is my celebration of being alive." -Fellow Traveler

Exercise 3: *Make a Big Red Book Cover*

Invite your inner child to create a cover (or bookmark) for your Big Red Book or other program literature. You can do this alone, with a fellow traveler or sponsor, or in a group. Some adult children use stickers, decorative paper, or collage to personalize their fellowship text. Others cut brown paper bags to fit, just like they did for schoolbooks. You can clip pictures of your younger self and create a collage with the words and recovery messages that inspire you. You can also visit a store and buy the cover your inner child delights in. Every time you look at your Big Red Book, you'll be reminded of your connection to your precious inner child.

Exercise 4: *Family of Origin Portrait*

Sketching your family of origin may reveal insights on how you felt growing up, but it can also show how you feel about your family now. You do not have to be a professional artist. Stick figures work fine. What you draw can help express what words cannot. The drawings can be done with your dominant or non-dominant hand. Use crayons, colored pencils, or colored paper. Or try painting, sculpture, or collage.

You might consider drawing an inner family portrait as well. When you're done, compare it with the portrait you created in Chapter 1.

Exercise 5: *Rediscovering Childhood Books*

Set a date to visit your local library. Let your inner child select a book to check out. Maybe they'll choose a children's book, a favorite chapter book, a nonfiction book, a graphic novel, or a comic book, or even something completely unexpected. Your inner child may like the idea of buying a book from a bookstore. Go to a bookstore, and let your inner child select something.

You can stay up late with your inner child, reading under the covers with a flashlight. Such experiences can help us reconnect to pleasant memories. If you didn't go to libraries or bookstores as a child, this activity is an opportunity to make up for what you missed.

For some of us, reading and homework bring up painful memories. If that's the case, get creative and find out what your inner child needs to make peace with the past. Maybe making peace means not reading. Maybe after taking time to grieve these painful situations, you'll feel more peace with reading.

The thing to remember about play and discovering our joy is that there is no right or wrong way to do it. That's the point! It's just for fun.

Your Key Chapter Takeaway(s):

Affirmation / Meditation

*I am integrating my inner child into my life by learning to play,
have fun, and by feeling the simple joy of being.*

A Day in the Life of an Inner Loving Parent

Meditation / Prayer
*May I remember that I walk together with my inner family through life. Help me
guide them with gentleness, humor, love, and respect as their loving parent.*

The more our loving parent can nurture and support our inner child and inner teen, the more ability we'll have as adults to navigate life calmly and seek out help when needed. We'll be more able to honor our inner children's needs in healthy ways.

Our inner child is the center of our feeling self, which knows how to love and trust freely. By making the effort, the child within can become a guide to feelings, creativity, and spirituality.

When our inner child is free to trust, they can express themselves to their inner loving parent and become part of our new inner compass. We will then "know" if a person we meet is safe, if we want to do a task we are asked to do, and be more able to express our feelings, needs, and opinions, such as what restaurant we prefer or what movie we want to see.

Unlike with flesh-and-blood children, there is no "day care" center available where we can leave our inner children. Whenever we go to work, face a tough conversation with a friend or partner, or even go out on a date, our inner children accompany us. They may not always agree with our adult decisions, or even be on the same page with each other. The loving parent will need to support and guide them with gentleness.

A Day in the Life of a Loving Parent

What follows is an example of real-time reparenting: ways a loving parent can lead the inner family to reach resolutions to problems in ways that satisfy all.

Kiran and Blake have a challenging day ahead. They face difficult conversations with bosses, siblings, and at dinner time tonight in their relationship with each other. Even as they wake up, their inner children are scared. They may have slept fitfully, fearful of some nighttime danger, or worried about the future.

Without recovery, Kiran and Blake would experience the insecurity of all adult children. They would try to "act like" and "look like" high-functioning adults, with no clear internal guidance of what they need and feel, or they might use their skills to keep difficult situations orderly and under control.

Fortunately, Kiran and Blake are learning reparenting skills. While challenging, their day will be a journey in recovery that affirms their progress. Their inner children will feel protected and whole; their inner teenagers will be able to relax and trust. Kiran and Blake will each take care of their "adult" business.

Kiran is scheduled for a performance review with their boss on how the new job is going. When they wake up with a nervous stomach, Kiran recognizes that Little Kiran feels anxious. They[1] realize that, of course, in this situation, a five-year-old would be frightened. Kiran connects with Little Kiran, whose needs for love, assurance, and safety are real and something Kiran wants to honor.

Kiran looks at a childhood photo beside the bed and says, "Hi, Little Kiran. I love you. I'm going to take care of you today." Kiran opens their journal and dedicates 15 minutes to connect with Little Kiran. With their dominant hand, Kiran writes, "What's on your mind?"

Slowly, Little Kiran's answers emerge on the page. "I'm scared. They're going to be mad at me. I made a mistake last week. They're going to fire us." Kiran pauses and writes back, "I'm sorry you feel so scared. The job is not your responsibility. They hired me, and it's okay to make mistakes and learn. No matter what my boss says, I love you, and we can trust a power greater than ourselves. When I have my conversation, you can hang out on my lap or in the safe space. Okay?" After a few more rounds, Little Kiran feels reassured.

Kiran serves up their favorite childhood breakfast and continues to assure Little Kiran. They call a fellow traveler and share their feelings. The fellow traveler validates Kiran's experience. "My inner child gets scared, too, because they think they're handling the meeting. I tend to their feelings and reassure them that I will handle the meeting for them."

By the time Kiran meets their boss for the review, Little Kiran no longer feels so frightened and alone. As a direct result, Kiran is able to hear the boss from a capable adult perspective. Kiran details their accomplishments in the new job. When the boss mentions a mistake Kiran made the week before, Kiran pauses and takes a deep breath to calm Little Kiran. Kiran explains what happened, and what they did to correct the situation. To Kiran's pleasant surprise, the boss isn't angry. "We all make mistakes. The important thing is to learn from them. You're doing well. Keep up the good work."

What if the boss had been unfair or critical rather than calm? Kiran could have remembered that the boss, too, may have had a dysfunctional family who criticized "little boss." If Kiran

---

1   As a reminder, we use "they" as a singular pronoun, rather than "he or she."

had felt anger arising, they would have recognized their inner teenager was ready to lash out and defend Little Kiran. Kiran could have let their inner teenager know, "Thank you for wanting to protect the little one. I've got this," while choosing not to react to the boss's criticism.

After the meeting, Kiran takes a 15-minute walk outside to enjoy the day, allowing all of Little Kiran's feelings to arise—fear, relief, even a special glow inside for being brave. "I am so proud of you," Kiran says. "I love you so much, Little Kiran." Kiran texts their sponsor to celebrate and returns to work.

With less than 30 minutes of the day dedicated to reparenting, Kiran is having an unexpectedly good day. And Little Kiran is delighted.

Across town, Blake meets with their older sibling over lunch. Like Kiran, Blake woke up with a scared inner child. Blake's sibling tends to dominate Blake, and Blake needs to set a boundary to no longer provide free weekend baby-sitting. During some non-dominant handwriting that morning, Little Blake said, "I'm scared and angry. Sissy always says mean things to me. I don't like them!! I don't even like their bratty children!" Blake took a moment to feel what their little one had written, then wrote back, "Thanks for telling me you feel scared and angry. This situation reminds you of those painful times when you had no power with Sissy. I'm here now, and I won't let that happen."

Before recovery, Blake avoided confronting their sibling, babysat whenever asked with no boundaries, and often left conversations in distress. But today, aware that Little Blake's well-being is at stake, Blake feels new strength from their loving parent. "I'm going to protect you, Little Blake. I will say what I need to say. If they are mean, we will leave."

Little Blake has never heard this before. They are still scared but hopeful. If Big Blake keeps their promise, Little Blake will trust more. Blake feels something shifting inside. When they leave their apartment for lunch, they're determined not to disappoint the precious little one inside.

Blake's conversation is challenging, and when their sibling's voice escalates, Blake holds up their hand, as in to say "Stop." Little Blake is listening, and this must go no farther. "I'm not comfortable with how you're speaking to me. If you can't treat me respectfully, I will leave." Their sibling shouts that Blake is unreasonable and ungrateful. Blake pays for their share of the meal and walks away.

Exiting the restaurant into a beautiful day, Little Blake is shaken with guilt feelings. Blake's loving parent addresses them. "It's okay to say no. We didn't do anything wrong Little Blake. It's okay to prioritize our needs, so that's what I did." Little Blake's loving parent has protected them. "Little Blake, you matter to me, and I won't let anyone mistreat you. It's okay to set boundaries."

That night, Kiran and Blake get together to resolve a recent conflict. Their inner children feel nervous about the conversation. They begin by talking about the day, including their conversations with Little Kiran and Little Blake. In sharing this intimacy, Kiran and Blake both feel closer. Their inner children realize they can be part of a family conversation and not have to hide.

After just a few minutes, Kiran and Blake realize their inner children are exhausted and decide to talk about the issue another day. They recognize they've each made progress in their recovery work. Before learning to reparent as part of their everyday lives, the couple probably would have ignored their feelings and plunged into a "serious talk" while exhausted and distracted by their difficult days.

Thanks to reparenting, Kiran's and Blake's day will end on a more nurturing note. Their loving parents both recognize that, in this case, the inner children are right. It has been a hard day. Enough is enough. Let's do a "fun break" instead.

Kiran and Blake choose to watch a TV show they both enjoyed as kids. They giggle like six-year-olds and the tensions of the day slide away. Gingerly, Kiran and Blake put their arms around each other. They feel safer and closer. There will be time to talk about their conflict another day.

The more we reparent, the more our internal process informs how we relate to others in the outside world. Before reparenting, our inner family members innocently chose our partners, tried to do our jobs, and played out family dysfunction. When our loving parent guides the inner family, these wounded and reactive inner family members will take charge less in our outer lives. Internal connection leads to external connection, making it possible to live as healthy adults aligned with our true selves.

"When I asked for a promotion, I stammered in fear and confusion. At first, I told myself to stay calm and 'act like an adult.' Then I realized my inner child felt terrified. I told him how much I loved him, and no matter what, I would still love him, and so would our higher power. I didn't get the promotion, but my inner child felt loved, and the boss and I work far more effectively together today." -Fellow Traveler

Exercise: *Taking Stock of Your Inner Family Relationships*

Like Blake and Kiran, your relationship to your inner family members has likely evolved since you began working through this guidebook. You might find value in journaling or otherwise contemplating the questions below and sharing your answers with a sponsor or fellow traveler(s).

- How has your loving parent become more a part of your life?
- How did you feel about your critical parent before working through this book? How do you feel about your critical parent now?
- How has your relationship with your inner teen changed?
- What was your relationship to your inner child like before working through this book? What is your relationship to your inner child like now?

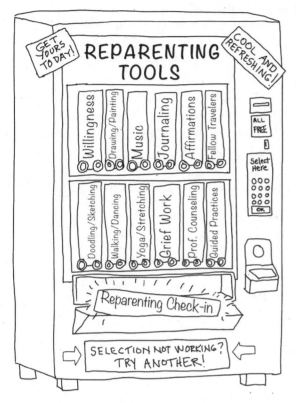

Creating a Daily Reparenting Routine

To see changes in our inner life, we need to make time to reparent ourselves regularly. Consistency (but not perfection) will make a difference. All of the tools you've learned in this book can help you maintain and build your relationship with your inner family members. Like a Step 10 inventory, these techniques can become something we practice each day to deepen our inner intimacy.

The "tools" and "techniques" we've been developing in this guidebook are all ripe for integration into our daily recovery work. We can use one of the techniques as a way to make conscious contact each day, or include one at the beginning of other spiritual and recovery practices. Perhaps if we start or end our day with meditation or prayer, we lengthen that period by ten minutes and use the extra time on reparenting dialogues. If mirror work appeals to us more, maybe we spend three minutes saying affirmations in the mirror before beginning our meditation or prayer practice. The reparenting check-in might be your tool of choice. It need not be lengthy—you can do shorter check-ins too. Some people form small groups to do 15-minute check-ins together; others pair up.

In an ongoing way, we can make our best effort to pause when we feel anxious, ashamed, or angry during our day and determine which inner family member holds the feeling. We can put their thoughts down on paper and see the false beliefs and distorted thinking more clearly. We can compare that to reality and guide them to new understandings. Reparenting can become less something we do, and more how we move through the world.

> *We can apply our reparenting work to parenting and relating to children. **We can be healthy role models** to children the more we take care of our inner children.*

Reflections: *Creating a Daily Reparenting Routine*

1. This guide has covered many tools to help you become your own loving parent. What are some of the tools that work for you?

2. What are some other tools you'd like to try out?

3a. What might get in the way of you making reparenting a priority?

3b. What inner family members might be involved? How might you work with that as your own loving parent?

4. What are some moments throughout the day where you could pause to check in with your inner children?

5. What does a daily reparenting routine look like for you?

Reflecting on the Promises

You may have heard echoes of The Promises throughout this book. If so, you heard accurately. Reparenting bears fruit—The Promises. Reparenting work—protecting, nurturing, supporting, and guiding—directly addresses each of the promises. The first promise of discovering our real identities becomes more real each time we love and accept our inner family members. Whether we choose mirror work, affirmations, or non-dominant handwriting as our tool to put that into practice, we strengthen the possibility of discovering who we truly are. When we do a reparenting check-in and tend to our inner child and inner teen, our self-esteem increases, because that care is a form of approval. Affirmations are another reparenting activity that support Promise 2. When our loving parent guides a triggered inner family member to see their distorted thinking and false beliefs, fear of authority figures and people-pleasing leave us. This is Promise 3, and on it goes.

You may want to turn to page iii and read The Promises—perhaps even aloud to yourself. Take time to reflect on their unfolding in your life, now that you've been gently reparenting yourself one day at a time. Consider each promise and what loving actions would support their appearance in your life.

Challenges are Opportunities for Continued Growth

The metamorphosis of a caterpillar to a butterfly is a magnificent transformation. Yet, from deep inside the chrysalis, it can look messy. We undergo a similar transformation on our reparenting journey. Challenges appear in a variety of ways, and at times these difficulties seem insurmountable. Still, learning anything involves periods of feeling awkward and ineffective. As we move through these stages, we can call on program principles like surrender, humility, patience, and love. We can reach out to the fellowship for security, strength, support, and connection.

Challenging times invite us to see ourselves and our spiritual journey as an ever-unfolding process, access our loving parent, and connect with our inner children.

There will be times of doubt and days we don't want to reparent. We won't be alone in feeling these ways; it is a natural part of the reparenting process, and these feelings don't define who we are. Healthy parenting takes time, patience, and a steady focus. Our parents couldn't model these skills, but ACA offers us a wealth of support.

As we continue on what could be seen as the most important journey in our lives, we can remember that reparenting isn't about getting better but about loving ourselves better. Rather than trying to be good, we can remember we already are good and that we are supported by a higher power. We are enough. We have always been enough, and we will always be enough. The more we remind our inner family members that our worth is not dependent on acts or deeds, the more we discover a wholeness we never knew was possible. We learn to expect the best and get it. These are the promises.

Your Key Chapter Takeaway(s):

Affirmation / Meditation

My greatest opportunity is to be the adult and loving parent my inner family needs me to be.
No other person in the world can be as consistently supportive of my inner family as I can.

Appendix A: Doubts, Misgivings, and False Loyalty

You'll find supplementary online guidebook resources at http://lpg.adultchildren.org.
Materials will be updated periodically as new resources are created and approved.

Doubts and Misgivings

"This is strange, weird, fake, unconventional."

Some of us can be skeptical or lukewarm about the notion of reparenting and the inner child—we can think it's nonsense. It can take time to be open to the idea of having an inner child and needing to strengthen an inner loving parent. It's also natural to feel awkward as we begin to talk to our inner children in loving ways. It helps to be aware of our judgments of the process, which stem from deep pain. We can acknowledge the discomfort and skepticism and ask ourselves, "What's the worst that could happen if I gave this a try?"

"I don't relate to "inner family members" or have any inner family members."

You might have a strong inner family member that keeps all of the others in line, such as a strong critical parent. You could tell them, "Yes, I know this seems a bit strange to you, but let's try it. We can keep what works and leave the rest." Your inner family members may not show up as voices or thoughts but instead through your body, emotions or images. Another way to begin is to view inner family members as representations of your past experiences. See if it's possible to stay open and see if anything shifts as you work through this guide.

"I should've gotten better parenting; I shouldn't have to do this now."

It's important to grieve the parenting we didn't get, which can begin when we reconcile with reality: "I got the parenting I got. I needed more, I needed better, and it didn't happen." Our parents could not pass on what they never got, so we can instead ask ourselves, "What can I do now?" This process moves us into The Solution to begin the spiritual work of healing our inner family and loving ourselves unconditionally.

"But I don't remember anything!"

It can be frustrating to face a past of vagueness and fragmented memories. No matter how much you don't remember, your body stores emotional memories as feelings and sensations. Those are places where you can begin to connect by becoming more aware of bodily sensations and emotions with the support of mindfulness, therapeutic body work/massage, and other practices in this guide. Feelings and buried memories will return as you risk moving out of isolation and when you feel safe enough to acknowledge and work with them.

"I had to be strong to survive. I can heal with just the steps."

In ACA, we believe connecting with our feelings and inner child are just as important as working the 12 Steps and sponsorship. Having a healed inner child allows us to live and act more from our true self. ACA's cofounder, Tony A. stressed the importance of learning to love oneself unconditionally; reparenting is ACA's suggested path to do so.

"Spending my time reparenting is navel-gazing. I don't want to be so self-absorbed."

Self-awareness is not self-absorption. People who are learning to love themselves more fully are often more available to love others. Navel-gazing happens when we stay stuck in self-pity and The Problem. Reparenting teaches us to proactively connect with our inner family to understand and heal the patterns that keep us trapped in childhood reactions and the false self. Becoming our own loving parent helps us be in The Solution of living life as healthy adults.

"It's too late for me. It's been too long and I'm too old to heal."

Being older can heighten our awareness of the fleeting nature of life, motivating us to do whatever it takes to recover. We can begin right now, one day at a time, and surrender the outcome to a power greater than ourselves.

"If I commit to doing this, how long will I have to do this? How long will it take?"

In the midst of falling in love, you wouldn't ask yourself, "How long will I have to love this person?" The same applies to reparenting. While it's true that recovery is neither fast nor easy, the rewards of doing this courageous work are life-changing, and some can be experienced early on. When you learn to love your inner child, you will be rewarded with a relationship that grows and blooms over your entire lifetime. It will become second nature, not a "chore."

"I began a daily reparenting check-in process at the age of 74. After spending a lifetime of reacting from early childhood trauma, I have a new understanding and connection with myself. I have a whole new set of principles and values, and I love myself. I feel safe, whole, and happy. I am home!" -Fellow Traveler

Reflections: *Doubts and Misgivings*

The following journal questions are intended to help you identify and explore any doubts and misgivings you have about reparenting work.

- What doubts, concerns, judgments, or misgivings do you have about reparenting yourself?
- What influences might your family of origin, adults around you today, or your culture have (or do you imagine them having) on your perspective of reparenting?
- If you're experiencing resistance to reparenting, what are you concerned would happen if you do this work? What needs might the resistance be meeting? Safety, protection, predictability?
- Reflect on what made you pick up this book. What might reparenting give you?

False or Misplaced Loyalty

A common reparenting barrier is false or misplaced loyalty. We may worry about our parent's feelings or reactions if they found out we're in ACA. We learned to be codependent early in our lives, so these worries are not surprising. Breaking the "Don't Talk, Don't Trust, Don't Feel" rule can trigger terror. To convince ourselves we were safe and loved as kids, we

*Parts of us that resist this work might do so because they **want to keep us safe** and help us function. They may not realize that **we're no longer dependent children.***

denied and distorted reality. We minimized or justified our parent's behavior or focused on the positive. Our stories and loyalty toward our caregivers are a way to escape pain, which helped us in the past.

Today, we can support our inner family members by being gentle as we take a closer look at what happened to us. They might fear that our caregiver will feel hurt or see reparenting work as a betrayal and retaliate somehow. They might fear abandonment and shame. Our inner child might worry parents will judge them as sniveling, weak, or dramatic. They fear caregiver messages such as, "You're making a big deal out of nothing," or "Others had it so much worse."

Our inner critical parent might downplay what happened. "What happened was for your own good." They might tell us it's just a normal part of the culture or that talking about family members is wrong. These inner family reactions are all coping mechanisms.

> **False loyalty self-talk:**
> "It wasn't that bad."
> "They did the best they could."
> "Maybe it's me, not them."
> "My childhood didn't affect me that much."

Looking at the effect of our parent's behavior doesn't erase their good qualities or happy memories, nor is it a betrayal. To recover, we need to look at what happened to us, so we're not doomed to repeat or reenact it. Hurt people hurt people. Our goal is to take a blameless inventory and heal in order to no longer feel compelled to hurt ourselves or others.

We can love our parents while still acknowledging that their behavior affected us. To transform something we internalized, we must bring it into consciousness. We can focus on our feelings and needs and remember our intention is to heal. We can release our loyalty to unhealthy family messages and rules and still be free to love and respect our parents and relatives.

It's important not to override the parts of us who have false or misplaced loyalty. Instead, we can learn about their concerns and meet them with gentleness. We may need help from a sponsor, fellow traveler, study group, or therapist. We can remember the Serenity Prayer and repeat supportive affirmations: *It's okay to love myself. It's okay to become my own person, with my own feelings, needs, and thoughts. It's okay to reparent myself with thoughtfulness.*

Confronting denial will give us freedom from the past. Getting to know and love our inner child and inner teen grows our capacity to see the inner children in others with compassion, benefiting everyone in our lives. We have much more love to give than we might realize. By practicing self-love, we don't subtract love from our parents or others. We increase the amount of love in our life.

Reflections: *Getting Curious about False or Misplaced Loyalty*

The following journal questions are intended to help you identify and explore concerns you may have about breaking dysfunctional family rules and becoming your own loving parent.

- What concerns did you relate to in the false loyalty reading? What feelings and thoughts arise when you think about doing reparenting work?
- What are you concerned would happen to your parent(s) or your relationship to your parent(s) if you reparent yourself? (Try answering this question twice, once with your dominant hand and once with your non-dominant hand.)
- What might your inner child, inner teen, and critical parent need to hear to help them be open to reparenting?
- If you don't do this work because of false loyalty, how might that impact your inner family members?

- How can you honor your caregiver(s) or parent(s) while still acknowledging how their woundedness was transferred to you?
- How could becoming your own loving parent benefit your parent(s), relatives, friends, colleagues, etc.?
- What would it be like to walk through the world with a loving parent inside?

It's natural to resist pain and new practices. An inner loving parent's response to pain is compassion. Rather than shame ourselves for having resistance or false loyalty, we have an opportunity to be gentle with ourselves. We can get curious about our inner family member's fears and concerns and reassure them the best we can. We can reach out for support and ask for guidance from a power greater than ourselves. And, if we need to take a break and instead work with a qualified therapist to address our inner family member's concerns, that's the sort of choice a caring and wise inner loving parent would make.

the power of sharing

Appendix B: Instructions to Prepare for Guided Practices

Guided practices can elicit a range of feelings and experiences, some pleasant and some unpleasant. Some people connect profoundly to the imagery or guidance; some don't. Sometimes, an inner family member can feel anxious when not feeling what the guided practice describes. Then other inner family members can get angry and react. You might find it best to let go of the guided practice if that happens or if you begin to move into your overwhelm zone.

At other times, an inner family member might feel strong, unpleasant feelings (anger or disgust) when encountering inner children. There is nothing wrong if this happens. It's merely a sign of deep childhood hurts and how much the inner child and inner teenager need your love and acceptance. This will lessen as you continue to reparent.

You might wish to repeat the guided practices from time to time or skip them altogether. Consider recording the script below in your voice, or have a friend record it and play it back once you're ready. Speak at a slow pace and pause at the end of sentences.

Sharing your experience and insights from doing these practices with someone you trust can help you feel your emotions more deeply. Doing these guided practices in a group and sharing together afterward can be a powerful experience. You might find it helpful to schedule a gentleness break in advance, so you can be with your experience and let it gently integrate after a guided practice.

[Begin recording – opening for each guided practice] To begin, find a quiet and comfortable space without distraction. Find a position that helps you stay alert, but comfortable. Your eyes can be open with a soft gaze on one spot, or closed. Please take care of yourself during this guided practice if it becomes too intense for you. If you move out of your challenge zone[1] try opening your eyes and looking around your space, listening to sounds in the room, or feeling how your body is supported by the chair or whatever surface you are sitting or lying on.

Take a moment to settle in and feel your breath or listen to the sounds in your space. If you choose the breath, pay attention to the part of your body where your breath feels most comfortable for you—that could be at your nostrils, belly, or the rise and fall of your shoulders. Pay attention to that one place, and take a few slow breaths, feeling your breath. Let any thoughts you might have fade away. (Pause) If your mind wanders, that's okay. Gently bring yourself back to the present moment and put your attention on your breath or sounds. Continue to breathe naturally.

[Note: record opening instructions and then continue with whichever guided practice you're recording.]

---

1   See also "Preface: About This Guidebook and How to Use It" on page 1.

Appendix C: Reparenting Check-in Worksheet

Please see Chapter 9 for detailed instructions and Chapter 10 for information on feelings and needs.*

After you read each question, pause. Allow your answers to arise from within, without judgment. It's okay if you don't have an answer.

1. Ground. What physical sensations, including your breath, and emotions do you notice? Allow yourself to experience them.

    a. My breath is: _____

    b. I notice (physical sensations): _____

    c. I feel (emotions): _____

2. Who. Who in your inner family needs your loving parent's attention? Check *all* that apply.

    ☐ Inner Child   ☐ Inner Teenager   ☐ Don't Know

3. What. What activated this part of you? Notice your self-talk. Check *all* that apply.

    ☐ Critical Parent / Distorted Thinking   ☐ People, Places or Things   ☐ Don't Know

    Describe briefly: _____
    Example: My critical parent projected a scary future. That scared my inner child.

4. Tend. Once you're feeling compassionate, curious, and connected toward the part of you that needs your loving parent's attention, how can you tend to them? Empathize with their feelings and needs (not the story or distorted thinking): _____

    _____

    Example: "I see how scared you feel and how you need some reassurance that you'll be safe."

    Reassure / Nurture: _____

    _____

    Example: "I won't leave you alone with these feelings. Let's breathe together, it's going to be okay."

    Do they need anything else? Comforting touch, guidance or a gentle internal boundary?

    _____

    _____

    Example: A self-hug. "This is not the same situation. Let's stay here in this moment."

Allow yourself time to be in conscious contact with this part(s) of you. Presence is also empathy.

Appendix D: Feelings, Needs & Physical Sensations Sheet

Feelings when needs are met

GLAD
happy
excited
hopeful
joyful
satisfied
delighted
encouraged
confident
inspired
relieved
touched
proud
elated

THANKFUL
grateful
appreciative

PEACEFUL
calm
conten
expansive
serene
loving
blissful
clear
respected

PLAYFUL
energetic
invigorated
stimulated
alive
eager
enthusiastic
excited

LOVING
warm
affectionate
tender
friendly
sensitive
compassionate
nurtured
trusting

RESTED
relaxed
alert
refreshed
energized

Feelings when needs are not met

SAD
lonely
heavy
hopeless
gloomy
grief
overwhelmed
distant
dismayed
discouraged
distressed
disheartened
disappointed

CONFUSED
perplexed
hesitant
troubled
torn
worried

SCARED
afraid
fearful
terrified
startled
nervous
panicky
jittery
horrified
anxious
lonely
skeptical
suspicious

TIRED
exhausted
lethargic
weary
overwhelmed
withdrawn

MAD
angry
annoyed
exasperated
agitated
furious
enraged
hostile
bitter
resentful
disgusted
frustrated

UNEASY
uncomfortable
pained
hurt
miserable
guilty

Universal human needs

TRUST
safety
security
understanding
honesty
love
to matter
community
play/fun
appreciation
freedom
meaning
rest

RECOGNITION
respect
validation
equality
reliability
predictability

COMPASSION
empathy
autonomy
choice
freedom
nurturance
comfort
warmth/caring
self-expression
contribution
creativity
effectiveness
growth
healing

INTIMACY
sharing
connection
companionship
support
cooperation

INTEGRITY
self-worth
authenticity
purpose
honesty
clarity
celebration
humor
passion
mourning
accountability
peace
ease
beauty

CLARITY
awareness
to be heard
to be seen

Physical sensations

achy	floating	limber	spacious
bloated	flowing	lumps	spinning
breathless	fluid	moist	stiff
bubbly	flushed	numb	still
buzzy	fluttery	open	strong
clammy	fragile	paralyzed	suffocating
clenched	frantic	pounding	sweaty
cold	frozen	pressure	tense
cool	full	prickly	thick
congested	fuzzy	puffy	thin
constricted	glowing	pulsing	tight
contracted	heavy	queasy	tingly
curled	heated	quivery	trembly
damp	hollow	radiating	throbbing
dry	hot	ragged	twitchy
dull	itchy	raw	vibrating
dizzy	jittery	restricted	warm
empty	jumpy	shaky	wobbly
expansive	knotted	smooth	
faint	light	spacey	

Appendix E: Partner Exercise–Translating Judgments into Feelings

We recommend doing this exercise with a partner or in a small group. Each person needs a copy of the Feelings, Needs, and Physical Sensations sheet in Appendix D. You'll want to allow at least 30 minutes for this exercise.

Choose a judgment or interpretation that is commonly confused as a feeling (list below). This list is not exhaustive. You might wish to practice with other judgments as they occur to you.

Judgments that we might confuse for feelings:

Abandoned	Provoked	Unheard	Attacked	Tricked	Threatened
Insulted	Invisible	Diminished	Guilt-tripped	Betrayed	Unwanted
Pressured	Manipulated	Put down	Abused	Blamed	Interrupted
Unseen	Rejected	Left out	Unwanted	Misunderstood	
Minimized	Bullied	Cheated	Used	Coerced	

Ask for a volunteer who can find a situation where they mistook that judgment for how they felt. This person will be the speaker. The partner or group listens for one minute as the speaker shares what triggered their interpretation. Listeners then offer, one at a time, a feeling and need (from the Feelings, Needs, and Physical Sensations sheet) that they heard underlying the judgment.

When you think you're being _____ (judgment), are you feeling _____ (emotion) because you need/value _____ (need)?

For example, "When you think you're being misunderstood (judgment), are you feeling angry (emotion) because you need to be heard (need)?"

The speaker receives each listener's question with a simple yes or no, without elaborating. If speakers begin to cry or feel emotions, avoid comforting or consoling them to allow them to be with their feelings.

Once every listener has offered a feeling and need, allow for a one to two minute debrief. Switch to a different judgment from the list and repeat the process with a new speaker until everyone has had a chance to be a speaker.

Listen for statements beginning with "I feel that…" or "I feel they…," which tend to be judgments, not feelings. The words "that," "like," "as if," or pronouns or names/nouns that come after "I feel" often express a judgment. For example, "I feel like a failure," "I feel as if it is useless," "I feel they don't like me," or "I feel Pat is inconsiderate."

Appendix F: Framework for The Laundry Lists Traits

The Laundry List describes the thinking and personality of an adult reared in a dysfunctional family. **The Other Laundry List** (also known as The *Opposite* Laundry List) points out that as adults, we might, in turn, "act out" those traits by becoming victimizers. In other words, adult children, by adopting their parents' behaviors, "become" their parents. **The Flip Side of The Laundry List** and **The Flip Side of The Other Laundry List** reveal what it's like to be free of these unhealthy patterns, through reparenting and practicing the 12 Steps. This traits framework is designed for adult children who have already completed the *Steps Workbook* and are ready to embark on advanced survival traits integration work.

TRAIT 1

The Laundry List	The Other Laundry List
We became isolated and afraid of people and authority figures.	To cover our fear of people and our dread of isolation we tragically become the very authority figures who frighten others and cause them to withdraw.
The Flip Side of The Laundry List	**The Flip Side of Other Laundry List**
We move out of isolation and are not unrealistically afraid of other people, even authority figures.	We face and resolve our fear of people and our dread of isolation and stop intimidating others with our power and position.

TRAIT 2

The Laundry List	The Other Laundry List
We became approval seekers and lost our identity in the process.	To avoid becoming enmeshed and entangled with other people and losing ourselves in the process, we become rigidly self-sufficient. We disdain the approval of others.
The Flip Side of The Laundry List	**The Flip Side of Other Laundry List**
We do not depend on others to tell us who we are.	We realize the sanctuary we have built to protect the frightened and injured child within has become a prison and we become willing to risk moving out of isolation.

TRAIT 3

The Laundry List	The Other Laundry List
We are frightened by angry people and any personal criticism.	We frighten people with our anger and belittling criticism.
The Flip Side of The Laundry List	**The Flip Side of Other Laundry List**
We are not automatically frightened by angry people and no longer regard personal criticism as a threat.	With our renewed sense of self-worth and self-esteem we realize it is no longer necessary to protect ourselves by intimidating others with contempt, ridicule and anger.

TRAIT 4

The Laundry List	The Other Laundry List
We either become alcoholics, marry them, or both, or find another compulsive personality such as a workaholic to fulfill our sick abandonment needs.	We dominate others and abandon them before they can abandon us or we avoid relationships with dependent people altogether. To avoid being hurt, we isolate and dissociate and thereby abandon ourselves.
The Flip Side of The Laundry List	**The Flip Side of Other Laundry List**
We do not have compulsive need to recreate abandonment.	We accept and comfort the isolated child we have abandoned and disavowed and thereby end the need to act out our fears of enmeshment and abandonment with other people.

TRAIT 5

The Laundry List	The Other Laundry List
We live life from the viewpoint of victims and we are attracted by that weakness in our love and friendship relationships.	We live life from the standpoint of a victimizer, and are attracted to people we can manipulate and control in our important relationships.
The Flip Side of The Laundry List	**The Flip Side of Other Laundry List**
We stop living life from the standpoint of victims and are not attracted by this trait in our important relationships.	Because we are whole and complete we no longer try to control others through manipulation and force and bind them to us with fear in order to avoid feeling isolated and alone.

TRAIT 6

The Laundry List	The Other Laundry List
We have an overdeveloped sense of responsibility and it is easier for us to be concerned with others rather than ourselves. This enables us not to look too closely at our own faults.	We are irresponsible and self-centered. Our inflated sense of self-worth and self-importance prevents us from seeing our deficiencies and shortcomings.
The Flip Side of The Laundry List	**The Flip Side of Other Laundry List**
We do not use enabling as a way to avoid looking at our own shortcomings.	Through our in-depth inventory we discover our true identity as capable, worthwhile people. By asking to have our shortcomings removed we are freed from the burden of inferiority and grandiosity.

TRAIT 7

The Laundry List	The Other Laundry List
We get guilt feelings when we stand up for ourselves instead of giving into others.	We make others feel guilty when they attempt to assert themselves.
The Flip Side of The Laundry List	**The Flip Side of Other Laundry List**
We do not feel guilty when we stand up for ourselves.	We support and encourage others in their efforts to be assertive.

TRAIT 8

The Laundry List	The Other Laundry List
We become addicted to excitement.	We inhibit our fear by staying deadened and numb.
The Flip Side of The Laundry List	**The Flip Side of Other Laundry List**
We avoid emotional intoxication and choose workable relationships instead of constant upset.	We uncover, acknowledge and express our childhood fears and withdraw from emotional intoxication.

TRAIT 9

The Laundry List	The Other Laundry List
We confuse love with pity and tend to "love" people who we can "pity" and "rescue".	We hate people who "play" the victim and beg to be rescued.
The Flip Side of The Laundry List	**The Flip Side of Other Laundry List**
We are able to distinguish love from pity, and do not think "rescuing" people we can "pity" is an act of love.	We have compassion for anyone who is trapped in the "drama triangle" and is desperately searching for a way out of insanity.

TRAIT 10

The Laundry List	The Other Laundry List
We have stuffed our feelings from our traumatic childhoods and have lost the ability to feel or express our feelings because it hurts so much (denial).	We deny that we've been hurt and are suppressing our emotions by the dramatic expression of "pseudo" feelings.
The Flip Side of The Laundry List	**The Flip Side of Other Laundry List**
We come out of denial about our traumatic childhoods and regain the ability to feel and express our emotions.	We accept we were traumatized in childhood and lost the ability to feel. Using the 12 Steps as a program of recovery we regain the ability to feel and remember and become whole human beings who are happy, joyous and free.

TRAIT 11

The Laundry List	The Other Laundry List
We judge ourselves harshly and have a very low sense of self-esteem.	To protect ourselves from self punishment for failing to "save" the family we project our self-hate onto others and punish them instead.
The Flip Side of The Laundry List	**The Flip Side of Other Laundry List**
We stop judging and condemning ourselves and discover a sense of self-worth.	In accepting we were powerless as children to "save" our family we are able to release our self-hate and to stop punishing ourselves and others for not being enough.

TRAIT 12

The Laundry List	The Other Laundry List
We are dependent personalities who are terrified of abandonment and will do anything to hold on to a relationship in order not to experience painful abandonment feelings which we received from living with sick people who were never there emotionally for us.	We "manage" the massive amount of deprivation we feel, coming from abandonment within the home, by quickly letting go of relationships that threaten our "independence" (not too close).
The Flip Side of The Laundry List	**The Flip Side of Other Laundry List**
We grow in independence and are no longer terrified of abandonment. We have interdependent relationships with healthy people, not dependent relationships with people who are emotionally unavailable.	By accepting and reuniting with the inner child we are no longer threatened by intimacy, by the fear of being engulfed or made invisible.

TRAIT 13

The Laundry List	The Other Laundry List
Alcoholism is a family disease and we become para-alcoholics and took on the characteristics of the disease even though we did not pick up the drink.	We refuse to admit we've been affected by family dysfunction or that there was dysfunction in the home or that we have internalized any of the family's destructive attitudes and behaviors.
The Flip Side of The Laundry List	**The Flip Side of Other Laundry List**
The characteristics of alcoholism and para-alcoholism we have internalized are identified, acknowledged, and removed.	By acknowledging the reality of family dysfunction we no longer have to act as if nothing were wrong or keep denying that we are still unconsciously reacting to childhood harm and injury.

TRAIT 14

The Laundry List	The Other Laundry List
Para-alcoholics are reactors rather than actors.	We act as if we are nothing like the dependent people who raised us.
The Flip Side of The Laundry List	**The Flip Side of Other Laundry List**
We are actors, not reactors.	We stop denying and do something about our post-traumatic dependency on substances, people, places and things to distort and avoid reality.

Appendix G: Working with Reparenting Challenges

Reparenting can be challenging. The first thing to remember when challenges arise is to be gentle. We want to support ourselves to return to our challenge zone, as mentioned in the preface, if we become overwhelmed or get stuck in our comfort zone. It can be helpful to review these sections of the guidebook when challenges arise:

Preface: "Finding Your Own Pace" (page 4)

Preface: "Learning to Reparent Yourself with Gentleness, Humor, Love, and Respect" (page 5)

Preface: "Reflections: Identifying Your Supportive Resources" (page 5)

Preface: "Expectations in the Reparenting Process" (page 6)

Chapter 4: "Navigating Our Challenge Zone with Mindfulness" (page 39)

Chapter 4: "Reflections: Creating Space when Triggered" (page 43)

Tools to Try with Any Reparenting Challenge

The foundation of our reparenting work is to give our inner children our time and attention consistently. Taking time to simply be—whether that's sitting in silence, looking out a window, having a cup of tea, or connecting with our inner children through listening—are ways to slow down and be present. Developing a relationship with our inner children makes life easier and leads to living into the promises.

Below are some tools to try when reparenting challenges arise. See also Appendix H.

Grounding Exercises

The Pause. Pause; take a few deep breaths. Feel the sensations of your feet on the floor or your hands touching. Focus on one of your senses—such as hearing or seeing—to ground yourself. Repeat an affirmation if it seems supportive. See also "Mini-Mindfulness Break" (page 39).

Touch. Place a hand on your heart (or on your arm, for example, if you are with others and feel self conscious). See also Chapter 12: "Exercise: Nurturing through Touch" (page 131).

Grounding Your Attention in Your Body. When you get caught up in distorted thinking and criticism, your body can ground you and return you to the present moment. With your eyes open or closed you can let your attention go to somewhere in your body that feels safe. You can then ask yourself, "What thoughts are happening that might cause these physical sensations?" See also Chapter 4: "Navigating Our Challenge Zone with Mindfulness" (page 39) and Chapter 4: "Guided Practice: Body Scan" (page 44).

Working with Takeovers

When we are not mindful of triggers, we tend to overreact. If that occurs, we experience what's known as a takeover. Identifying your feelings, thoughts, physical sensations and impulses helps you better recognize what a takeover feels like so you can begin to create space and get perspective. Revisit Chapter 8, "Reflections: Recognizing Takeovers" (page 90) to better identify what part of you has taken over.

Check Who is in the Driver's Seat. Are you allowing or resisting what's happening? Turn toward the emotion and remind your inner child or inner teen that it's okay and safe to be with whatever they're feeling. You don't need to push yourself to feel the emotion's full intensity but you can slowly build your capacity to be with your feelings.

Gentle Internal Boundary. Ask the critical parent or another part of you to take a break to make space for your loving parent. See also Chapter 8: "Managing Takeovers in a Loving Way" (page 91).

Other Tools

See Appendix H for a larger list of guided practices, exercises, worksheets, and tools. Here are a few foundational tools to try when you encounter a challenge.

Steps 1, 2, and 3:

1. "I am powerless over having a critical parent (distorted thinking, etc.). My life becomes unmanageable when I believe them or fight with them."
2. "I believe I can be restored to clarity, to unconditional love, and acceptance of myself."
3. "I am making a decision to turn the critical parent over to the care of a power greater than myself."

Prayer and Meditation. Many forms of meditation and prayer exist to help you improve your conscious contact with something greater than yourself and your inner family. Which type you choose isn't so important but rather that you choose something to help you connect spiritually.

Non-dominant handwriting. In non-dominant handwriting, you write out a question to your inner child with your dominant hand (the hand you normally use to write). Then you write the response to the question by placing the pen, pencil, or crayon in the opposite hand (your non-dominant hand), giving your inner child a chance to answer. If you're ambidextrous, you can assign one hand to speak for the loving parent and the other, as the inner child. See Chapter 14: "Reparenting Dialogues: Connecting through Writing" (page 149).

Journaling. Journaling can help you get in touch with your inner family and help resolve inner conflicts. It's also a way to reach the other side of your grief. See Appendix H: "Guided Practices, Worksheets & Exercises" (page 230).

Seek Support and Perspective. Sometimes you need help identifying what's going on in your inner world. Talk it through with a sponsor, fellow traveler(s), or a therapist. Letting a trusted person contribute to your well-being is a loving action you can take for your inner family.

Appendix H: Techniques, Practices, and Exercises

Toolkit

The columns below represent some of the tools we can use alone or with others—consider it a quick reference for program guidance and actions coming from love. Some adult children use an inventory like this to help them remember to take care of themselves, as a loving parent would. Remember the slogan: Easy does it. The goal is not to check all boxes in a day but to use this reference sheet to help you to support your recovery.

							Toolkit								
Date	Step 10 Inventory	Step 11 (mindfulness, etc.)	Affirmations	Reparenting, Check-in	Mirror Work	Journal / Non-dom	ACA Literature	Play, Fun	Physical Movement	ACA Meeting	Sponsor / Fellow Traveler(s)	Step Work, Steps 1-3	Service	Grief, Family of Origin Work	Managing Takeovers

Guided Practices, Worksheets & Exercises

Guided Practices

Worksheets

Exercises

Appendix I: Sample Meeting Scripts

Scripts for public Reparenting Check-in and *The Loving Parent Guidebook* (LPG) meetings are available at http://lpg.adultchildren.org and are updated periodically based on feedback. There, you'll also find information on LPG Study Groups. See also Big Red Book, page 568 for information on study groups.

The Loving Parent Guidebook Study Group Sample Script

(This script is intended to support study groups where membership remains the same. See above for public meeting scripts for *The Loving Parent Guidebook*.)

Welcome. This is a study group meeting of Adult Children of Alcoholics and Dysfunctional Families. My name is _____ and I am chairing today. The focus of this meeting is recovery through the study, application, and practice of reparenting. The Solution named in our program is to become your own loving parent. Working in *The Loving Parent Guidebook* helps us act as adults grounded in the present rather than reacting from childhood coping mechanisms.

Please check that all cell phones are turned off and put away. Let's open the meeting with the serenity prayer (either version) followed by a three-minute silent guided reparenting check-in.

Reparenting Check-in

(Note: a slow, steady pace with pauses at the end of sentences and gentle tone supports this guided meditation. Consider reading the reparenting check-in guided practice in Chapter 2 of the guidebook at your first meeting and then switching to this abbreviated version moving forward.)

(**Ground**) Please adjust the intensity if needed during the check-in. You're invited to close your eyes or soften your gaze. Notice your breathing where it's most comfortable for you, without changing it. (Pause 5-10 seconds.) What emotion are you feeling? (Pause 5-10 seconds.) What physical sensations tell you that emotion is here? Let yourself feel, as best you can, whatever you're feeling.

(**Who**) Notice silently to yourself who needs the loving parent's attention now or in the recent past – the inner child, inner teenager, or both? It's okay if you don't know. (Pause 20-30 seconds.)

(**What**) What brought this state about? People, places or things? The critical parent or distorted thinking? Some combination? If you're feeling more "pleasant" feelings, perhaps the loving parent has been present. It's okay if you don't know. (Pause 20-30 seconds.)

(**Tend**) Once you're feeling connected, curious, or compassionate toward the part of you who needs your loving parent's attention, tend to them while focusing on their feelings and needs. What do they need to hear or need you to do, (which may be offering words, comforting touch, or silence.) (Pause for up to a minute.) As we close, I invite you to take a moment to ground yourself back into the present moment. (Pause) When you're ready you can open your eyes or lift your gaze, and reconnect with the world around you.

Working with The Loving Parent Guidebook

Meeting Boundaries

(Chairperson notes: If study group membership stays the same, read this at the first few meetings and then when necessary. For study groups with changing membership, read each time, adapting to your particular meeting type-online, phone, or in-person.)

We ask that everyone respect the following meeting boundaries:

- Please indicate that you've finished sharing by saying "Pass."
- Please use the words "I, me, and my" to share your personal experience. Please avoid the use of "you, we, and us" except when speaking directly to your inner child or teenager, since it takes the focus off your unique perspective.
- We do not 'cross-talk,' which means: we do not refer to, negatively or positively evaluate, or comment on anyone else's sharing. We do not touch, hug, or attempt to comfort others if they become emotional or cry during the meeting. We allow the person to feel their feelings without interrupting their process.
- Anything heard at this meeting stays at this meeting. Please respect the privacy and vulnerability of those who shared here today.

Guidebook Work

Let's take turns reading one or two paragraphs of the Loving Parent Guidebook starting on page____. Who would like to start the reading?

[Before reflections, guided practices, or exercises[1]]: Before we begin answering the questions [or doing the exercise or guided practice], I'd like to read this reminder: How you feel answering the reflections [or exercise or guided practice] is as important as what you answer [experience]. You may not have answers [or experience anything in particular]. That's okay too. If that's the case, include how you feel and what it's like to not have an answer (experience) or to dislike your answer (experience). Who would like to start/continue question/exercise/worksheet__?

Ending The Chapter

Now that we've completed all questions and exercises in the chapter, let's take three minutes to review the chapter on our own, noting down our key chapter takeaway(s). After a few minutes of silence we'll open it up for brief sharing on our key chapter takeaway(s).

Closing the Study meeting:

(5 minutes before ending) Thank you all for sharing tonight. In keeping with our 7th Tradition, let's pass the basket. In closing, what we hear at this meeting should remain at the meeting. Please respect the anonymity and confidences of those who have shared here today.

Would someone please read the ACA Promises? (page iii)

Let's take the next minute in silence to transition as we each wish. (1 minute) Let's close the meeting with the ACA Serenity Prayer.

---

1   For guided practices consider having a participant record the script ahead of time. You might wish to make time to debrief the guided practice. Some groups use cross-talk guidelines and time each share.